THE LAST
PLANTATION

THE LAST
PLANTATION

COLOR, CONFLICT, AND IDENTITY:
REFLECTIONS OF A NEW WORLD BLACK

Itabari Njeri

HOUGHTON MIFFLIN COMPANY

BOSTON   NEW YORK

1997

For information about this and other Houghton Mifflin trade and
reference books and multimedia products, visit The Bookstore at
Houghton Mifflin on the World Wide Web at
http://www.hmco.com/trade/.

Library of Congress Cataloging-in-Publication Data

Njeri, Itabari.
The last plantation : Color, conflict, and identity:
Reflections of a new world black / Itabari Njeri.
p. cm.
ISBN 0-395-77191-9
1. United States — Race relations.   2. Afro-Americans — Race
identity.   3. Afro-Americans — Relations with Korean Americans.
4. Social conflict — United States.   I. Title.
E184.A1N5 1997   505.8'00973—DC20
96-41466   CIP

Book design by Anne Chalmers

Printed in the United States of America

QUM 10 9 8 7 6 5 4 3 2 1

For

ART BERMAN AND JOHN BROWNELL,

two very different kinds of newspaper editors,
who made a difference in my career and
whose talents are increasingly rare
in American newsrooms

My discussion of the concept of race and of the white and colored worlds are not to be regarded as digressions from the history of my life.

— W.E.B. Du Bois

It doesn't take a conspiracy to be racist in America. It takes a conspiracy not to be.

— Andrew Sarris

ACKNOWLEDGMENTS

LIFE constantly got in the way of this book. Neither I nor many others thought it would ever see the light of day, no matter how much time I spent in writers' prison. That it has is due not merely to my tenacity in the face of hostility from many quarters to some of the subject matter and my approach to it, but also to the friendship and support of numerous people. Linda Williams is first among them. My agent, Miriam Altshuler, has never wavered in her faith in my talent, and I thank her for that, as well as for her gifts as a skilled negotiator. To my editor at Houghton Mifflin, Dawn Seferian, who leaped at the chance to publish this manuscript, I wish to thank you for affirming the compelling nature of this project and its execution. Thank you, too, Mom, Peter, and Reg, for material support at crucial times, as well as for words of encouragement, and to Kervin for being a true friend when my moods hit rock bottom.

As is often the case, this book underwent a series of metamorphoses. And while I am sure to omit unintentionally people who influenced the book at various stages, let me thank those who stand out as early contributors to the effort before the book took a different direction and I was forced to exclude them from the text: Donald S. Will, Alex Norman, Halford Fairchild, Victor Valle, Ed Paik, and Patty Yoon.

This work, and the previous incarnations that influenced it, benefited greatly from my conversations with, among others, Barbara Love, Michael Lerner, Cornel West, Charles Lewis, Yvonne Ziegler, Monica Walker, John Lee, Marcia Choo, Ron

Wakabyashi, Steve Perry, Ibrahim Sundiata, and Billy J. Tidwell. I plan to use in a separate collection of essays some of the golden material many of them provided but that I was compelled to omit from this work.

I am indebted to several people who read the manuscript at a crucial juncture and whose thoughtful comments renewed my faith in my initial vision of the book: Samuel G. Freedman, Barry O'Connell, David Lionel Smith, and Fahamisha Brown.

Finally, despite the tensions that inevitably arise in a subjective account of social conflict and, in particular, the tragedy of a child's death, I maintain unflagging respect for the courage and dignity of the family of Latasha Harlins — whose killing is at the center of this narrative — and their willingness to let me into their grief-stricken lives.

THE LAST
PLANTATION

INTRODUCTION

I AM your ordinary, everyday, walking-around Brooklyn Negro. That is to say, I am African, East Indian, French, English, Arawak, and more I don't know about. In other words, I am a typical New World Black. That self-perception — especially my comfortable, prosaic embrace of its contents — is part of the particular alchemy of biography, history, and place that brought me to the issues in this book: conflict among people of color in a White-dominated nation.

Not only was I born into a family that represented the diversity of the African diaspora in microcosm; I have lived and worked in some of the most diverse, ethnically engaged, as well as divided, cities in the country — environments that prodded me to think about my personal identity, that of the groups from which I come, and how it all fit into the fabric of American life. It fit very well, thank you. Defined it, largely, I felt.

But historically carved out of White-imposed myths under political duress — the ethos of the plantation, Jim Crow, and more — Black identity seems more and more constricted each moment, descending, as the masses of Blacks struggle for economic survival and respect, into a compensatory nationalism that defines as the only authentic Black the functionally illiterate brother with a hood over his head, hands sunk in his pockets against a chill wind as he stands on a desolate urban corner waiting for a bus to the unemployment office   if he hasn't totally given up hope. Beyond class, in the era of Afrocentrism as interpreted by too many homeboys, he is also a displaced pure African; culturally still a

stranger in a strange land at the end of the twentieth century. To
such a person, especially but certainly not exclusively, in a widely
xenophobic nation, the world is full of hostile strangers. Many of
them running the corner store.

"Go home. Nobody asked you to come here. Who asked you
here? No one. Go." The irate Black man paced the Brooklyn
subway platform. The oblique object of his hostility — he did
not actually look at the man — was someone of Asian descent, a
Southeast Asian, I guessed. He was already seated, waiting for
the train as I approached. I sat next to him. Another, older, Black
woman sat on the other side of him, though she had other options. We said nothing but silently seemed to conspire. If the
brother attacks, he'll have to hurt us too. He walked our way, this
time stared directly at the Asian man between us, but did nothing.
Meanwhile, above us, police barricades lined Church Avenue in
the Flatbush section of Brooklyn, the scene of a bitter, much-pub-
licized boycott of Korean greengrocers by Blacks in 1991.

My mother, until recently, owned a home in that neighborhood. Several blocks from her former street, a Vietnamese man
was bludgeoned by a Black man who mistook him for a Korean
immigrant. The horror of that incident, however, paled in com-
parison with the massive violence soon to erupt on the other side
of the country.

The Black-Korean relationship in L.A., and the role it played in
the 1992 uprising, remains an underreported story. Thirteen days
after the videotaped beating of Rodney G. King by L.A. police,
on March 3, 1991, a Black teenager named Latasha Harlins was
killed by a Korean immigrant merchant named Soon Ja Du. The
shooting, the trial that ensued, and particularly its aftermath underlay much of the devastation of Los Angeles in the spring of
1992 and is the central story of this book. I view it as a metaphor
for ongoing and looming tensions among people of color, who are
expected to become the nation's majority in the next century. The
lives of Latasha Harlins and Soon Ja Du put flesh on the issues
of structural inequality that generate these intraminority group

tensions and the psychological pain and alienation — springing from those inequalities — that make conflicts among historically subjugated groups so incendiary. To be successful, any approach to conflict resolution among these groups must, I think, be a holistic one, addressing the structural issues of economic, political, and social inequality while it attends to the societally induced sense of inferiority that haunts oppressed people and the universal problem of hostility toward dehumanized "others."

Intertwined with the tragedy of Latasha Harlins and Soon Ja Du are two other stories that drew me deeper into the arena of intraminority group conflict and the backdrop against which I viewed the Black-Korean-*White* relationship.

In the early 1980s, as a reporter for the *Miami Herald,* I began writing about the rise in *interracial** marriages and the new sociology that debunked the myth that these were all pathological

---

* Except in direct quotations, I place *racial* references in italics or quotes, unless the context in which they appear already makes clear my challenge to the use of such terms.

As many social scientists have acknowledged for years, *race* is a pseudoscientific category that has been used to justify the political subordination of non-White peoples based on superficial physical differences. *Race,* of course, remains a social construct of enormous political significance. But there is one race, *Homo sapiens,* and the physical variations that characterize the species do not amount to fundamental, qualitative differences, as the popular use of the term suggests. Indeed, as a classic 1972 study by Harvard geneticist Richard Lewontin found, there is greater genetic variety within *racial* groups than between them. He showed that only 6 percent of the differences between groups were attributable to *race*. Updating his study, the Human Genome Diversity Project at Stanford University concluded in 1994 that the differences within a *race* overwhelm the differences between *races*. One is likely to find greater similarities between any randomly picked "White" in Manhattan and an African American than between two African Americans, the overwhelming majority of whom are *multiracial*.

The cultural and physical variations among humans are perhaps best contained within the concept of ethnicity, a term that can encompass shared genetic traits, culture, and history — real or perceived.

Further, no one's skin color, obviously, is literally black or white. Phenotype is not a definitive indicator of one's genetic background. However, recognizing that social identity in the United States is based primarily on this color divide, I acknowledge it but treat Black and White as ethnic terms and therefore as proper nouns.

unions, simply theaters for the expression of larger *racial* hostilities. By the end of that decade, I was at the *Los Angeles Times,* documenting the concerns of children born to those unions and parental demands that these children be acknowledged as *multiracial.*

This so-called multiracial population could, of course, be any amalgam of groups. But the most problematic unions include the genes of America's most stigmatized group, Afro-Americans, because any known or perceived African ancestry has historically made one Black in the United States.

In his 1972 book, *Neither Black Nor White,* Carl Degler asserted that as intermarriage between Blacks and other groups increased, there would either be more Black people in the United States, because that's what the one-drop rule creates, or people would try to change it.

People are trying to change it.

The one-drop rule, the definition of who is Black, is the linchpin in the United States system of *racial* classification and social stratification. To challenge it is to alter — perhaps for good, perhaps for ill — social alignments based on perceptions of *race* and color in this country.

Consequently, a bitter battle has been brewing for decades between the traditionally defined Black population and a new generation of *multiracial* Americans of partial African descent who do not want to be defined solely by their African ancestry. They want the United States government to create a *multiracial* category and put it on the federal census by the year 2000. This will foster social acceptance and pave the way for political representation of *multiracial* Americans, proponents argue. But it threatens to siphon large numbers from so-called parent minority pop-

---

Both the accepted meanings attached to *race* and ethnicity in our current social lexicon, and my challenges to them, are imperfect. However, my hope is that by challenging our *a priori* acceptance of *race* and the social classifications that result, I will prompt discussion of *race* as a concept, *racism* as an ideology, and the false reality they create in our daily lives.

ulations — Blacks, Latinos, and Asians — resulting in a loss of political power and civil rights protections, all linked to the census count.

Eschewing any new *racial* classification schemes but always interested in challenging the deceptions surrounding the fraudulent notion of *race* in the United States, I years ago seized the debate over *multiracial* identity as an opportunity to do so.

A confluence of scientific hostility to the concept of *race,* massive immigration of people to the United States for whom single-*race* identity rather than ethnicity is foreign, as well as a burgeoning home-grown population of multiethnic Americans demanding recognition has moved this politically explosive issue closer to center stage since I began writing about it in the eighties. My essay "Sushi & Grits," published in the anthology *Lure and Loathing: Race, Identity, and the Ambivalence of Assimilation,* has been a major resource for teaching about *multiracial* identity in universities and for reporting on the subject; it reflects my thoughts on the *multiracial* debate through the early nineties. I continue to write about it because, among other reasons, there is a dangerous, divisive attempt to exoticize *multiracial* identity; to act as if African American identity is not already mixed, to deny that Black, by definition in the New World, is essentially *multiracial.*

As I explore in this work, the tensions between traditionally defined Blacks, *multiracial* Americans, and their *interracial* families cannot be understood unless we examine the unresolved issue of colorism — color conflict within the African American community. The well-documented economic and social preferences accorded lighter-skinned people in this society are the source of deep, continuing resentment in the Black community. The multiethnic population often possesses a complex of characteristics preferred by the dominant Euro-American culture — lighter skin, straighter hair, thinner lips, slimmer noses — triggering that resentment and adding a sometimes harrowing level of hostility to the antagonism between Blacks and *mixed-race* Americans.

The Black-White-Korean issue, colorism, and the "Black"-ver-sus-"multiracial" struggle are wedded in my perception and in this book not just because Blacks are central players in them. They all symbolize to some extent the dangerous politics of dis-traction, diverting attention from the larger issues of social injus-tice that plague people of color and masses of White Americans.

Despite loud protests to the contrary, attitudes about color in the Black community remain a source of concealed resentment and an impediment to building coalitions within our own com-munity. Those attitudes not only spill into the "multiracial" de-bate, alienating potential allies in a nation increasingly hostile to the progressive social agenda of most Blacks. They also make most African Americans turn a deaf ear to any of the positive im-plications of the *multiracial* debate, namely, the need to move be-yond narrow interpretations of identity based on imposed, mar-ginalizing notions of culture as well as on *race*.

I consider myself part of a heterogeneous, panethnic group of African-descended people linked by history, culture, and blood, despite the tenuousness of those ties and disruptions engendered by the Middle Passage and slavery. And viewing them as generic ethnic categories, I treat Black and White as proper nouns.

Further, as a writer, I detest any limitations placed on my use of language and often use Negro, Black, African American, and Afro-American interchangeably in the New World context. Afri-can American and Afro-American most properly refer, I think, to the descendants of those enslaved Africans who were brought to the American South and were transformed — as much as they ultimately transformed the United States — by their contact with Europeans and Native Americans. Depending on the context, I sometimes use African American more broadly to refer to people of African descent throughout the Americas. And it is in this last sense, as the product of a United States–born-Black and Carib-bean-immigrant community, that I call myself an African Ameri-can, too.

Like others before me, I believe that Black identity in the

United States is shaped by the memory of slavery, the awe of surviving it, the hopes attending emancipation — usually betrayed — and the persistent, life-threatening, occasionally rewarding struggle to extend the application of American democracy — and in doing so to inspire world admiration and emulation. This history — alive in song and food, story and motion — is the launching pad for my open-ended, ever-evolving New World identity. Its contours do not erect a static prison of the self.

Too, my romance with jazz and James Brown and Bermuda nights on precarious cliffs draped across a motorbike while hanging on a tree limb as the unmistakable high, round, deeply padded curves of a dark man's moonlit posterior undulates above me to the Godfather's declaration, *I'm superbad,* intoxicates me with all its endlessly inventive pleasures and cannot but make me healthily ethnocentric. Such emotional attachments, however, are no ground for asserting cosmic moral, aesthetic, and intellectual superiority. I am no Afrocentric.

That African Americans have profound difficulty psychologically embracing — not just stating as fact — the reality of our complex identity and, most significantly, intellectually constructing its meaning in a manner that serves our political interests in the twenty-first century is, I believe, increasingly problematic.

Late-twentieth-century America is a place of unparalleled diversity, ethnic competition, and a shrinking Black population relative to other minorities. How functional, in such an environment, is the enforcement of a false, marginalizing *race*-based identity? America at the millennium demands internal coalitions that transcend differences of color, culture, and class, as well as those beyond the limits of group identity, to ensure political and economic advancement. How confident, how sustainable is a solidarity forged by denying internal color, class, and cultural resentments that are often projected psychologically onto our relationships with others — particularly other people of color, the twenty-first century's predicted majority?

We need to foster, I believe, a sense of identity that maintains the integrity of Afro-American culture in all its complexity and uniqueness but expands our psychological and, ultimately, our political capacity to reach out and connect with other communities. This book explores some of that territory. But the reach cannot be unilateral.

On the plantation that America remains, Blacks continue to be the demonized other. But even as we are victimized by the ethos of slavemasters and their descendants, we often define ourselves and operate in terms that speak to the psychological slavery that leaves the mind the last plantation.

Finally, historical forces and self-will have placed Blacks at the center of struggles over ethnic identity and power that continually redefine the character of U.S. society. The subjects of this work and the writer presenting them address you, therefore, not from the margins of U.S. life, but from its central nervous system.

CHAPTER 1

In a chilling and widely unreported coda to the Los Angeles apocalypse of 1992, a woman sat in a banquet room of the stately Biltmore Hotel, violently thumping her fingers on a dining table . . . slamming down her silverware . . . trembling as she threw back a cocktail — apparently for courage — as the then mayor of Los Angeles, Tom Bradley, spoke.

He came, said the stiff, legendary politician, who often looked like an escapee from Madame Tussaud's Wax Museum, to pay respects to his friend of thirty-five years and former law partner, Charles Earl Lloyd.

Lloyd, a man who exuded a spirit of generosity and seemed possessed by even more generous ambitions, was being honored that May night by the Criminal Justice Section of the Los Angeles County Bar Association as trial lawyer of the year.

It was not a universally welcomed event, as a placard held by one of the handful of Black and White protesters outside the hotel announced: CHARLES LLOYD WHITE FOLKS NIGGER. The allegation, if true, was not necessarily bad — depending on one's political objectives.

Lloyd's long career as a win-'em-against-the-odds defense attorney was justification enough for the honor. That's what William Thornbury, president of the Criminal Justice Section at the time, defensively declaimed in my face. Declamatory had clearly been deemed the night's official tone.

The veteran counselor, whose past included the boast of trying more murder cases than any other lawyer in Los Angeles County, once defended a local television sportscaster charged with fatally shooting another reporter in the presence of the dead man's estranged wife. Despite having pumped the victim with twelve bullets, the sportscaster served only eighteen months for the crime.

Another time, thanks to Lloyd, Danny Young — a Black man — "charged with murdering a 12-year-old West Covina White boy, was convicted of second degree murder instead of first degree," reported the *Los Angeles Sentinel,* the largest Black-owned weekly in the West. Reading like the ads paid for by ambulance-chasers and slip-and-fall lawyers, the paper's profile of the attorney bragged that over the past two decades "Lloyd has literally freed thousands of people charged with serious crimes."

Michael Stewart was among them. The son of a wealthy Alabama industrialist and a classmate of former Alabama governor George Wallace, Stewart got off narcotics charges, thanks to Lloyd. Another client, packing fourteen thousand pills, seventy-five balloons of heroin, and five pounds of marijuana, was set free after Lloyd got the case dismissed on the grounds of illegal search and seizure.

When Judge Everett E. Ricks let loose a Lloyd client who pleaded guilty to attempted murder — firing eleven shots at a bound security guard, then, with a partner, filling a shoebox with $1.3 million worth of diamonds before being apprehended — furious prosecutors charged, "This is totally out of character" for a judge habitually tough on violent criminals. The sentence, claimed Deputy District Attorney Jeffrey C. Jonas, seemed "to be a favor to" the defendant "for whatever reason or to his attorney." Such a notion was not uncommon in relation to the well-connected Lloyd, better known for deal-making, said a former associate, than for stellar legal arguments.

However he did it, apocrypha has it that when one Mrs. Henrettia Perkins exclaimed, upon the demise of her mate, "Oh, my God, I killed my husband," friends and relatives instructed the hysterical woman, "Don't call the Lord; call Lloyd."

Despite Lloyd's notable record, the association of trial lawyers had not seen fit to acknowledge the fifty-nine-year-old attorney in previous years. But it did so now, at a time when he'd actually lost the case that had brought him the most notoriety and to this ballroom in the Biltmore on May 28, 1992 — a month after Los Angeles became the scene of the worst domestic uprising in the twentieth century: 16,291 arrested, 2383 injured, 500 fires set, nearly a billion dollars in property damage, 52 dead. An uprising precipitated not only by the acquittal of four White Los Angeles policemen in the videotaped bludgeoning of a man whose international appellation became "the Black motorist Rodney King," but another painful and, in its social implications, more complex case: *The People* v. *Du*. That case, and the fallout from it, did as much as the King beating and the initial acquittal of his assailants to set the stage for the class and ethnic warfare that erupted on the streets of Los Angeles in the spring of 1992.

On March 16, 1991, a forty-nine-year-old female Korean immigrant-merchant named Soon Ja Du shot a fifteen-year-old African American girl named Latasha Harlins in the back of the head after a dispute over a quart-size plastic bottle of orange juice worth $1.79.

Captured on tape by the store's surveillance camera, Latasha's shooting took place thirteen days after the videotaped assault on twenty-five-year-old Rodney G. King.

The Black teenager's death, Judge Joyce A. Karlin's decision to sentence Du to probation instead of prison, and the rationale Karlin offered from the bench for that decision sparked outrage across Los Angeles and ignited bitter controversy and debate within the city's legal community.

Feelings of anger and loss were certainly most intense in the African American community. But the dead teenager's ghost seemed to haunt the entire city; a vision derived from the few photographs that existed of the girl — a dewy-eyed, plump-faced child with full lips that yearned to widen into a smile but, for some reason, could not. Nine months after the shooting, four months before the riot, Al Martinez, a Latino columnist for the *Los Angeles Times,* wrote of her spectral visage:

You sense its presence on the streets and in the stores, in office buildings and churches.

Each time its name is said, the ghost's presence is enhanced and its longevity assured.

They say it in anger and they say it in grief. They say it in rallies and they say it in sermons. They say it in writs and they say it in petitions.

The ghost hovers with the persistence of sunlight and the power of a gale. Its existence is a shout for justice and a battle cry for atonement.

Its name is Latasha Harlins.

Latasha's killing and the trial's outcome represented the nadir, nationally, of the long-simmering hostilities between many Korean-immigrant merchants and the Black, often impoverished, customers they serve in the country's inner cities. This interethnic strife has generally, and mistakenly, been characterized as the Black-Korean conflict, with White Americans as merely *tsk-tsk-tsking* bystanders. It might better be described as the bitter brew of White power, Asian middlemen, and Black rage. And even that formula for social dynamite obscures the underlying class conflict that extended the strife to other ethnic groups.

Many Latinos — particularly Central American immigrants concentrated in neighborhoods such as Pico-Union, just west of downtown L.A. and merging into Koreatown — complained that they felt exploited by Korean immigrants as both landlords and employers. They claimed to suffer the same disrespect in dealing with them that Blacks continually alleged.

In what one White policeman tagged a "rainbow coalition of rage," more Latinos than African Americans were arrested during the uprising. Latinos accounted for 36.9 percent of those jailed, Blacks, 29.9 percent, Whites, 6.8 percent; the ethnicity of

26.4 percent of those arrested was described by authorities as unknown.

Many Latinos empathized with the anger Blacks felt over the death of Latasha and the slap on the wrist her killer received. Like many African Americans, they used the shooting and its aftermath as excuses for the vicious, systematic, and disproportionate targeting of Korean American merchants during the unrest. Korean-immigrant businesses suffered an estimated four hundred to five hundred million of the one billion dollars worth of property damaged during the rebellion.

"This is for Latasha," claimed a Latino looter encircled by man-made coronas of torched buildings on the first night of the uprising.

In Korean, the start of those nights of rage, which would tragically define a crucial time in the early immigrant history of Korean Americans, would be labeled for the ages Sa-I-Gu — April 29, 1992.

Charles Lloyd defended Soon Ja Du.

And when Judge Karlin's actions stirred multiethnic outrage throughout the city and a bitter, Black-led recall effort to remove her from the bench, Lloyd was among her most vocal supporters.

The big, boyishly handsome former high school football player from Indianola, Mississippi, could be seen in the Biltmore lobby outside the ballroom, rushing, arms outstretched, toward the petite blond judge as she entered the building, accompanied by plainclothes security guards. (There had been reports of threats to her life, as well as to Du's and Lloyd's.) Lloyd embraced her, and while television cameras captured the moment, he called out, "Judge Karlin!" as if it were a declaration to a nonexistent balcony.

The klieg-lit moment was apropos not only of the need of a deal-maker like Lloyd to stay in the good graces of incumbent judges, but of the seventy-year-old Biltmore's history as birthplace of the Oscar statuette's design — sketched on a napkin in the hotel's dining room — and site of the early Academy Award ceremonies. Lloyd's manic buffoonery seemed straight from a silent movie.

"Andrea," Thornbury said — mistaking me for Andrea Ford, a Black *Los Angeles Times* colleague to whom I bore no resemblance — in no way was this night meant to "aggravate" social tensions in the city. This event had been planned months before the riots. He was aware, however, that "there had never been a Black lawyer honored by the association before." And it was certainly, he declaimed, "long overdue."

The seventy-four-year-old mayor — soon to leave the office he'd held for two decades and relinquish thirty-six years of Democratic control of City Hall to a White Republican who ran on a law-and-order campaign in the aftermath of the riots — had asked to address the crowd early in the evening so that he could leave for another engagement.

I recalled tales of his tenure in office as Bradley, a man of calculated inscrutability, approached the podium:

"You look at him and you wonder if he has been chiseled in stone," said an advocate of the homeless, who met with him repeatedly. "He has dreams; no one knows them. He has opinions; no one knows them . . . There's a life span to that kind of governing."

The son of a Texas sharecropper, Bradley once cautioned a reporter, "I am a very complex man in my reactions, emotions, and in the way I do things." Simplistic approaches, he warned, would yield no understanding of him.

When the end of his reign was tainted by allegations of unethical conduct, reporters asked: Why does every big-city mayor in the country except him recognize a potential conflict of interest in accepting a paid position as an adviser to a private corporation? The color rose in his waxen face, as did the pitch of his usually monotonous voice, and he snapped, "I'm a very unusual person, and I don't want you comparing me with somebody else in some other city . . ."

Yet this man — so much an enigma to even his closest associates that he was known as the Sphinx of City Hall — enjoyed immense popularity during most of his twenty years in office. Los Angeles was already the nation's third largest city when he was elected, in 1973. But it was on Bradley's watch that Tinseltown got respect: he energized culture and the arts, turned the moribund downtown into an international trade center, expanded the airport and the harbor, making the latter the nation's leading port, and laid the foundation for a commuter rail network.

In a city only 13 percent Black, Bradley accomplished all this with a remarkable, now tattered, coalition of Jews from the city's West Side and Blacks that lasted for years.

All the while, the city's ethnic mix grew larger and more complex. Los Angeles — gateway to the Pacific, the new Ellis Island — became the latest social laboratory for testing the promise of democracy and the limits of assimilation and accommodation.

Many said the riots made a mockery of Bradley's greatest claim — that he was able to unite the inhabitants of the nation's most ethnically diverse city. That may be, but Bob Gray, a long-time aide, remarked harshly, "His legacy is going to be that his friends got enormously wealthy during his tenure."

At this moment, though, in this room, he towered as he long had: an aloof, admired father figure to a sprawling metropolis. The former jock and cop assumed his customary stance before the night's audience — a ramrod covered with taut, brown skin draped in the best threads.

"Everyone in this audience admires Charles Lloyd," he began. "I have known him since he was nineteen years old. He so impressed me that I began following his career as he went from Los Angeles City College to Cal State Los Angeles, then to the University of Southern California Law School while working a full shift —

eight-hour-a-day shifts — as a member of the Los Angeles Police Department. I hadn't seen anybody that bright, that committed, that could concentrate on a full workday and then wind up with top grades in his class in school. And I said to myself, 'This guy is going somewhere. He's going to be a tremendous voice.'"

Then Bradley recalled the day Lloyd passed the bar. The mailman dropped the notice in the box. "Charles stopped to read: 'We are pleased to . . .' and he didn't bother to read the rest." The crowd laughed. "He raced down to the city attorney, where he signed on and rose to become the chief trial lawyer. In the course of a brief but meteoric career there, he tried 145 criminal cases and got 140 convictions."

He was an "intense young man, one who had an eager, active mind," Bradley said with passion. "The only thing I couldn't figure out about him was that I learned he had been born in Indianola, Mississippi, and I had never known *anything* good to have come out of Mississippi." The mayor's voice had a chuckle in it, his face was deadpan, and he got a laugh. "Charles destroyed that myth . . ."

As His Honor spoke, I could understand the kinship between these two men. Legend had it that Lloyd, now among the richest Black men in the city, had arrived in Los Angeles in the 1950s with a hole in his pants and twelve cents in his pocket. Those on the street below, and in the corridors of the courthouse during the Du trial, who alleged that Lloyd was an Uncle Tom were often generations removed from him and Bradley. These were men who'd pulled themselves up by bootstraps attached to thin air, and were the survivors of an even more cruel and circumscribed world than the one protested in the spring uprising, Sa-I-Gu. Such generational polarizations were hardly new.

In their time, in their way, Lloyd and Bradley were dangerous men escaping a certain fate — the fate of Black peasants whose life was unprotected and whose labor was bought so cheap as to equal servitude in the rural South of their time. "Tomming," and

other improvisations on the Black art of psychological subter-
fuge, were the stratagems employed to navigate the social prisons
of their pasts. Such devices could, of course, become crippling,
reactionary patterns difficult to abandon even if one had the
consciousness to try. And if these patterns served one's ambitions,
if these ingrained impulses could be transfigured as the art of
political and social compromise — well, with Montaigne, Lloyd
and Bradley would no doubt assert "ambition is not a vice of
little people."

Bradley went on: "Most of the people who have any knowledge of him think he's the best. Well, Charles thinks he's the best,
so it follows." The crowd laughed. Applauded.

When he was elected to the Los Angeles City Council in 1963,
Bradley said, he gave up the legal practice he shared with Lloyd.
"But in no way has that interfered with our close friendship and
my love and admiration for him."

He is a man who "doesn't run away from controversy. In fact,"
Bradley said, edging toward the desperate and absurd quality
that would characterize most of the evening, "he is one of the
most controversial figures of our time.

"Someone said to me, 'You going to that dinner for Charles
Lloyd? Well, they'll be picketing outside. Because,'" Bradley
added cryptically, "'of events of the recent past.'" There will be
people who will be critical of Lloyd's decisions and his perform-
ance, he was warned. There's going to be a lot of controversy. "'I
think you just ought to ask him to let you off for tonight.'" And
this advice came from many people from diverse walks of life, the
mayor told the audience.

His friend would have let him off the hook, he said. "But I
would shrivel up inside if I were so small as to say that because
he's been involved in some controversy lately I should not come
to honor him tonight."

And then the Sphinx of City Hall, his voice turning stentorian,
declared: "I honor this man because I know him. I honor this

man because I respect him. I honor this man because I love him as a human being and a friend. I'm proud to present this commendation to him now, Charles Earl Lloyd . . ."

A loud round of applause was followed by a sudden "Boo, boo." The lone voice belonged to an elegant White woman seated at the same dining table as the muttering woman banging down her silverware.

Hearing the heckler, Lloyd commandeered the microphone. "After you're comfortably seated, would you now give the greatest mayor this or any other city has known a standing ovation."

Chronically sounding like a man about to have a stroke, the high-strung attorney, his voice cracking slightly, said, "Mayor Bradley, I love, admire, and respect you. And I love, admire, and respect each person present here tonight. I need you. Do I have you tonight?" he asked, as if it were a pep rally for the Indianola high school football team. The audience applauded on cue. "Thank you," boomed Lloyd. "I'll talk to you later."

"Anything for a buck," yelled that lone voice again.

On the other side of the ballroom, a Black man who called himself Brother David, a member of the Latasha Harlins Justice Committee, shouted at the mayor, "This is a mockery. All of you should be ashamed of yourself."

Thornbury, the master of ceremonies, commandeered the stage again. "Sir, if you don't sit down, you'll be asked to leave and you could be subject to arrest."

"Arrest me then. I have more to say." Security guards obliged his request, and throughout the ballroom people clapped and laughed as he was removed.

The mayor left and the room calmed during a lengthy and boring speech, several awards to judges, which included honoring a little-known jurist named Lance Ito as the Los Angeles Superior Court Judge of the Year, followed by the group's official recognition of Lloyd.

Of the night's honoree Thornbury said, "In spite of the rampant racism that characterized his life [Charles Lloyd rose to great success as a] man who worked within the system. A man who surmounted the barriers without succumbing to the rage or yielding to the prejudice that surrounded him. If all of us were as color blind as Charles Lloyd, our city would be a far better place in which to live. Charles Lloyd is a defender; judges and juries decide guilt or innocence." So, please, Thornbury declaimed, "join me in saluting this great-grandson of a slave, the former football captain of Indianola Colored High School, former Los Angeles policeman, former city prosecutor and trial attorney extraordinaire . . . Los Angeles County Bar Association attorney of the year, Mr. Charles E. Lloyd."

Amidst applause, Lloyd stood at the microphone and said, "I love you. I am grateful to the LACBA for giving me this prestigious award. I accept it because I know I deserve it." *Thud.* The muttering woman banged her glass on the linen-covered table. "This has been a year of growth for me," Lloyd continued in an adrenaline-soaked voice. "People do not want justice; they want to have it their way. The judiciary must remain free and independent," he said, affirming one of the evening's mantras. The group applauded. "I have always supported incumbent judges and I am not going to stop this year. You've been patient, I love you, I am not going to take any more of your time." Then he took more time to list the other judges honored during the evening, and offered special congratulations to the "greatest judge of them all, the honorable Judge Joyce Karlin."

"Oh, please," shouted the White woman heckler. "This is outrageous. You are applauding the vindicator of murder."

"No," someone in the crowd shouted back.

"Boo," someone else yelled at her.

"You should be ashamed of yourself!" the elegant White woman shouted. Then, with a skillful display of outrage contorting her body, the obvious plant, who later revealed she was a part-time actress as well as a member of the Harlins Justice Committee, stormed out.

A shaken Lloyd prodded: "Let's give Judge Karlin — I'm very

proud — let's give Judge Karlin another hand." And then I saw, standing up, the muttering, trembling, angry woman with golden skin and slick brown hair snatched back in a smooth bun. She was Denise Harlins, the aunt of Latasha. Her voice was surprisingly steady.

"Charles Lloyd, how can you have the unmitigated gall to — the audacity to celebrate the death of my niece? Over the bloodshed of her, to get what you're getting right now." She turned from the stage to face the seated diners. "All of you people sitting applauding over a child, all of you who have children, fifteen-year-old Latasha was defenseless." Her voice spiraled to a shriek: "She didn't do N O T H - I N G !"

Her fractured wail elicited a threat. "Sit down, or we will have to arrest you," Thornbury yelled. "You are disturbing the peace. Police officers will remove you."

More quietly but firmly, she began again. "Let me tell you something —"

"You will have to leave," the MC boomed again, cutting her off.

"You arrest me," she responded defiantly, then turned once more to the seated crowd. "Latasha left a brother and a sister, nine and eleven. They have lost their mother, their father, and now their sister. The videotape don't lie. She was defenseless. You can have all the money in the world . . . but this whole system is going to come tumbling down," she warned the stunned crowd. People looked embarrassed. They looked as if they wanted to find the nearest exit. The rage that leveled large swaths of the city, skirting mostly White enclaves of privilege, had invaded the Crystal Ballroom. "ALL YOUR MONEY IS NOT GOING TO COVER WHAT'S GOING TO HAPPEN. GOD BE WITH ME AS I STAND HERE RIGHT N O W W W W W W W W W . . ." The police took her away, her voice a human siren of pain piercing the hotel corridors.

The shrieking aunt's voice was still audible in the distance when Lloyd again commandeered the stage to introduce a representative from the county supervisor's office. "Mr. Brad Pye, who is going to give me an award, too. Indulge me a few more minutes," Lloyd begged.

Reaffirming that Lloyd was an outstanding attorney and a "personal friend," Pye told them that the county supervisor, Kenneth Hahn, were he present, would invoke the words of a poem this night:

"*I am proud,*" Pye recited, "*of people who are proud they're Black / but intelligent enough to be oblivious of that / I'm proud of people who are proud they're White / We all have to be some color / And God knows any color should be all right / I'm even prouder of people who truly understand / It's the character that makes the difference / And color never did a woman or a man.*"

"Charlie," said Pye, "congratulations." The pained, frozen smiles and stiff applause suggested that those untouched by Denise Harlins's desperate and useless demonstration did seem offended by the banality of this moment.

Again, Lloyd's tremulous voice was heard. "I promise, one more minute. Celes King will make some comments about me on behalf of Governor Pete Wilson."

"Charlie, I'm certainly pleased to say a few words about you tonight. And I've been admonished that they should be a very few. I knew him when he was a cop . . ."

When he finished, Lloyd told them, "Again, I thank you from the bottom of my heart. I needed your support this evening and I have it. God bless you."

"Thanks, Charlie," said Thornbury; "a well-deserved award."

There was something else that the Criminal Justice Section did this term, besides deciding to honor Charles Lloyd, Thornbury told the crowd. When the effort was begun to recall both Judge Karlin and her supervising judge, Ricardo Torres, because he refused to reassign her to civil court, the Criminal Justice Section wanted to take a stand in support of an independent judiciary.

Basically, Thornbury explained, "a group of people disagreed with one decision of Judge Karlin's — not a pattern — but one decision. The Criminal Justice Section took the position that the entire Los Angeles County Bar should oppose the recall effort. But the board of trustees disagreed, which they are entitled to do. They are the governing body. However, due to our strong commitment to the independence of the judiciary . . . the Criminal Justice Section is giving a certificate of support to both Judge Torres and to Judge Karlin."

A representative for Torres accepted on his behalf. And then Karlin was introduced. She made her way from the rear of the ballroom to the podium to subdued applause.

While Karlin clung to the philosophical life raft of judicial independence, assorted legal scholars and the city's African American bar association argued that the real issue was abuse of judicial discretion. She was an inexperienced judge who had overstepped the sentencing boundaries in the Du case, many in the legal community contended. And her rationale for doing so signaled to some a combination of naïveté and bigotry that rendered her unfit to sit on the bench. Even some of Karlin's supporters, though protesting the recall effort, publicly criticized her sentence as too lenient.

The district attorney, Ira Reiner, denounced it as a "stunning miscarriage of justice" and vowed an appeal. Issuing a "blanket affidavit," he ordered prosecutors essentially to boycott the judge, disqualifying her from all criminal cases. That controversial move ignited its own firestorm of criticism in the legal community. Eventually, the grandstanding D.A., who was seeking re-election and who had tried to control the judiciary before, backtracked and instructed his deputies to decide on a case-by-case basis whether to remove Karlin.

It was Reiner who asked Karlin's supervisor, Judge Torres, to transfer her from criminal to civil or juvenile court. Judges who'd suffered similar fates often labored in obscurity, shuffling motions.

That was not the future the forty-year-old Karlin had in mind when the Republican governor, Pete Wilson, appointed her to the bench in July of 1991.

She was a tough, highly respected U.S. attorney who helped develop and prosecute some of the government's most important drug cases — among them the case against defendants in the kidnaping, torture, and murder of U.S. drug agent Enrique Camerena. She also prosecuted child pornography cases.

When, in the course of what Torres called the usual reassignment of judges, she was transferred to juvenile court, Karlin said that was in accord with her desire. She had a long-time interest in the welfare of children, evidenced, in part, by her aggressive prosecutions as a member of an intergovernmental Task Force on Child Pornography.

By accepting the reassignment, she seemed to be lying low. When the political dust settled, she might be reassigned to the criminal court. But for now, her reputation was so seriously challenged by the Du case that she feared professional death.

No California judge had evoked as much controversy since the brutal 1986 campaign to recall Rose Elizabeth Bird as chief justice of the state's Supreme Court. Now leading an isolated life, and — incredibly for a former chief justice — struggling to make a living, Bird was removed by voters convinced that her personal opposition to the death penalty distorted her legal rulings.

The Los Angeles County Bar Association refused to take a position when Bird and other members of the state's Supreme Court were threatened with removal. To take a stand now, many cautioned, would send the wrong message to members of the African American community. Those supporting the campaign to unseat Karlin were not rioting; they were appropriately exercising their constitutional right of recall.

It surely stung Karlin to know, as she made her well-guarded way to the podium, that she'd received an unenthusiastic endorsement from the bar association in the upcoming judicial elections. Instead of "well qualified," the label that the bar's Judicial

Evaluation Committee usually bestowed on incumbents, they merely found her "qualified" to do the job.

"I want to thank all of you for your support and encouragement in these very difficult times," Karlin said firmly. "There are those in the community who demand that we define justice by what is politically correct. I think that we must unanimously reject such demands," she pronounced to applause. "What's politically correct today may not be politically correct tomorrow or the next day. But what is justice today is justice always." The evolution of American jurisprudence clearly suggested otherwise. Nonetheless, she went on indignantly, lowering her voice for effect: "I for one am sick and tired of less than five percent of this community trying to tell the rest of us what to do, what to think, and what to say. We have, today, politicians, bullies, and gangsters who are exploiting racial tensions in our community for their own personal gain. It's time to tell them that we are not going to be intimidated and we are not going to be bullied. And one way we can do that is to vote for judicial independence" — vote for her next Tuesday, Election Day 1992. "Thank you all very much."

As I stood in the emptying ballroom, Denise's wail lingered in my mind, and I shook. I'd been sitting opposite her at the dining table when she rose to disturb the fabricated peace of the ballroom. I'd been shadowing her and her family for over a year. I was a fly on their wall whenever they'd allow it. And I had not been untouched by their complicated, anguished lives.

For several years, I'd been writing about them and two other instances of minority-group tension in which Blacks were central players — color conflict among African Americans and tensions between supposedly pure Blacks and the country's growing *multiracial* population. *Race* and its manipulation were central to all of these hostilities — nothing new regarding conflict in the United States. But immersed for what stretched into almost seven years of writing about these tensions, tensions in which anger and death were lead characters, I fell into a deepening depression.

I walked around the ballroom writing furiously, eyes glued to the reporter's notebook I sometimes used as a psychological shield when a story unleashed a pain too familiar and familial. Latasha could have been one of my cousins; I'd already lost too many of them to violence or drugs on America's urban reservations. And that the particular branch of my family most susceptible to these mortal assaults fit no physical stereotype of Blacks — suffered rejection from multiple camps because of it, yet reflected not just my family's ancestry but the denied *multiracial* reality of Black identity in the New World — drew me to issues of color, identity, and ethnic conflict while I worked in the contentious "melting pots" I made my home for years, New York, Miami, then Los Angeles.

My sense of the familial, however, encompassed more than my ethnicity and class. I felt in that ballroom, as Denise Harlins screamed of a coming class and color cataclysm — a miniversion of which occurred during the uprising — a rage and pity for my ignorant and manipulated White citizen-kin.

Manipulated by a Euro-American elite who use the ideology of White supremacy socially, politically, and culturally to divide poor, working-class, and middle-class Whites and lighter skinned people from a demonized Black population, masses of Whites still imbibe, at the end of the twentieth century, a diluted portion of the original poison that tainted the Declaration of Independence and the Constitution. And if it's not the poison of rejecting Black humanity as the Founding Fathers did by refusing to denounce the slave trade in the Declaration of Independence and then giving constitutional sanction to slavery, there is, in a nation of citizens deliberately left ignorant of its often cruel racist history, the 1930s Capra-esque mush agreed to by many Whites and uttered by the logy-brained Rodney King: "Can we get along? . . . And just, I love — I'm neutral, I love every . . . I mean we're all stuck here for a while . . . Let's try to work it out." (At least when the great Frank Capra's cinematic John Does triumphed against corrupt politicians and capitalist barons, there was no denying that the struggle was over power and privilege in terms of class. But the fraudulent notion of *race* always trumps class here, undercutting the struggle for social justice across the color divide.)

"I thought what he said was really moving," a White editor at the *Times* soulfully said of King's halting, elliptical plea before the *click-flash* of cameras. The slop made me sick, I said, even before I heard it had been scripted by the jacked-up motorist's handlers.

We are in this together, but in more complicated ways than the country's institutions usually teach. Connected by history, culture, *and* blood, we're all, as Ralph Ellison put it, "mammy-made" in America. Of course, the dichotomized Black-White rhetoric that passes for meaningful social discourse in the United States makes an embrace of the nation's true miscegenated character — genetically and culturally — difficult if not impossible. But as early as memory serves me, I was conditioned to do so.

I was born at Crown Heights General Hospital, not far from what was Ebbets Field. But my family's ancestors had been unloaded from slave ships that stopped in ports throughout the New World, melded with the Chinese and Asian Indians to come, the Amer-Indians already there, and the French and English and the Irish settlers who imposed their bodies and their names on the anonymous African women they enslaved and raped. To my mind, there was nothing exotic about my ancestry. What was rare was that I embraced it as one does the rose despite its thorns.

My Guyanese-Jamaican-American mother's encompassing sense of identity, shaped outside the bifurcated racial myths of the United States, was largely responsible for my own. But so was my father, a Georgia-born philosopher and Marxist historian. An inconsistent presence in my life, my pale father never went around pronouncing himself anything as awkward in casual conversation as a New World Black. Stinking up the house cooking poorly cleaned chitlins, breaking suddenly into a chorus of "Shortening

Bread" as he shuffled in his boxer shorts across the room to his work table, laden with the writings of Lincoln, Plato, and Marx, he didn't have to.

The rare, overtly *racial* comment I distinctly recall him making was about a White judge who spotted a male Negro spectator in his New Jersey courtroom talking intimately to a White woman, his arm draped around her shoulders. The enraged judge reprimanded them publicly, then threw them out of his courtroom. I can still hear my father telling the story in a tone that, were it bottled as a scent, some slick marketer could push as Derision: Dab it on and stay pissed. "Stupid White sonofabitch. The woman was my friend's wife. She was a light-skinned Negro."

It took my father's aunt, when she was a hundred years old, to give up the 411 that daddy's mother had been raped by either a "mulatto preacher" or a "White one."

Among most contemporary Blacks, especially given the Afrocentric mood, mum was the word on those connections. But I could not look at any of the players in that ballroom and not feel those ties, not just because I knew my history or saw its consequences in the daily life of my family, but because I had lived a cosmopolitan life on intimate terms with Whites. Consequently, at that moment in the Crystal Ballroom, I felt a contempt for them that familiarity breeds. I was disgusted with the White establishment and their surrogates' attempt to discipline Blacks with hollow accolades for a hack: "*In spite of the rampant racism that characterized his life,* [*Charles Lloyd rose to great success as a*] *man who worked within the system. A man who surmounted the barriers without succumbing to the rage or yielding to the prejudice that surrounded him. If all of us were as color blind . . .*" There wouldn't have been the carnage that caused death by the dozens, millions in damage — Sa-I-Gu — if the nation's majority was not intent on using *racial* differences as a means of determining power and privilege, to the detriment of darker-skinned people. The uprising was the product of man-made forces, and humans had the power to change the institutions that generated it.

But even as I raged inwardly at the color-based institutional bias that generated the material poverty of United States *bantustans* and contributed to its intellectual and spiritual decay, there was a more particular alchemy of anguish at work for me, a psychic propane fueling my writing and distress.

My grandfather was killed by reckless White youths in a small Georgia town. Drunk and speeding, they rammed into his car late one night as he drove home from an emergency call. He was a doctor. Thrown from his Ford, he cracked his skull when he hit the pavement; his neck broke. When my pale stepgrandmother, her face made more ghostly by fear, her nightgown and hair flying in the Georgia breeze, ran to the scene, a White man told her not to worry. It was just a nigger.

It was a Klan town. The year was 1960. My grandfather was a troublemaker, a subversive. That meant he was a member of the NAACP. He was for integration. He demanded the same textbooks for Black children and White. And he'd been doing so almost from the day he arrived in the town, in 1935. From the start, the Whites were leery of this dark immigrant from British Guiana with the strange accent and the pale wife. Wasn't from around here, the Whites constantly said of him. Didn't understand our ways.

When, pretending to be a disinterested journalist, I tracked down the man responsible for my grandfather's death more than twenty years later, a doctor who boasted he was the "oldest living White man in the town" told me better my grandfather died that way "so we didn't have the bother of a trial for whoever shot him." It was on that trip that I began the habit of digging my nails into my reporter's notebook and scribbling with indecipherable fury when a story stirred the vestige of the deep, unassuageable pain that exists, I believe, in the life of every Black American.

The boys in the car that killed him were never charged with anything, and for years I'd been told nobody knew their names. But their names were known, I eventually discovered, and learned, too, that my stepgrandmother had filed a civil law suit, demanding $100,000 in damages. She was awarded $6000.

When I asked one of the surviving jurors from the 1961 case how they had decided on the sum, he said that point was tossed around quite a bit. Finally, the jurors — they were all White; Blacks weren't allowed to sit on juries then — agreed that they "never saw a hundred-thousand-dollar nigger."

My grandfather was the only male in my family I remember openly loving me as a little girl. The year he died, I was taken from a joyful childhood in Brooklyn to live with my father, for the first time, and began to sleep with a knife under my pillow.

A brilliant scholar best known for his elucidations of Plato in Harlem barbershops, and the liquor store bills that fell out of his copies of the *Republic*, my father had self-destructive impulses that fit neatly with the maze of deadly traps set carelessly and casually by a White supremacist culture. He spent most of his waking hours at a folding conference table in the living room, dressed only in his boxer shorts, writing his Platonic-Marxist analysis of liberty in the United States, which was finally published and remaindered under the title *The Tolono Station and Beyond.*

There were few places for a Black man in his twenties with a doctorate in philosophy from the University of Toronto in the America of the Depression years — or for decades after. My father's leftist sentiments and general arrogance did not help. So he drank himself to death. On the way there, his frustrations made my childhood a perch from which to frame daily domestic madness, and I will never forgive this country for his destruction.

I certainly brought this emotional baggage to my work as a journalist writing about the peculiarities of *race* and racism in America — determined to challenge its insanity yet haunted by it and resentful. But even if, decades after the death of my father and grandfather, I accepted that White supremacy at the end of the twentieth century is the rock-hard ideology of extremists only, I saw a causal relationship between the fog of White racism that creeps and settles in the crevices of the national unconscious, diffusely engulfing the land like an uncontrollable mist, and the grief I intimately associated with the psychological and actual murder of colored people by colored people. Against the landscape of America's color hierarchy, I'd seen these assaults on my own family, and it was the backdrop to the tragedy of Latasha Harlins and Soon Ja Du.

When my tears dried and I thought my eyes and nose no longer red, I walked, notebook in hand, toward Lloyd to ask him a few questions. We were acquainted from the Du trial, and I had written an op-ed piece in the *Los Angeles Times* hostile to Karlin's sentence. He slapped backs, grabbed friends and acquaintances in a bear hug while veins bulged at his temples — he'd already had a heart attack or two, I'd heard — and studiously ignored me.

Finally he responded, "Please don't send me the book when you've finished. I know what you are going to write."

"You think so?" I actually thought him a rueful figure, and something in my eyes must have conveyed this because he suddenly pulled me into one of his viselike hugs and said, "God bless you."

I walked away, wondering who could have invented such an evening. Orson Welles, maybe. Lloyd's manic buffoonery may have seemed straight from a silent flick at the start, but the night had become a cliché-riddled talkie, descending into a brand of sentimentality James Baldwin once called the excessive and spurious display of emotion that betrays an arid heart and signals a secret and violent inhumanity.

And there was no daily newspaper reporter in the ballroom to record it. I was on leave from the *Times* to write my book. Television cameras captured the melodramatic Lloyd-Karlin hallway show, but there were no reports of the demonstration inside the Crystal Ballroom from the broadcast media the next day. And not a word in the *Los Angeles Times*. In the main, if the *Times,* the city's newspaper of record, didn't report it, it didn't happen.

CHAPTER 2

WEEKS PASSED after that night at the Biltmore, but more than time and space separated the absurdities of that evening from a Saturday morning in the basement of Saint Cecilia's Catholic Church in Koreatown, near the center of the city. A group of African American and Korean American Catholics were seated in the same room. Their shared faith, they hoped, might help them navigate tortuous emotional terrain. But in postrebellion Los Angeles, ideas like "common ground" and "healing" were alien notions. People had staked out tribal positions and circled the wagons. Perhaps the least aggressive act in this atmosphere was the display of a bumper sticker on a car spotted on a Los Angeles freeway: IF I KNEW THEN WHAT I KNOW NOW, I WOULD HAVE PICKED MY OWN COTTON. But in different corners of the city, many were trying to find some common turf.

Horace Williams, a Catholic activist, professor of bioethics, and member of an international peer-counseling movement known as Re-Evaluation Counseling, was one of them. A mustachioed, dark-brown man with salt-and-pepper hair, a slight build, gentle manner, and formidable persistence, he'd donned the familiar hat of facilitator this Saturday. And it was a hard hat to hold on to. He was trying to encourage honesty among the participants *and* contain their impulse to bludgeon one another. "Please, let him speak," he told two elderly, muttering Black church women ready to pounce on a Korean American while he spoke.

He had watched his friend get shot in the leg by a Black teenager while defending his store during the riots, Kenny Son, a
twenty-two-year-old premed student, told the mostly Black
group seated on metal chairs in a circle. "If I were to tell you what
the African American has done within the Korean community,
you'd be outraged. My neighbor's mother — excuse me, I might
get emotional" — he sighed deeply — "was pregnant. She was
managing an apartment building. Two African [American] men
came in saying they'd like to see the apartment. They raped her.
Then they set her on fire."

The nuns in his neighborhood parish "are always having their
cars stolen" by Black kids in the neighborhood. Son had to chase
down such a thief himself recently. "And the list goes on and on,"
he insisted.

"I came here with my mother in 1981," he told the others, his
strained civility a frayed veil barely hiding his rage. "We lived in a
single-room apartment with rats and roaches. With the grace of
God we were able to move up, literally move up the rungs of the
ladder. A lot of African Americans condescend because they were
born here and we are immigrants. If anything," he said with a
sudden explosive rasp, "we are more American than you guys are
because we earned it. We came here seeking American democracy. We weren't forced here. African Americans say they were
forced here because of slavery. If you don't like it, leave! Go back
to Africa. Koreans feel very much hatred against you right now."

Go back to Africa. That phrase, like *nigger* — learned by generations of immigrants before they know the Pledge of Allegiance
— was the surer sign of their Americanness.

Not many months before Kenny Son's civility hung in shreds
around him, I stood in the DuSable Museum in Chicago, looking
at its permanent exhibit of African American stereotypes — images intended as fixed, derisive statements about Blacks. Visual
propaganda in the service of White tribalism, many, historically,
were retouched, cut-and-paste compositions or staged photos,
like the infamous 1897 "Honey Does Yo Lub Yo Man," shot in

the studios of Knaffle and Brothers in Knoxville, Tennesee. In it, a bedraggled old Black man in dirty clothes presides over a wedding ceremony in which the bride wears a soiled dress and the drunken groom looks old enough to be her father. In the background, signs on the wall proclaim "De Lawd Lub De Churfel Giver" and "Lebe Yo Razzer at De Do."

Other images were trademarks, with a global impact, hawking American products. Consider "Darkie" toothpaste, made in the U.S.A. and sold for decades in Japan with the picture of an impossibly dark Black man in a top hat, with bulging eyes, printed on the box. Thanks to cable and American films, no corner of the globe is immune to such distortions of Black humanity. Is it any wonder that a Korean American store manager, whose parents grew up under Japanese occupation, would admit, when considering his immigrant community's negative image of Blacks, that "the glass was already dirty when we got here." *Go back to Africa!*

Latasha's family had no country to go back to. This one was theirs. But their place in it was very different from that of Tom Bradley or Charlie Lloyd, people they felt were indifferent to or uncomprehending of their world. The class divide between them and the Harlins family — all the Harlins-like families of L.A. — fed the rage that erupted on Sa-I-Gu. It was class, too, that alienated them from the striving group of Korean immigrants they knew mostly as merchants, immigrants whose ambitions they often shared, though not the means to achieve them.

I'd been hearing about tensions like those exposed in Saint Cecilia's basement for years by the time Kenny Son exploded. When I came to the *Times*, the story that set the tone of my reporting to come was about colorism — discrimination among Blacks based on skin color. Of course, the historical context for it was the preference accorded lighter-skinned, European-looking Blacks by slavemasters on the plantation and Whites in postbellum America. But I thought the issue marginal among most Blacks by the late 1980s — until Gloria.

At a camp in the woods of Massachusetts she stepped to the front of a room, bathed in harsh fluorescent light, and took the hand of Barbara Love, a peer counselor who used her skills in a variety of settings. "So, tell us who you are." The woman shifted from side to side. She flashed a nervous smile. Knowing she was here to heal, knowing it was a setting of anonymity, knowing she had the complete, respectful attention of a community of people who, no matter their disparate origins, had lived some piece of her psychic terror, she spoke her name.

"Gloria." She said she was of Creole ancestry, born in Louisiana. About forty-five, she was handsome and statuesque, with a hint of gold in a complexion that was brown like the crown of a well-baked biscuit. "I was the darkest one in my family. All my life I heard my grandparents, my cousins, my — everyone — whispering 'nigger-nigger-nigger-nigger . . .'" The more she said it, the more it became an aspirate hiss: "nihhger-nihhger-nihhger . . . NIHHGER!'" She laughed. "Errrggg." It was the sound of someone gargling with gravel. She shivered.

"When I had my first child, it was a beautiful mahogany-colored boy. He was so beautiful. Errgggg." She shook again. "Then I had my daughter." The woman moaned.

Love caressed her hand and smiled encouragingly. "Then you had your daughter," she said. They stood silently for seconds. All that was flesh and wood in the room seemed to breathe with them. Gloria looked at the gathering of Re-evaluation Counselors — Puerto Ricans, Chinese Americans, Colombian natives, Japanese Americans, and the seemingly endless variations on *Black*. All of them were members of the Re-evaluation Counseling community, an international peer-counseling movement founded in the early fifties by Harvey Jackins, a White labor union activist from Seattle. Drawing on psychoanalytic theory and the work of analysts of the oppressed, such as Frantz Fanon and Albert Memmi, RC theory basically assumes that the psychic wounds we carry — whether from physical injury, illness, or various forms of social oppression — can lead to rigid, irrational patterns of thought and behavior unless the painful emotions are expressed systematically in a safe, supportive environment.

Here, Gloria felt the safety to speak. She squealed, "Blue eyeeees. My daughter, she was vanilla-colored, like ice-cream, with red hair and blue . . . eyes." She pulled her shoulders to her ears. "And I freaked out."

"Why?"

"Why? Why?" Her voice was singsong. "Because . . ." Then, from some boxed-up corner of her soul, she let loose a scream so primal it seemed to reach back thirty thousand years . . . pierce the room's thin, dry wall . . . echo through the woods . . . shake the leaves and scar the trees. "Because . . ."

And then this biscuit-brown woman revealed that she'd spent the past twenty-five years of her life in mortal fear that her vanilla ice cream–colored child would hate her, reject her because . . .

"I'm a nigger. Oh, God, because I'm black, because I'm so black . . ." And then, on a spring day nine years shy of the twenty-first century, she screamed that ancient scream again and fell to moaning for what seemed, by the unyielding knot in my gut, an eternity. I heaved and thought of Jeffrey, my cousin. He looked like Ricky Nelson and always wanted to be the baddest nigger on the block.

Like me, he was African American and Caribbean American. When he was being sent to prison, the judge, examining his record, called him a White man. My cousin protested and pointed to our brown-skinned grandmother in the courtroom. "If she's Black, I'm Black too." Then he demanded he be treated just like any other "Negro." The judge obliged, adding a year to his sentence.

Trying to prove how bad he was in the eyes of other Black men, my cousin bought into the street life, absorbing, as they had, an oppressor's definition of a Black male — a thug   confusing patterns of survival with culture. And since Jeffrey was a Black man growing up in Harlem during the late fifties, he saw few options but the street life. But his looks made the price of admission exceedingly high.

When they found his bloated, bullet-pierced body on a Harlem rooftop, it was because he'd spent his too short life trying to prove how Black he was.

I could not hear this golden-hued Creole woman's story without thinking of Jeffrey and his sister — pale, golden-haired, and hoping desperately that her next baby is *black black black* — wishing out loud that she could give her first child to somebody else to raise 'cause he's so *light light light.*

I wondered if we'd ever escape the shifting, irrational nuances of a seldom acknowledged but constantly reinforced color hierarchy as I spoke to a twenty-three-year-old warehouse dispatcher named Sean, who'd called into an L.A. radio show and stated his preference for light-skinned women.

"My sister has two beautiful light-skinned children," and that's what he wants too. "I don't want to marry a woman who's African dark, even if she's really nice. Uh-uh. Nope, I'm going to be truthful. I don't want to walk into the room at night and be scared by just the whites of her eyes." No daughter of Japan's favorite "Darkie" on the toothpaste for him.

A controversial 1988 article I wrote about colorism, in which Sean was among those quoted, encouraged a Black-Japanese–Native American woman named Velina Hasu Houston to seek me out, thinking I would be sympathetic to the concerns of "multiracial" people like herself who had a beef with "Blacks."

Asserting what she called her "biological truth," and seeking a separate identity from Blacks, she said: "What I don't appreciate about the African American community is this mentality of annexing anyone with one drop of African blood . . . I don't know why African American people seem so obsessed with annexing other people." Yet when *multiracial* people want to voice their unique concerns, they are told to shut up and "just carry out the political and cultural agenda of African Americans. African Americans want us to be their political slaves," she said with the intensity of water at a low boil. "They are saying, 'Come join us.' But it's not because of some great brother or sister love — it's political." If the U.S. Census shows their numbers decreasing, their chances of getting public funds decrease, as does their political representation, since both are based on the census count. "To me, that's a totally unethical way of saying that you want people to be a member of your community. As far as I am concerned, all slavery is over — whether it's physical slavery on the plantation or political slavery that gives one group, like African Americans, the audacity to say that they own people because they have one drop of African blood."

I put my face muscles in the relax mode while feeling clubbed upside the head and kicked in the guts, listening to her ahistorical Black-bashing. The Little Dab'll Do You School of Genetics was the creation of slavemasters, not Blacks, of course. But I was not interested in debating her at the moment. Besides, this was an interview strictly for the *Times,* and I needed to maintain a professional distance. We'd have other encounters.

About the same time I began a series of interviews with Velina, I was invited to meet with a group of Blacks in L.A. whose attitude signaled to me, years before Kenny Son's contemptuous outburst, the magnitude of the Black-Korean violence to come.

"You stupid, you don't do nothing, don't work, you stupid. Get out of my store." From a menacing squint, Iola McClinton's eyes opened and her jaw loosened. She'd just retold the encounter with a Korean American storeowner that had pushed her to the edge. Slowly, she regained her customary relaxed but serious expression. She was in her early thirties, a legal secretary for the county's Workers Compensation Department, single and without children. On a fall night, a little more than two years before Sa-I-Gu, I sat in her living room in the Mid City section of Los Angeles, just a few miles east of what some dubbed low-rent

Beverly Hills, or the Beverly Flats — expensive, but not mansion-status, homes surrounded by Neiman Marcus, Saks Fifth Avenue, and I. Magnin. Mid-City held mostly Black and Latino residents and many mom-and-pop stores run by Korean immigrants. It contained attractive, single-family homes often built in the region's varied plays on Mediterranean style, small apartment buildings of similar design, immigrant-packed tenements of no particular architectural interest, and walls of commercial and private edifices bearing the tribal graffiti of various gangs.

What was to be a one-on-one interview with McClinton, sparked by a letter she had filed with the county Human Relations Commission charging mistreatment by a Korean immigrant merchant, turned into a mini-community forum. She'd informed others I was coming, and they wanted to vent their concerns.

She avoided all Korean American businesses now, McClinton said. "I've had so many negative experiences with them." The last time, she'd tried to return a dress given to her as a gift.

The dress was too big. The purchase had been made three days earlier. She had the receipt. She gave it to the storeowner and said she wanted to exchange it. The storeowner told her, "'No refund after twenty-four hour,'" she mocked in broken English.

It was outrageous to enforce a twenty-four-hour exchange policy, she told him, and pointed out that it didn't say that on the receipt. That's when he told her to get out and began calling her stupid.

"I've heard them call Black people all kinds of stuff under their breath," another area resident claimed. Claire Ausbie, a medical claims examiner about the same age as McClinton, was among the eight people gathered around McClinton's coffee table. All of them had the steady, clean-cut, solid-citizen demeanor one would have expected to find among a group in Rosa Parks's living room in Montgomery, Alabama, in the 1950s.

Three of the eight were members of a nascent grass-roots association called OMNI, Organization of Mutual Neighborhood

Interest. They planned to boycott merchants accused of unfair business practices and discriminatory behavior toward Blacks. The boycott was planned for mid-November, the start of the 1988 holiday shopping season, explained a man with an earnest, commanding presence. He was thirty-six, named Ward Wesley, owned a Los Angeles janitorial service, and worked as a maintenance supervisor for the U.S. Postal Service. His authoritative manner conjured up a bit of Martin Luther King, Jr., and a bit of Malcolm — the latter, he would admit, an idol he consciously emulated.

"The system is allowing drugs into our community," he said in an intense but even voice. "Then you've got gangs. That makes it an already volatile situation, and when you bring in another element, merchants taking a person's money and treating them as less than human no matter how green your money is —" He stopped himself and breathed deeply. "I mean, some Black people, after years of struggle, are making $70,000. They may stop in a Korean merchant's store, get disrespected, called a name, and after years of all that hard work, they really feel ready to kill somebody. We are already killing each other in the Black community; we are just one step away —" He caught himself again. "I do not believe in violence, but that's how bad the sentiment is running. I *know* these young Crips and Bloods running around feel that way. And, dangerous as they are, no telling what they may start doing."

"I'm from a Black-White society," added Ausbie, who grew up in Texas. When she was a little girl and went to buy clothes, Blacks couldn't try them on. It's the same thing with the Koreans in their stores. "And I'm telling you," she boomed, "we don't need any new Massa's."

Go back to Africa!
Nihhger nihhger nihhger . . . NIHHGER!
African Americans want us to be their political slaves.
No new Massa's.

For several years, at great psychic cost, I'd been writing about these tensions in a manner that challenged accepted notions of *race,* ethnicity, and culture in an environment uncomfortable with such challenges — the mainstream press — and sometimes overtly hostile to them. For me, the '92 "riots" were a numbing anticlimax.

CHAPTER 3

I STRUGGLED FOR BREATH and watched death in slow motion . . . watched death enlarged . . . freeze-framed. I watched death move forward too fast . . . The remote control fell from my limp hand to my lap. A thin shaft of air whistled through my left nostril, the right one hopelessly congested. L.A. had the smell of lurking social morbidity and impending destruction when I arrived in 1986 from Miami, a city similarly inclined. But in L.A., the air had literally threatened my life. A cold became a lung infection, thanks to the city's notorious air pollution, which hung with a particularly heavy, bad brown attitude downtown where I worked. And the place where I worked, the *Los Angeles Times,* was a particularly sick building. Reporters chronically complained to each other that the bad air outside surged through the puffing knots of *Times* nicotine addicts huddled at back, front, and side entrances, mixed with the viral-plagued (and, we laid odds, asbestos-tainted) air inside, then recirculated among sneezing reporters and editors hunched inside their partitioned pods, adding their atomized mucus to the stale milieu of the paper once dubbed the Velvet Coffin. This notion of comfortable death referred to the belief that one could do little, for long periods of time, and be well paid for it, at one of the revered institutions of American journalism.

Most of the reporters I knew at the *Times* worked long and hard, but did so in an atmosphere too often hostile to genuine creativity, intellectual rigor, and — most sadly — journalistic enterprise. There wasn't much street reporting at the *Times* during my five-year, full-time tenure there, not even freeway reporting. Journalism by phone was lazy reporting, and I saw more of it at the *Times* than I'd witnessed at other news organizations. Admittedly, I had never wanted to be a reporter in my hometown partly because of the horrors of Manhattan gridlock and the nightmare of rushing along snow- and ice-covered streets to meet a deadline. Sun Belt cities enticed me, and the expanse and speed of off-peak freeway driving were comparatively pleasant. Undoubtedly, after several decades, it becomes a drag to travel sixty miles on Southern California's packed, polluted freeways for the telling gesture or unintended revelation inspired by eye contact, personal chemistry, and mere persistence. But good reporting required it and a concomitant wealth of energy that made all but the celestial tier of journalism the playing field of those usually under fifty-something — unless one wanted to be an editor. I had no such interest. And despite a successful fourteen-year run, I stayed at newspapers longer than I'd intended. If the *Miami Herald* was merely the *last* plantation for which I struggled into armor daily, adjusted my helmet, grabbed my lance, and clanked into the newsroom to joust another round, the *Times* would be *the last*. The phrase would evolve to have psychological and political implications more significant than I'd initially conceived. At the time, I just meant I was determined to free myself from daily newspapers before I was forty. Shuffling to my kitchen, I didn't think I was going to make thirty-six.

I lumbered through the galley-like space, much as I'd seen my colleagues do in the corridors of the *Times*. While there were always exceptional journalists, often working at the margins of the paper, I found the *Times* an overly cautious, intellectually bland institution, inhabited by large numbers of reporters and editors who seemed permanent residents of Donna Reed's world. Post-Ike, pre-late-sixties' radicals, they seemed to dwell psychologically in the fabricated world of early sixties' ads for Congoleum vinyl floors with a built-in cushion "so springy it even recovers from spike-heel dents!" And a buxom blonde in a red

dress and spike heels twirling on the floor — sans Donna Reed's
pearls — proved it. The ad caught my eye in an old copy of *Life*
magazine resting on a bureau in a hundred-year-old vacation
home I'd rented in the mountains. It was the magazine's date that
first struck me: May 1963. Just months before President Kennedy
was assassinated, shattering a manufactured national innocence
about the violence at the heart of the society, an innocence challenged on national television for several years, even then, by the
hosing, burning, and bombing of civil rights activists. There was,
as well, the war in Vietnam. But the impact of the graphic depic-
tions of that campaign would not take effect for several more
years. As I fingered that well-preserved issue of *Life* in the cen-
tury-old house, it seemed a sign of the last epoch of easy social
denial: Congoleum U.S.A. It was to this world that a disproportionate number of my White male colleagues seemingly longed to
rush at day's end, particularly middle-management types pushing
sixty. Perhaps this crew struck me as overrepresented because of
my five years at the *Herald,* which had a justified reputation for
chewing up, spitting out, and replenishing their young regularly,
while showing little respect for veterans who'd "failed" to become stars or managers.

At what was allegedly the top tier of the profession, one expected to find a more mature group of reporters and editors, with
long-established careers. But I sensed the drag of dead weight
everywhere at the *Times* — journeymen and superior women
and men burned out and tired of managerial ineptitude and journalistic blindness. Congoleum U.S.A. seemed a salient, competing ethos at the *Times,* if not, arguably, the prevailing one. From
appearances, the spirit also seemed to apply to certain management wanabees vacating their twenties and aiming for vertical
blurdom. Long-observed corporate phenomena, vertical blurs
were young White men with rocketlike career advances often
attributed to serendipitous encounters with an executive editor at
the health club while power-lifting.

But this ethos probably lived most among a particular type that never made it into management, just on to the copy desk in seeming perpetuity. Though more than one had saved my butt from embarrassing errors and lawsuits, these men and women could be dangerous. Among the last lines of defense between reporter and reader, some copy editors were ever ready to sabotage point of view, prose — even facts — with the meat axe of their frustrations. For some reason, again, the men stuck out among them, perhaps because they bore their lot with such enormous literal and psychological volume. I'd occasionally spot one waddling through the newspaper's corridors, sometimes grim-faced, sometimes grinning, head bent toward the floor, mumbling to himself about some private, distant pleasure. Perhaps the memory of that Jet Smooth 1963 Impala Convertible, "Body by Fisher," and the "doggonedest collection of automotive virtues," so the ad of the day went, waiting for him in the parking lot when fantasies seemed an accessible future. Perhaps that dervish of a blonde in red dancing on Congoleum to a Sinatra cut. "Songs for Swingin' Lovers," no doubt — the essence of hip for such guys. I imagined those Sinatra songs blowing from the radio as they drove their Impala convertibles home from the *Times*, the swinging orchestral swell of Nelson Riddle's arrangement a propelling force as formidable as the horsepower under the Impala's hood:

> It happened in Monterey, a long time ago
> I met her in Monterey, in old Mexico
> Stars and steel guitars
> and luscious lips
> as red as wine
> broke somebody's heart
> and I'm afraid that it was mine
> It happened in Monterey, without thinking twice
> I left her and threw away the keys to paradise
> My indiscreet heart longs for that sweetheart
> that I left in old Monterey

Bitterly and audibly complaining that they'd been passed over professionally in favor of women and colored people, these guys played time for pensions maybe two years away and the more immediate reward of a steak on the grill in the backyard of a suburban home as isolated as possible from the polyglot immigrant communities that gave Los Angeles its status as the new Ellis Island but belied its more heartfelt persona: Iowa on the Pacific.

These men rarely spoke to me, though I was told they could be heard to mutter in elevators and near water coolers, "Why is she always stirring things up." But I knew the lure and loathing I symbolized to them: *My indiscreet heart longs for that sweetheart that I left in old Monterey.* Was this a brown passion left below the border? Above it or below, these conscious and unconscious longings and their realizations were at the core of American identity, its culturally and genetically miscegenated soul. This was the variously veiled and deliberately denied narrative of American life. And I talked and wrote about it often. It made people squirm. But I had loved and loathed too many of these men and their sons not to understand their contradictory impulses and leave the tale unwritten.

There were variations, of course, to this pale, waddling stereotype haunting the halls of the *Times,* evidenced by the cosmopolite who'd hung with Hemingway in Europe and wrote for the *International Herald Tribune.* Sauntering toward me one day, he gallantly expressed his own veiled desire: "My dear, had you lived in another time you'd have been a great concubine of the de Medicis."

A presumed *royal* whore or not, I would not have railed at him under any circumstances. And, despite his rakish manner, aware of his failing health and incomprehension of the sexist and ethnic insult easily inferred, I stopped, acknowledged him with a slow, imperial nod congenital among the Caribbean women in my family, and informed him that "in another life, I *was* a de Medici."

The female variants of these men could often be identified by the penciled slash above each eye masquerading as a brow, their equally fifties cardigans, and their icy acknowledgment of me in the ladies' room. Younger ones, cloaked in Liz Claibornes, would simply blurt perkily, "You're so exotic."

In an editorial conference, when I pitched a story about changing cultural perceptions and suggested that, while plants and animals might be called exotic, it was worth questioning the appropriateness of the label for fellow human beings, one young female editor exploded: "Well, why can't I call someone exotic? They're exotic if I'm not used to them. What's wrong with that?" Which emboldened another editor, who liked to tout her New Age consciousness by telling me of her ability to swallow a towel and pull it out of her ass, to say how disconcerting it was to drive through her once White, English-speaking neighborhood and be bombarded by signs to the right, left, front, and back of her in Korean, Chinese, and Japanese characters — only. I agreed, it was uncomfortable.

I recalled returning to my Brooklyn neighborhood from college one night. I approached my home and the Orthodox synagogue two doors away, then stopped abruptly in fear. I saw a white cross, suspended in the air, burning brightly near our brownstone. The Klan, I gasped. My body tilted forward over frozen feet. Gradually, I realized the cross was lit by neon and had been attached to the former synagogue by the Baptists who'd just bought it. It was most disconcerting, as was the loss of the best bagel shop in Brooklyn just a block away and the proliferation of mediocre Caribbean bakeries. I was half Caribbean American. I got the best "West Indian" cooking in town from my own family. But we couldn't make bagels.

Change was hard, I reiterated. But she persisted. It was as if she didn't count anymore. And with a melancholy ache in her voice, or perhaps a raw throat from her peristaltic feats, she remembered with longing when Southern California was a purer "Iowa on the Pacific."

It was not long after that I heard about the civic-minded driver whose bumper sticker lamented the historical blunder of White folks not picking their own cotton: IF I KNEW THEN WHAT I KNOW NOW, I WOULD HAVE PICKED MY OWN COTTON. This was the stuff of America, not just L.A. But I wanted out. I was profoundly homesick. I'd been away from New York for fourteen years and longed to be back in a city where dogs were prescribed antidepressants so that they could face leaving their apartments. Compared to home, there was insufficient intellectual stimulation in L.A. to mitigate the horrors that resided in both places. The *Los Angeles Times* had been good for me professionally because it brought my work to a larger audience. But I had to get out of the business before it squashed my spirit and the city killed me.

The lung infection had led to asthma, the doctor told me. Acute. My lung capacity had diminished by 60 percent. Steroids were rejected as part of my treatment because of the possible nasty side effects. Consequently, my recovery was slow, several months of feeling helpless, depressed, and near death just as I began work on a new book that, more than most, demanded a life of its own, because it conjured up so many personal ghosts, and thrust me into writers' prison for several years just as I was planning to escape the plantation of newspapers.

I dragged myself from the kitchen to my recliner and eased onto the seat. I parted my lips to steal a shallow breath and fell back, limp, from the spasm of coughing that triggered. My fingers crawled toward the remote control buried in a crevice of the chair I pressed a button and in real time death played on . . .

A young boy, hands clasped behind his back, waddles into a store. In blurred, grainy, black-and-white silence he reaches his sister, already at the counter. She is paying the merchant, a Korean woman. Someone else approaches the counter from the rear of the store, a Black teenage girl. She stands waiting her turn. In the mute video, the merchant speaks to her and points to her backpack. The girl turns sideways to show her the contents of the bag. The children watch, then slowly back away as the quarrel escalates. The merchant leans over the counter and grabs for the girl, catching the left sleeve of her black sweater. The girl tries to slap her hand away. The merchant holds on, pulling harder. The boy hops sideways toward the door. His sister backs away too, her arm springing up in a defensive reflex when she sees the girl swing at the shopkeeper's head with the backpack. The merchant snatches it. The girl swipes the woman's chin with her right fist, then slams her fist into the merchant's eye. The woman's body crumples toward the floor, but the girl tugs at the bag, pulling the merchant toward her, punching her in the face again. The merchant falls but comes back hurling a stool at the girl. The girl dodges the flying stool. The shopkeeper reaches under the counter, comes up with a holstered gun, and seems to scream for someone as she fumbles with the weapon. The girl picks up the bottle of orange juice and hands it to the merchant. But the woman knocks the bottle away. As the girl turns toward the door to leave, the merchant grips the gun with two hands, aims at her, and shoots. Literally dead weight, the girl drops to the floor. The merchant's left hand flies free, revealing the glinting barrel of a .38 in her right palm. Her knees seem to buckle. She leans over the counter, looking for the body. She presses a hand to her injured right eye, still screaming for someone. Seconds pass; she reels backward, on the verge of collapse. A man enters the picture, the merchant's husband. He rushes to his wife behind the counter, then looks over it, staring at the fallen girl. He picks up the phone and dials 911, then paces behind the counter and peers over the divide at the girl's body. A customer walks in — a Black man with a doo-rag wrapped around his head. He stops when he sees the body, then moves closer. He is waved away but comes closer still, stares at the child's body, turns, then shambles out the door, muttering to himself in apparent disbelief.

The silent images ceased on the screen, but not my vision of the fifteen-year-old's corpse as it lay in her coffin just months before. I'd gone to Latasha Harlins's funeral. I'd seen her teenage girlfriends weeping in the packed-to-overflowing church. And I remembered, particularly, the grim, caramel-colored face of an adolescent boy who sat rigidly upright in a corner seat and refused to cry as he chewed violently at his lower lip.

I'd been to too many funerals in recent years. In the church, I thought about my cousin who'd turned his life around too late. He'd left the street life and drugs, determined to be a good father to his young daughter, whose mother was an addict. As a little girl, I'd adored Jeffrey. He was not only handsome but gentle — a Catholic boy with an angelic countenance who could fix anything electrical, the nuns said. But in my eyes he fell from grace by committing the mortal sin of stealing from our grandmother to support his habit.

When I last saw him, he'd just been released from the penitentiary and was living with his mother. He did not look like Ricky Nelson anymore. His face was pasty and pocked. His hair was sandy and thin. Though I did not want it to be, my voice was cold and formal when I said, "Hello, Jeffrey." Between puffs on a cigarette, he glanced at me sideways and said, "Hi, Jill," my childhood name, then averted his eyes and stared again through a window of the sprawling, half-inhabited tenement he maintained in exchange for rent. Among the cityscape of Harlem rooftops before him was the scene of his approaching death — a payback shooting for an old drug deal gone bad. His younger brother, Frank, would self-destruct from alcohol and drugs a few years later, his truncated existence spent trying to prove how bad he was in the eyes of other Black men, too. And Bobby, their gray-eyed junkie brother, who gave up explaining he was Black long ago and just passes for what people want him to be, calls me irregularly from prison, trying to get money. I never accept the calls. Their struggle to be accepted as Black, and the compensatory bad-ass nigger profile they often assumed, might have been unnecessary had their mother not also been a casualty of the urban reservation.

Spotted by a neighborhood madam during the Depression in

Harlem, my alabaster-complexioned Aunt Glo was a teenager when she was snatched and set to turning tricks that filled the erotic fantasies of Black men seeking the forbidden flesh of White women, and Northern White men hungry to indulge themselves with a local octoroon look-alike on the cheap. For one night, they could savor the illusion of being Rhett Butler when his kind was after the *real* action, far from the likes of Scarlett, and paying handsomely for it — a house, servants, the whole elaborate system of concubinage that existed in Rhett's Charleston and known as *placage* in New Orleans.

In her salad days, a fun-loving gangster's moll who arrived, to my prim mother's disgrace, at the airport one Saint Patrick's Day wrapped in ermine, with her hair dyed green, Aunt Glo was a useless disciplinarian and undoubtedly laughed off debates about the substance of a Black identity she never denied or elaborated for her children.

My grandmother, who lived to see Glo, her youngest child, die, was a foreign dignitary without portfolio. Her ample bosom would heave when, still outraged after fifty years, she told me she was ordered to step off the curb and into the street to let White women pass on Lenox Avenue in the Harlem of 1919. A privileged Creole princess with servants of her own in Jamaica, she was, with her bearing, education, and British colonial accent, a perfect candidate for scrubbing toilets in America. When my grandfather finished medical school and decided to practice in the South, she refused to join him, fearing Ku Klux Klan terrorism. It was the thirties. Lynchings were very popular. They divorced. But up North, she and her four children almost starved to death during the Depression. And she didn't have a clue what to do with Aunt Glo, except turn her back out of embarrassment.

Granddaddy tried to reclaim Aunt Glo, forcing her to join him in Georgia. But in exchange for something other than cash, I suspect, she got a White taxi driver to take her out the state, out the region — all the way to the Apple. Then, Granddaddy was merely furious. Years later, she would break his heart.

Arriving in New York alone on business, he checked into Harlem's Teresa Hotel. When my proud physician grandfather was comfortably ensconced, the departing bellman mentioned that if he got bored he could arrange some company for him, then rattled off all the available entertainment, among the list, the name of his own child.

To some of my family I am an annoying *griot,* an unending repository of tales told in the daylight or overheard in the night. They are always trying to forget and I want always to remember and understand the web of human frailty, calculated social action, and the corrosive posture of "benign neglect" that culminates in the pain I see so close to me. I thought of this when I wept at my Aunt Glo's funeral, watching her obese form, which never left the house for years except to attend the funerals of her children, who lay in the same spot as she just a few years earlier, and where my grandmother's casket would rest afterward. I pondered this web upon all their deaths.

Of course, others distilled my motives to something more base, more human. "You really hold a grudge," the managing editor of the *Miami Herald* once told me.

"What makes you think that?"

"Well, twenty years later, you tracked down the man who killed your grandfather."

I could not deny the element of vengeance. In tracking down my grandfather's killer, I was tracking down a thousand anonymous bigots whose acts would never be known, whose guilt or innocence would never be judged. Men who killed a Black man and laughed. Even men who, without malice, killed a Black man and sighed, knowing it ultimately did not matter. I wrote this at the time. And I felt a similar sense of urgency about Latasha; that the circumstances of her life and death must be revealed for whatever they were. Though other events were rapidly overshadowing her shooting, Latasha was not insignificant to me. The corpse of a murdered Black child before me, her peers trembling with a sense of loss and the knowledge that her future may be theirs tomorrow, made memory — individual and communal — a deep well easy to access.

At the tape's end the VCR clicked off and the local news flashed across the television screen, broadcasting, once again, the videotaped bludgeoning of the man whose international appellation would become "the Black motorist Rodney King." I watched, again, Police Officer Laurence Powell, up at bat, strike some of the forty-something blows against the insufficiently submissive King on a March night in 1991, thirteen days before Soon Ja Du would kill Latasha Harlins. As if prompted by some mystical, levitating force, my right hand rose slowly, my last three fingers curled toward my palm, my index finger eased into position, I aimed at the screen — and heard the hiss of a speeding bullet dragged from real time into slow motion pass my lips, *Phewwwwwwwwww.*

Just a year before, an acquaintance offered to teach me how to use a handgun. The man, whom I'd been interviewing for a prescient piece on the combination of police brutality and Black-Korean tensions leading to the fire next time, reached for the top of the china cabinet in his dining room and came down with a .38-caliber handgun. He placed the gun on the dining table and suggested I pick it up. I froze. Even when it was unloaded, I could not bear to touch the weapon. Its capacity to snuff out life angered and frightened me. Cars evoked similar emotions. Several tons of metal hurtling down the road were a machine of destruction. And at about the age of seven, when I moved to Harlem to live with my father, the alcoholic who thought himself an intellectual behemoth among mental midgets, I began to have a recurring nightmare. I was trapped in an automobile rocketing straight down 129 Street, smearing babies in strollers across the pavement beneath its wheels, felling the maze of edifices called the Manhattanville Projects, and plunging me to the bottom of the Hudson River. Automobiles were symbols of potential destruction familiar to me. Guns were not. They struck me as an alien, as well as dangerous, monstrosity — but one that would become

enmeshed with the careering horror of cars disturbing my childhood nights. So, the suggestion of a date with this guy and his
wife on the firing range repelled me, as did the accompanying
advice that a woman, particularly one whose work took her out
and about as much as mine, needed a gun for protection.

Despite the T-Birds and Mustangs that threatened my childhood sleep, for years I drove around the country alone and unarmed for the solitude, for the excitement of exploring places
and people as alien to me as I was to them, and for perverse
amusement when I realized that my self-assured charm, palpable
intelligence, and "strange" African hairdos intimidated my fellow Americans along interstates and back roads. And alone and
without a gun, I'd tracked down Larry Harper, the man who
had been drunk and drag-racing when he killed my grandfather
and was let go without the bat of a lash by the Bainbridge, Georgia, cops. I found him, an insurance agent struggling to make
ends meet by selling vitamins on the side, two decades after he
thought no one would care or remember. Answering my knock,
his wife opened the door while he hid behind her and his son, a
young boy, maybe sixteen, bare-chested, wearing blue jeans and a
pained expression.

When the *Miami Herald* sent a disinterested Southern White
reporter down to Bainbridge after me to question him further,
Harper ran into the men's room of his office building and hid in
the stalls, bleating, "Leave me alone; you better leave me alone."
Though my grandfather had been targeted by the Klan, I believe
Harper killed my granddaddy accidentally. Still, the death was of
no consequence to him or the system of justice that existed in the
town then.

After I found Harper, my aunt told me that Granddaddy would
have said to forgive him. "We can't live in this world with hate."

I felt no such charity. I wanted a thousand anonymous bigots to know that somebody's grandchild might knock at their
door too.

Knowing the monstrous and minor indignities Black people

survive each day, I found that the act nourished and satisfied me the way a dish of hot cheese grits do on the coldest, hungriest day of a Black woman's life. One could be victimized as a historical fact without internalizing a sense of victimization. I was not tragically colored, as Zora Neale Hurston once put it. "Even in the helter-skelter skirmish that is my life, I have seen that the world is to the strong regardless of a little pigmentation more or less. No, I do not weep at the world — I am too busy sharpening my oyster knife."

But something had happened to me. I felt a creeping paranoia. Possessing a gun now seemed a viable option. Watching Rodney bludgeoned and Latasha fall, I heard the whistling of that imaginary bullet escape my lips, and a gun seemed necessary. A gun suddenly seemed a requirement of my United States citizenship.

I was approaching as many years on the planet as the number of blows Laurence Powell is estimated to have landed on the prone Rodney King, and I felt vulnerable in a way I'd never known before. It was a sense of *racial* vulnerability that had been gaining psychic momentum, I would realize, for a decade, tied to emotions I had staunched in my search for Granddaddy's killer. And all the psychological and intellectual brakes a woman like me — middle class, born to an intensely assimilationist family, with strong doses of Catholicism thrown in — uses to control both the anger and the fear that define the life of Black folks in America seemed to give way one day on the Pacific Coast Highway.

I'd jogged to my rented vacation home just short of the timberline among the sheep and felt my body sway as I tipped a bottle of water to my mouth. "I thought I was in better shape than this," I said out loud. Then I fell sideways, holding on to the edge of the counter for support. I soon discovered there'd been an earthquake about a hundred and forty miles south, in San Francisco, the October 17, 1989, big one. Driving up to Mendocino had been a pleasure until I left the lovely winding inland roads and was confronted by the Pacific Coast Highway and the narrow, undulating shoulder separating me from the cold and misnamed Pacific. Navigating the precipitous drops along the band of road as locals and truckers, hauling lumber to and from the Pacific Northwest, bore down and around me impatiently, unearthed every automobile-associated fear I'd possessed but had constrained since my childhood nightmares of plunging into the Hudson.

My sweaty hands clamped the steering wheel as I crawled back toward Los Angeles, taking detours compelled by earthquake-damaged roads. For seven hours, the usual several it took to reach Sacramento from Mendocino was a slow-motion defiance of destruction as traffic crept toward the quake-ravaged city and one driver panicked as a rock fell, causing a chain reaction of swerving cars, mine braking short of the road's edge. By the time I reached the main freeway, nothing could draw me to the right side of the road. My body had decided that the edge of every road led to the cold waters of the Pacific or a mountain-shielded abyss. And every hill, even bumps on city streets, paved the way to a fatal fall. Within months, I panicked on every freeway, suddenly intimidated by its vastness and the fear that my car would speed out of control at any second — and at moments I felt my hands would willingly fly free to let it. Such feelings were not unfamiliar to me; I'd known them off and on since the tranquillity of my early childhood in Brooklyn was disturbed by my father's violent outbursts. Because of him, order, control were all the more important to me. But they fled in the Harlem nights of my childhood, sinking in the Hudson's murky waters. Like a shell-shocked veteran, I felt my sweaty hands put a deathlock on the steering wheel as a rush of adrenaline compelling me to fight or flee overcame me, this time three thousand miles from the dark river.

        *   *   *

He came in late, just as the group at a peer-counseling conference paired off. I was the odd number in the row and without a partner. He saw me and beckoned.

Within minutes of my telling Mike about my highway panic attacks, he said, "Let's go." We were in the woods of western Massachusetts and he took me to his jeep and said, "You drive." The road had narrow shoulders, over which the drop was deep. Not the craggy coast of Mendocino but close enough. The speed limit was forty-five miles per hour. I crept along at thirty until the inevitable impatient tourist bore down on me and forced me to speed up. At forty-five miles per hour I felt out of control on the undulating road and put that deathlock on the steering wheel, decelerating to fifteen. I pulled over to the narrow shoulder and stopped, my hands still gripping the wheel.

"The shoulder's too narrow. I'm in the way."

"You're fine," Mike told me. "They can go around you."

Staring straight ahead at the cars coming toward and going around me, I sat as if rigor mortis had set in. He asked me what I was feeling. Shocked at my own words, I blurted, "Someone took my grandfather's car and was driving around town in it." I'd been told that long ago, but had forgotten, until then. Larry Harper hit him . . . skull cracked . . . hit the pavement, I said. The bashed 1953 Ford was carted off and retrieved by some White man, without my stepgrandmother's permission, I'd been told, and fixed up. "The mother fuckers just took it!" I suddenly screamed. Old memories, fragments of overheard conversations spilled out, "White-men-driving-round-town-grinnin'-at-my-grandma-from-Granddaddy's-car. Nigger's-dead-why-waste-a- good-auto . . ."

On a moonless night in southwest Georgia a photographer and I had searched for the house of Larry Harper. Lost along the narrow unfamiliar paths, we found ourselves surrounded by miles of farmland set afire. The farmer's torched fields flared toward the tall pines. There were no hooded men surrounding me in pickup trucks, just the setting for them and the amused voice in my head of the ancient White juror: "Never met a nigger worth a hundred thousand dollars."

I had written of all this, then carefully locked away the memory, even forgetting, unless I looked it up in my files, the name of Larry Harper. It was the vise of terror that gripped me on Pacific Coast Highway that seemed to loose this boxed-up fear and rage.

I wanted to scream, but I clenched my teeth. "We gotta go."

"No, we don't," Mike said calmly.

"They'll see us."

"Who?"

"And they'll hurt us."

"Why?"

"We're not supposed to be here. You're White." I panted, and started heaving. "They'll hurt us." He reached for me and wrapped his arms around me tight. I sunk into him, sobbing, but would not stay. I looked over my shoulder. It was not safe, I insisted.

When I was better, or at least when my lungs healed, I drove a straight shot down Figueroa Avenue, a main north-south drag that, to the north, led to L.A.'s downtown skyscrapers and genteel emblems of the city's past, like the Biltmore. To the south was the bleak Black and Latino neighborhood Latasha Harlins last called home. This unsettling city that had become my temporary home, this country — brutal and unwilling fully to confront its past so that it could be liberated from it — had never disturbed my sleep so much as in these few years before and after the "riots." Still, I dreamed, and despite my psychic distress could remember technicolor nightmares. But Latasha's family was summoned early to that dreamless sleep occasioned by the grave.

CHAPTER 4

THERE WAS DEATH in the family. It plagued theirs like cancer, heart attack, diabetes, or stroke in other families. It was not the consequence of some deadly pathogen or organic breakdown, but seemed a disease unto itself. Unnatural, violent death. "R. L. Harlins — I don't know what the R.L. stood for — we just called him R.L. — he died 1968, shot in a lounge in East Saint Louis," said his sister, Ruth. "I remember talking to a White man on the phone. He gave me information how to get to the hospital and where the back door for colored was."

"In 1968?" I asked.

"No . . . no, " she recanted slowly, searching for the details of a distant and unwelcome memory. "I guess it was before then. He got shot one time before he was killed." The shot that killed him was April 15, 1968. "May 24, 1968, I received Christ in my life."

Before that, her half-brother, Lionel, was hit by a car when he was eight years old. "Yes," she said, breathing deeply. "Oh-Lord, he passed too."

Curtis, another brother, "he got killed the same day as Crystal," her daughter. Curtis went into an East Saint Louis bar and never walked out. Shot. "I-ah, errr, I, oh," she struggled, tortured by expression though her small, pretty face remained strangely placid and incongruously attached to a five-foot, six-inch frame carrying too much weight. The burdensome flesh seemed to hide a physique that once was Hollywood's image of an exotic, statuesque siren circa 1950: that Abyssinian-looking Neapolitan Sophia Loren — her African proportions still the object of desire.

But the comfort food — potato salad, cornbread, and fried-to-the-depths meat — Ruth Harlins loved to eat had buried that likeness. She was the mother of four and grandmother of four — one from each of those generations dead before her — and she moved laboriously at times, short of breath, at fifty.

Thanksgiving of 1985, as her brother Curtis lay dead two thousand miles away, her child Crystal was found shot to death on the floor of the B and B Club on Florence Avenue, now home to the Greater Resurrection Church, a short drive from Ruth's home. The family said Crystal Harlins was sitting at the bar doing her nails when she and Cora Mae Anderson got into an argument. Anderson shot her in the chest. Crystal, relatives insisted, had simply gone to the club to celebrate her boss's birthday. But witnesses told police she was also a regular customer, known for her boisterous behavior. Anderson, who contended that Harlins had threatened her, was sentenced to five years in prison.

Six years later, Crystal's daughter, Ruth Harlins's granddaughter, Latasha, would be killed by Soon Ja Du inside the Empire Liquor Market at 91 Street and Figueroa in South Central L.A. — just around the corner from her grandmother's apartment.

She sat there now, a back three-bedroom flat on the first floor of a two-story beige-stucco building. Hers was a garden apartment without a garden, only concrete. In the narrow, always dim living room, she recalled how she had left her home in East Saint Louis in 1980 to escape the infamous poverty and crime of that Mississippi River city. But her family seemed unable to escape the ubiquitous and fatal happenstance of days and nights on America's urban reservations: *A five-year-old-boy was shot in a Chicago playground yesterday . . . A Brooklyn mother of eight was killed in the crossfire of gang violence while . . . A beloved teacher in the Red Hook section of Brooklyn was murdered while walking through a housing project on his way to see a student who'd missed class . . . An eight-year-old Korean American girl was shot point blank in the chest after a robber held up her parents' Los*

Angeles convenience store, turned to leave, then, as an apparent afterthought, fired at the cowering child . . . The reservation's economic prisoners knew the pattern well, and sojourners, like the merchant class of immigrants Soon Ja Du represented, learned it too.

"The police came to the door. The first question they asked me was 'When was Latasha's birthday?'" the girl's aunt recalled. "Mama just started crying; she already knew too. But I just said, 'This can't be true. I don't think this is Tasha they talking about.' I started shaking and trembling. And Mama, she didn't fall out, but she was at that breaking point. She didn't scream. She wasn't loud. She just kept saying she couldn't believe it was Tasha. Shay, that's my little girl, she just went chargin' off." She and Tasha were the same age, like sisters. "She took it real bad. She had a real bad attitude. She went running up and down the street, screaming, 'It can't be Tasha, it can't be Tasha, I know that bitch didn't kill my cousin.'

"The police said they couldn't identify her, she had no ID on her, so they went knocking on everybody's door, showing them a picture they'd taken of her body. There was this gang of people in front of our house. They kept trying to tell the police where we lived 'cause they took so long to come to us.

"They wouldn't let us identify the body immediately. They wouldn't let us even go to the coroner's office," Denise Harlins recalled in a hoarse, weary voice two months after the shooting, a dazed look in her eyes. Latasha's aunt still seemed suspended in fog as she sat in a booth at the venerable Pacific Dining Car eating lunch on a Saturday afternoon in May of 1991. The weekday power-breakfast-and-lunch contingent of downtown lawyers, judges, and stockbrokers was absent. The quiet, clublike converted dining car, known for its simple, good food and unobtrusive service, seemed a suitably untrendy and closeted atmosphere for the conversation. The only other diners in a back corner of the restaurant proved to be a white-haired matron and her attorney discussing heirs to the woman's apparently substantial estate.

"The coroner had the body but we couldn't see it until it was taken to the mortuary, but we never got to the mortuary," she said, because things were so confused. "We did not see Latasha until the wake. I couldn't understand why we couldn't see the body at the coroner's," she said, shaking her head. "They just told us we couldn't.

"When my sister died, none of us had the strength to go down and see her. None of us wanted to. Crystal's best friend ended up ID-ing her. It was a big shock when Crystal was killed," she said, her sad eyes widening. "When Latasha passed away, I was better prepared to handle it." Still, inevitably, she wonders out loud, "Who will be next?

"When Crystal died, it was especially hard because I never told her I loved her — I'm just not that type of person. I never even told Mama I loved her. We was always in church. Mama was always saying the Lord is going to do this and — she makes me mad. She is extremely religious." She suddenly laughed. It triggered a phlegm-filled smoker's cough. "One time, she backslided for about three or four months. Boy, she was somebody else. I never seen her like that. We argued the whole time. We stayed in a constant battle. I had never seen my mother change in so short a time. She started smoking cigarettes, drank a beer here and there. Mama is a sweet, sensitive person. She doesn't let anything get to her. But she started cussing and stuff. I ain't never seen Mama do this. I said, 'Uh-uh, this ain't my Mama.'"

"Was that back in East Saint Louis?"

"Here, in L.A.," Denise said. "About two or three years ago. She had stopped going to church for a while. She hadn't found a church that she liked, and in the process, she'll tell you, the devil gotta-holda-her. I got my own opinion what the devil looked like —"

"And what car he drove." We both laughed. She coughed again, then settled back in the thickly upholstered booth.

"After Crystal passed, I started kidding and hugging Mama and telling her I loved her. When Tasha died" — her tone turned to disgust — "I said, 'I'm out of here.' If Blacks owned that store instead of the Dus, I don't think this would have happened. I'd like to get out of the neighborhood, but the family can't afford to move now. We're totally broke." Silently, she picked at the salad in front of her, then ate a little.

"I get scared thinking about my little girl Shay. She has a heart condition and —" She stopped abruptly. "I had a dream one night, suppose something happened to my daughter? That would really be the cracking point. I would really lose it. Shay has an enlarged heart and a heart murmur. She has to be particular about what she eats. She loves hot sauce, spices, and stuff that's bad for her health. You instill in a child that her life depends on her eating the right stuff, and it seems that she's been paying more attention. But Shay kind of hard-headed. I can't be there 24-7 and monitor the way she eats." Even if it's not her heart, what else might take her life, she wondered. "Crystal, now Tasha. I'm just left wondering what have we done to deserve this kind of punishment? Why," she asked an unresponsive universe, "is this happening?"

She breathed in deeply and offered a weak smile. She resembled her mother, though shorter. As she approached thirty, she was edging toward the same burdensome weight her mother carried, but, like her, possessed a pretty, poreless face whose natural bronzed beauty seemed subcutaneously lit by the sun.

"The children need some counseling to get through what has happened. Mama is always talking about God will heal up all the hurt and pain. And I say you got to do for yourself and God will come along and help you. I know he is the complete healer, but sometimes . . ." Her voice trailed into a deep pit of annoyance. "At no point can I discourage her from that attitude. Though she did say she would try counseling for a month."

"What about you?" I asked. She was not only depressed but

exhausted from her nonstop efforts to organize the Latasha Harlins Justice Committee.

"Me, I try to work my anger off through stuff like the Justice Committee, making sure Latasha is not forgotten, that her killer is punished, and maybe start a recreation center or foundation for children in her name. But the kids, I been checking them real close lately, especially Joshua, Latasha's brother. I saw him staring at the picture."

"Of Latasha?"

"Uh-uh, the lady's picture, Soon Ja Du." He had picked up a newspaper with her photograph plastered across the page, one of the hundreds of articles about the case Denise had been methodically clipping and pasting into bound notebooks since the killing. She found the boy still as stone, sitting on the sofa in that living room where blocked sunlight and inadequate lamps submerged the space in an endless twilight. "He was just looking with this anger in his eyes and I said, 'Why are you looking at that, Joshua?' And he said, 'I don't know.' But he just kept looking at this woman's face. That's what started me checking him out real good. He never cried. I mean, he cried at the funeral, but he never cried no more. He is a strong little boy. But as strong as he is, it scares me. He has never talked about his feelings except to say that he misses his sister. But the way he kept staring so hard at that picture — I have a real fear about that. When he grows up, I don't know what his attitude will be like.

"Ronnie, on the other hand, she'll cling to you. Anybody comes in the house, she'll hug you and stay up under you."

"That's Veronica, right?" She nods and says Latasha's youngest sister is eight. "My daughter is more easier to talk to than Joshua. Shay will let her feelings out. I'll sit with her one-on-one and we'll discuss it. And sometimes she'll break down and say how much she misses Tasha. I went through that experience with her a couple of nights ago. Whereas Joshua, he has no parent, particularly a father, here to help him."

"Could he help, even if he were?" She rolled her eyes at the thought of Sylvester Acoff.

"If it wasn't for Mama, his children would be in a foster home 'cause nobody in this family would have been able to take care of them — a large family with three kids in it. Mama's got a big heart. That's a lot for someone to take over unless they truly love the children. He had the opportunity to take those children many times. Mama never had anything against Vester. If she did, she could have filed custody papers after he abandoned them. But she said those are his kids, and he's more than welcome to come and visit them. I was the one who asked her why don't she file custody papers in case he comes back and tries to claim his kids after she done the best she can."

Since Ruth Harlins was not the children's legal guardian, she could not file a civil suit against the Dus on behalf of Latasha's estate. But Latasha's father — a convicted felon living in Illinois — could and did. Acoff filed a $10 million wrongful death lawsuit against the owners of the Empire Market. And he was being represented by Geraldine Green, the attorney who initially represented the Harlinses in their civil suit against the Dus.

"I am telling you, when the *Los Angeles Times* reporter called me up and told me that this man, out there in Illinois — who begged and borrowed $800 from his own people and several hundred dollars from Mama to come to Tasha's funeral, yet never showed up — is trying to profit from her death with our own attorney's help" — she sucked her teeth — "I think there is a conspiracy going on over our heads, and everybody is going to end up getting rich and the family is going to end up in the slum house just the way it usually is set up."

Denise would sound this conspiracy theme often. From the infamous Tuskegee experiment in which the government deliberately let Black men with syphilis go untreated from the 1930s through the 1970s, to the unproven genocidal plot of White scientists to infect Blacks with the AIDS virus, and the undocumented certainty that Church's Fried Chicken restaurants, so popular among Blacks, were secretly owned by the Ku Klux Klan, which put something in the chicken batter to make Black men sterile — living in the margins of a racially oppressive society provided fertile ground for such an attitude. With the kind of rationality that betrays middle-class smugness, however unintended, I quoted the critic Andrew Sarris to her: "It doesn't take a conspiracy to be racist in America. It takes a conspiracy not to be." She got it, but was unimpressed. There was, in fact, more going on over our heads than either of us knew.

I reminded her that she'd dismissed Green.

"Yes, and she went and tracked down Vester and filed the $10 million suit on his behalf. She dumped Mama 'cause she wasn't the legal guardian, instead of helping her get custody. She didn't give a damn about the family. And Johnny Cochran" — the most prominent Black attorney in L.A. — "sold us out," she claimed. "He said he'd fight to get Mama declared guardian. He said it could be a landmark case because so many women are in her position — grandmothers taking care of children without having legal custody. But I'm totally depressed now, 'cause he tells me yesterday we can't win the case. But that's a damn lie. He told us we could. But he went to Seoul, Korea, on a business trip with a lot of other high-profile Blacks, and it's only after he got back that he's handing us this line. I believe some kind of dirty deal was made between him and the Koreans, and I told him so. But all he said was, 'Denise, you could do all the hoop-lahing you want, but you are not going to win that custody case.' I haven't told Mama yet; I don't want to upset her."

Ruth Harlins would, one day, take a closer look at Latasha's birth certificate: Latasha Lavon Harlins . . . born January 1, 1976, 3:30 P.M. . . . Christian Welfare Hospital, East Saint Louis . . . Mother: Crystal Harlins, 16 . . . But the father was not named — though Sylvester Acoff's name was on the birth certificate of Crystal's two other children. Whether Acoff was even Latasha's biological father was soon in doubt.

Denise went on. "I'm the most strongest one in the family right now. It's me who has to work things out for the family. Mama is all with the Lord God Jesus and I am looking more at the reality part of it. Something needs to be done more than that." I asked her what she felt the family needed most now. She gave me a what-don't-we-need look.

Her mother worked as a clerk for the Department of Social Services. "She's only able to bring home $1600 a month," Denise volunteered. "Two of the kids she gets welfare for. I was working until June 1990, but I had to take off 'cause of my daughter's heart problems. I was about to return to work when Latasha was killed. Trying to organize the community around her death — I'm telling you, I keep getting myself kicked in the butt. There's a lot of stuff I just don't know about. My family doesn't know about a lot of stuff. And all that's going on is just hitting me in the head like a hammer."

"What do you mean?"

"There are all these people trying to make money off Latasha's death." She named Danny Bakewell, for one, a well-known Los Angeles activist and wealthy landowner who ran the Brotherhood Crusade, one of the nation's leading Black charities. He was known for his confrontational style and mastery of both boardroom and street politics. There were, as yet, no reports of him parting the Pacific, but if he couldn't do it personally, chunks of Black L.A. happily believed he could arrange it.

He and others, she said, "talk about opening stores in the Black community and perhaps buying the Dus' store, now that it's shut down, and letting Black people run it. I asked Danny if he would allow a percentage of the profits from the store to go to Latasha's brother and sister and a foundation in Latasha's name. I ain't heard from him no more. And I don't even consider him the worst. I'm learning that Danny's always looking out for Danny. But in the process, he was the first to at least act like he was supporting the family publicly, and he helped to get the Dus' store closed down."

A week after Latasha's death, at a rally in front of the Empire

Market, Bakewell declared, "This store will never reopen," and taped butcher paper to the front door with a message on it: CLOSED FOR MURDER & DISRESPECT OF BLACK PEOPLE.

When she was looking for help in organizing that rally, Denise said, she called the local offices of the Urban League and the National Association for the Advancement of Colored People. "I tried to reach Joe Duff [president of the Los Angeles NAACP chapter]. I couldn't get past his secretary.

"Politicians and all these community organizations are focused on getting Gates out of office," she said, referring to Daryl Gates, the Los Angeles police chief on whose watch Rodney King was battered. "I'm not saying that's not important. But this is a child that got killed. Daryl Gates and Rodney King is big news now, and folks got on the political bandwagon. But they need to show some leadership about this too. This is not something that is going to pass over. This is a big situation. These Koreans ain't going to change without some big action. It's all about big trade-offs, people way up there," she said with a generalized but deep bitterness. "It all goes way back, businesswise, political, economical."

People, she said, were using Latasha's name to promote their own political and economic agendas. If everybody else was making money off Latasha, she wondered, why not her family? It was part question, part demand, and full of hurt . . . not mercenary.

"Sometimes I just say forget it and go on back to work. But if I do that now and court is coming up, I know I can't keep no job with all that back-and-forth to court. And I have no intention of missing a court date. So I'm thinking, maybe I'll work for a temporary agency — once I go and get me a car — and just work it that way. But by me being on welfare it gets complicated." The right corner of her mouth twitched upward — it could hardly be called a smile — as she elaborated on the poor person's social maze. "If I work part time and they find out, they'll cut me off. So I got to get a job that pays enough to where I can just cut off from welfare. Because I don't have a car, friends take me and Mama to court. My mama got to take a bus back and forth to work every day. Why?" Then, "I had to put in an extra phone to handle the Justice Committee work. I had to open a post office box. This takes money we really don't have. The family is totally broke."

Latasha would have wanted her family to be financially stable, "that's one thing I do know." That's one reason she wanted to become a lawyer. "All of our lives we had to do without. Why should we constantly have to go through a struggle when a child has paid the price of her life and not reap something? And I just feel like everybody is getting rich off her. Why? Because we don't have the knowledge, the education behind us, to know the loopholes and what's really going on out there."

"Who are you looking for to help you?"

She said she hoped someone would organize a major fundraiser that would benefit Latasha's brother and sister — "that's what I mean when I say Latasha's family, and Mama, since she is responsible for the kids." But it's not all about money, she insisted. "If it was, we would have taken money from those Koreans who wanted to come see us."

"Which Koreans, the Dus?"

She shook her head. "Leo Terrell was calling me for two weeks — he's counsel for the local NAACP — he called us after Latasha was shot."

"What did he want?"

"He was trying to hook me up with some Koreans so they could offer their condolences."

"Did they offer you money?"

"Yeah, it was all kind of confusing. I don't know how much exactly, because I told Terrell to call our attorney. We didn't want it to look like we were just after money, and we really are not, then or now. But Terrell never did call our attorney, and we didn't pursue it. So it really wasn't just about money. But why should my family be catching the bus all over town while these big political leaders running around in their Cadillacs and limos?

"Every time I look around something different is going on and we are the last to find out about it." Exasperated, she grabbed the sides of her head with both hands and smoothed her hair pulled into a bun.

"I know if I let this stuff get to me, I'll drive myself crazy. Mama's attitude is: 'I'm not letting my hair get gray over people.' She's always talking about her hair turning gray — Mama has this beautiful hair but she keeps it covered up with a wig 'cause it got gray in it — 'and it's in the Lord's hands and he'll do the best for the family.'" She stabs a piece of steak on her plate.

"If nobody gets nothing but Latasha's brother and sister, that would be okay. But that daddy, he didn't give a damn, in my opinion. He don't care nothing about his children. Instead of everybody in the family joining forces, like we asked him to on this lawsuit, he's out here scandalizing the family name."

He's been in and out of jail, she said. He was sitting in an Illinois prison convicted of burglary as we spoke. "He was in trouble out here in California because of something to do with drugs. He came running into the house one night like a crazy man, grabbed his things, packed his bag, and was out of here in five minutes, trying to get away from some gangsters who pulled up outside the house.

"Joshua says he loves his daddy 'cause that's what his grand-mama taught him. But once, when his daddy was in town, I asked him if he wanted to go live with him, or at least visit him. He said no, he'd rather go play ball. He knew what was up with his daddy. 'My daddy hasn't been here for me' is what he said. 'He hasn't taken care of us.'"

And Latasha didn't particularly care for him. "She was old enough to see and understand what her daddy did to her mother in front of them. He beat Crystal up one time out there in public. Tasha wanted to have a party for Joshua at Chuck E. Cheese's. And after they came home, they all went up to the liquor store and then a gang of them went up to the house. On the way, he really did Crystal wrong in public. And they saw all that." Vester

Acoff beat her even worse on other occasions, court records
showed. Crystal eventually had to get a court order to keep him
away from her.

Still, Denise's mother told the kids, "'Your daddy loves you
and he'll write.' The only time he wrote was when he was in jail
and had nothing else to do. He sent one letter to Latasha last
year."

I asked her about early news accounts of Latasha's death that
suggested she was a runaway. Police found a change of clothes in
her backpack.

"Latasha and me argued the night she went out. Latasha and
me had a problem," Denise acknowledged, an unguarded response that would become increasingly rare from any member of
the family in the months and years ahead. "I had a problem with
Latasha. By that I mean she wanted to spend the night out at a
friend's. I said, 'No, you don't need to spend the night out.' And
Mama, being the way she is, trying to keep us from arguing and
stuff, not arguing but disagreeing, she went on and let her spend
the night out."

"It sounds like the problem was deeper than one night out.
Was it?"

"Mama was responsible for Latasha, but I played a big role,
too. She was my sister's child. I loved her like she was my own
child, and I didn't want her to make the same mistakes I made
when I was young."

"Having a child?" She nodded. She'd had her own child when
she was Latasha's age.

"I went to the ninth grade and had to drop out." Later, she
received a high school equivalency diploma and then attended
secretarial school.

"I feel like every parent should know what the kids their child
hangs out with are like. Tasha had her own style, her own way.
She would never let no one take advantage of her if she got her
eyes open." But some girls in the neighborhood jumped her recently because she wouldn't join a gang. And there was one girl in

the crowd Tasha hung with who particularly concerned Denise.
"She let these guys pull a train on her."
"Pull a train — you mean a gang bang?"
"Yup."
"Was that the girl Latasha spent the night with?"
"No."
"Who'd she spend the night with?"
"I think it was Marcolette."
"Marcolette who?"
"You know, I don't know the child's last name," Denise told
me, though I didn't believe her. I made a mental note to track
down Marcolette.

In a tired, musing voice, Denise said, "She wanted to be with
her mother."
"Latasha?"
"Uh-huh. She had this empty feeling inside her." She rarely
talked about Crystal, but whenever she passed the Inglewood
Park Cemetery nearby, she cried, even though her mother wasn't
even buried there.

"But Latasha also wanted to be an example for her brother and
sister," Denise said. "She was kind of the leader of the family. She
was very protective of her brother and sister. But she really cling
to her grandmother."

A waiter interrupted. I said no to dessert. She asked for coffee
and a chance to think about what else she wanted. I was afraid
the momentum had been broken. Respectful of their grief, cogni-
zant of their distrust of the media and concern for their privacy, I
had been very careful not to push Latasha's family for informa
tion but to let them tell me things at their own pace. I wanted to
cultivate a relationship with them that could be sustained over
time. It was frustrating and too often unrewarding, but this time
Denise continued with no prodding.

"If me and Latasha had not had a long heart-to-heart about
five days before she died, I'd be on a big guilt trip now." Several
days before that, they'd had a big "falling out," said her aunt. But

they made up. "I thought you wanted to be an attorney," she'd reminded Latasha that night. "I thought you wanted to have things for yourself." And Tasha had said, "I do," and had promised to try harder in school. She did well in junior high school and was an honor student in earlier grades, but she was doing poorly at Westchester High, where she was in the ninth grade when she died.

"She was very strong, very positive" in that last conversation, Denise recalled. "She told me she was going to talk to her counselor at school about bringing her grades up. We laughed and we cried for two hours. Then she went into Mama's room and sat on the floor and told her we had made up and what she was going to do."

She was not the average fifteen-year-old, Denise said admiringly. "She could conversate on any subject. She could see the future, so to speak. But you know, she was naïve about certain things, too. Tasha had this big old thing — this smile. This love thing. She had a big heart," she said softly. Her tone suddenly changed, as if her saliva glands were pumping vitriol that coated each word. "This was a child shot in the back of the head. And that woman who shot her in anger is now playing half-sick in some wheelchair."

Days after the shooting, news photos of Soon Ja Du showed a dazed woman in a wheelchair. Stories about the shooting tended to present a fuller, more personal picture of Du's life than they did of Latasha's. Perhaps, because she was the one still breathing, there was a more human dimension to the stories about Mrs. Du. Too, there was simply more to tell. Soon Ja Du was forty-nine and Latasha fifteen.

"You don't pull a gun out of a holster, aim, and shoot it as the girl turned to walk away," her aunt spat out. "If she wanted to hurt Latasha, do something else. Say, 'Get the hell out of here. Don't come back again.' And then you got this Black attorney of hers trying to say it is an accidental death. That hurts even more. And the Du son, Joseph, he has a real nasty attitude. I have this article saying that he told police Latasha came in the store trying to rob them. Tasha had no weapon," she said emphatically. "I guess they must have forgot about that videotape that the police confiscated.

"How can Charles Lloyd defend those people? He saw the tape. Is money so important to him? I wouldn't care what kind of background Latasha came from or what she did her entire life. What that woman did was cold. If that tape gets released, I just know that the public will go stone crazy."

CHAPTER 5

IT WAS an August afternoon, and the light then, in this part of southeast L.A., was a sorrowful brown. The city's infamous smog always hung heavier on the east side of town, but to the south the cloud of pollution met urban grime and economic desperation in the desert heat, generating a grimmer haze. Here, near Central and Florence, where the city line met county streets, a knot of unemployed Latino men stood drinking on a corner . . . there, five blocks away, two carless Latino women juggled children and grocery bags on the long walk home . . . at a stop light, an old woman with Mayan angles to her weathered brown face pushed a shopping cart holding all her worldly goods through the busy intersection . . . and every few blocks there seemed to be a church . . . Not much changed farther west along Florence Avenue, except that the faces grew a deeper brown and some of their myriad ancestry could be seen in Ruth Harlins's face and form: Akan, Hausa, Wolof? Choctaw, Creek, Cherokee? German, English, Irish?

"I don't know," she said, as I drove her home from work. In her hometown, one could pick from any of those columns, stir 'em up, and come out with Ruth Harlins. She was born in Tuscaloosa, Alabama. Her people came from there and nearby Aliceville. All she could remember was that they were sharecroppers and domestics as far back as anyone knew — at least until her mother took her to East Saint Louis when she was eight and started driving a taxi.

"They broke up," she said of her parents. Her father's people raised her in Aliceville. "Lula Thomas was my father's mother and Ed Thomas was her husband. He was my stepgranddaddy." She was particularly close to him. "When he was dying, my relatives kept calling me: 'Please, please try to get here.' I didn't have nothing to get there with. I asked my landlord to take the rent late," she recalled without emotion. "'Two weeks and I'll pay you.' But he wouldn't do it." Ed Thomas finally died, without seeing her, in a convalescent home in 1984.

"Is your father still alive?" I asked.

"He's dead."

"What was his name?"

"Emmett Harlins."

In 1956, when she was Latasha's age, she boarded a Greyhound bus in East Saint Louis bound for Cleveland. When she got to the Cleveland depot, she placed a phone call.

"Hello," a woman answered.

"I'm Ruth Harlins, and I'm here to see my daddy," she blurted to the surprised woman on the other end.

"You stay right there," the woman told her. "Somebody will be right over to get you."

Emmett Harlins was living in Cleveland with his new wife and her daughter. "I had a nice time," Ruth recalled. "He drank, maybe like an alcoholic. But I loved my daddy. I kind of look like him." He took her around town, showing her off to friends. "We were on the bus and we were supposed to get off and I wasn't sure which way to go and ended up running to the back door while he went out the front. He laughed and told everybody on the bus, 'That's my Little Margie.'"

"You know who Margie was?"

"Oh, yeah." I'd been attached at birth to the television like most baby boomers and had seen every rerun of the comedic perils of Gale Storm on *My Little Margie*. She was a younger Lucy kind of character, whose father, instead of husband, got the emotional pie in the face each week.

I took my eyes off the road to catch Ruth smiling girlishly and wagging her index finger in a gentle scold. "I can hear him now: 'That's my little Margie.'"

We reached Figueroa and turned south, away from the city's skyscrapers. She recalled Tasha and Shay walking home from elementary school along their section of Figueroa. Even then, Latasha had been a strong, athletically built girl. And Shay, then as now, a frail pretty one. Sometimes, because of her heart, Shay would become so weak and tired that Tasha would scoop her up in her arms and carry her for blocks, past the neighborhood's ubiquitous liquor stores, past the knots of unemployed dark men conversing near them, past the grim glitter of unswept gutters, till they reached their destination.

Shay's ninth-grade English teacher remembered how difficult Latasha's death was for her. She was already having comprehension problems in school and was reluctant to get help, Terry Mernin told me. "And just as she was about to get it, Latasha was killed. Shay missed a lot of school. She told me she was unable to sleep." People around her kept talking about death. "Her house was always full of people having meetings and talking about Latasha late into the night. But she seemed lethargic even before then," he recalled. "I thought she might have been malnourished. She was so thin." He didn't know, he said, she had a heart condition.

English teacher by day, rock musician by night, the thirty-three-year-old Mernin had taught Latasha too. He was her favorite teacher, Marloe Alexander told me. She was a classmate and close friend of Tasha's. But another classmate described Latasha as a "teacher's worst nightmare."

"Hmmmmm." Minnie Crews considered her answer. Now retired, she'd been the dean of students at Westchester High for fifteen years. And during the six months Latasha was there, "she was in my office more than the average student. I tell you one thing that was strange to me. When a student is in trouble in school, I would get in contact with the parent." In Latasha's case,

"I found it unusual that I could not make contact with some adult who was responsible for her consistently." For one thing, "there was no telephone at the home. And the number I was calling was the grandmother's job. I'd talk to the grandmother, and then out of nowhere, the aunt — what's her name?"

"Denise."

"Yes, Denise would appear. It was hard to tell who was responsible for the child."

Deeply offended by the suggestion that no adult was supervising her grandchild at home, Ruth later told me that Denise responded to calls from school when she was at work. "I was responsible for all my children. That's a cruel thing for that woman to say and it's untrue."

"Now," Crews threw in, "Denise has a daughter at Westchester. And what's really sad to me is that she is being neglected so the mother can be in the limelight. Her mother is dealing with the Latasha issue in the media when she has a child alive she should be dealing with. But that would take her out of the limelight. That child is lost. It's so sad."

I asked her if she ever met Latasha's grandmother.

"Yes, and I felt she showed genuine concern. But I was very surprised to find out the grandmother was as young as she was. From talking on the telephone to her, I'm thinking I'm dealing with an older person. A matter of fact, the grandmother's younger than me! And here I thought I was dealing with this tired old woman — and she might have *been* tired, but it seemed like she should have had more energy or a little more time to deal with whatever was going on. But she *was* open to hearing what I had to say and trying to rectify Latasha's behavior — even though not too much happened with the child."

"Who is this Minnie Pearl person?" Denise exploded when she heard what the former dean of students had to say.

"Minnie Crews," I told her.

She sucked her teeth. "That woman don't know nothin' about my mama, me, or Latasha. Who is she to say anything about this family? If I'm not out here trying to get justice for Latasha, who's going to do it? You think I want to be out here doing what I am doing?"

When, again, I asked Crews why anyone would say Latasha was a nightmare, she responded: "Well, when I met her, she *was* a teacher's nightmare. I don't mean she'd jump on a teacher physically, but she did cut her classes, her academic work was poor, and she was maybe a little bit of a smart-mouth — she was disruptive. But I can't remember precisely why she was sent to my office. Just two weeks before she died, she stole her folder out of my office. We keep a folder with a record of the student's visits — when the student came in, what action was taken. And she just took it. So there's no record now of why exactly she was brought to me."

Crews didn't sound particularly fond of the child, so why, I asked, did she attend Latasha's funeral?

"Well, I was concerned that this had happened to a student from my school. And I felt Westchester was so White-oriented that not too many were going to show respect and attend. I'm a Black person and this was a Black child, so I said let me do this to show I care." At first, she admitted, she didn't connect Latasha to the teenager who'd been killed that Saturday morning in the Empire Market. "Before I realized who this girl was that got killed, all the students would describe her to me as the girl who was always smiling this beautiful smile. That's when I said, 'Oh, God, yes. She was just here in my office last week.'"

Latasha the nightmare. "I didn't see that side of her," said her friend Marloe, a soft-spoken, doe-eyed teenager who aspired to be a dancer. She had no telephone, so I tracked her down one Sunday morning outside her house in Compton, just as she drove away to church. Her father, a part-time gospel musician, and her mother, a laid-off teacher, said they'd have to discuss whether they'd allow her to be interviewed. The father said he'd call me but didn't, and I found her one afternoon between classes on the sprawling Westchester campus. We sat in my car in the parking lot, away from the bells and thousands of milling students.

"Latasha," she told me, "was real attractive too, with a really nice figure. You can't tell that from the pictures of her in the paper."

"No," I agreed. In fact, she looked rather homely.

"No, no. Latasha was really cute and she had a lot of boyfriends." Both girls had had Mernin for ninth-grade English. "I knew Latasha could be tough, and she would speak up if she didn't feel she was being respected." But Marloe never saw it.

There was little doubt in my mind that a very White, very middle-class school like Westchester could be a tough place for a girl like Latasha — very dark, poor, and made to feel, consciously or not, defensive about it. In a school essay, explaining why she wanted to become a lawyer, the ninth-grader wrote: *The most important thing to me is that my family is always protected by a shield so that they won't be harmed by dangerous, ruthless, uncaring people.* In that same essay, written for her history class a few weeks before she died, Latasha said she hoped to graduate from high school with a perfect grade-point average and go to college. Perhaps that was why, knowing that neither her academic record nor behavior had been stellar in her freshman year, and having promised her grandmother and aunt she'd get her act together, she stole her file from Crews's office.

But Marloe reiterated that she never saw the defensive, hostile side of Latasha, because her friend had needed no emotional shield with Terry Mernin. "A lot of teachers don't respect students, but that would never happen with Mr. Mernin, and that's the only class I had with her, so I didn't see any negative behavior. He respected all his students and tried to relate to them. I guess it was easy for him to do, 'cause he was young, too."

"I'm still not over her death," Mernin said hoarsely, the sound of late nights and the tough streets of Boston's Irish neighborhoods in his gravelly voice. He wore a mustache and short beard. His dark hair was brushed back off his face and fell just below his earlobes. He had attended Latasha's funeral, too. His own brother had died in an accident at the age of sixteen. "How can you get over seeing a fifteen-year-old girl in a casket? Yeah, she was a tough kid. Really rough around the edges. But she was intelligent. She could do good work. But she was absent a lot. I thought she might have problems at home — I don't know. She also lived a long way from school." Westchester High was on the opposite side of town from where Latasha lived. "She had to take a lot of buses to get here; maybe it was too much. But I really liked Tasha." When I asked why, he seemed indignant. "What's not to like about a fifteen-year-old kid? In many ways, she was just a naïve little girl. And she had this smile, this wonderful smile."

Latasha's grandmother pointed to a bus stop. "I try not to do too much thinking about it, but I get sad when I get off the bus from work. Before that, I be okay. Then, it just comes to me. I remember how in the morning, sometimes, I be running a little late for work and I'd run to catch the bus. Latasha would be on the other side of the street and she'd watch me run a little bit, jog a little bit. Then I'd have to stop. Her eyes were right on me, real steady. And then she'd jog a little — you know, to give me a little encouragement 'cause I'd be out of breath."

And when she came home from work on payday, "the fifteenth of the month, check time, she and Shay and the other children be waiting on me at that bus stop and I'd go to the store to cash the check. Yes," she said with a sigh, "they'd all be there, smiling, waiting on me."

Just a block before the Dus' market, we turned off Figueroa and pulled in front of the Harlinses' apartment house.

The neat living room was still and, as always, dark in the midsummer afternoon. I noticed a package of hamburger meat sitting on the kitchen sink. "This beef is out here getting warm," I called to her. She'd headed for the bathroom. When she came out, she grabbed a mop. The toilet had run over. "Richard must have left it out to thaw," she called out in a strained voice while she mopped. She'd told her son she'd make a little spaghetti for dinner.

"I don't know why the children aren't here," she said, a bit winded as she talked and mopped. "They're supposed to be home. When I come in" — she walked toward the living room — "I generally just come on in and rest" — she leaned on the mop — "and have a cup of coffee." She put the mop away and walked to the rear two bedrooms shared by five people.

"Nobody done any work back here," she complained loudly. "They should have had the house cleaned. I tell Denise they should help me out a bit. But" — she approached me with sudden, quiet animation — "what I'm going to do on my vacation is get my floors together and get me some pictures and things — 'cause I really don't have the place the way I want it." She toed the shag carpet. "I was going to get a washer and dryer and put right there," she said, pointing to a space along the wall of the small doorless kitchen a few feet away. But that would have to wait. "When I wasn't working I could keep my house better than this." She opened a sliding door that led to the concrete back courtyard. "Let some air come in here."

"Please," I told her, "do whatever you would usually do. Have a cup of coffee."

"Will you have some?" she offered.

"No, thanks. But some water would be fine."

She put her coffee cup on a cocktail table that separated two sofas facing each other in the living room. "I like to sit here, when it's quiet like this, and listen to my gospel music."

"I'd love to hear some."

"Okay." She stood to sort through some cassettes and put one on.

"I accepted Christ into my life over a year now," she told me as she sat back down.

"But you backslid a little bit," I teased. "Denise told me." She didn't respond. "You're only human," I said gently.

"I came back to Christ, uh-hum, yes. At times like these and places like this you really need the Lord."

Mama, I wrote this song for you . . . not because time has colored your hair white . . . but because one day brought us together and one day will take us apart, but we will be together again. The song's oppressively saccharine soliloquy filled the room as her son came through the front door. A tall, slightly stoop-shouldered figure with gangly arms, he had a childish manner that belied his twenty-six years.

"Hi you doin'?" I asked.

"I'm doin' okay," he said gently, his voice high-pitched and Southern. "The man upstairs says he works for a cable station and he's doing a show about Blacks and Koreans."

"What's the show?" I asked.

"I don't know 'cause I don't have cable."

"You look like you've been up to mischief today."

"Who-what?"

"Mischief."

"Mister what?"

"Up to mischief."

"No, uh-uh."

"I'm teasing." He didn't respond.

His mother sighed. "I guess nobody did no work around here today, but that's okay."

"I did — I did," he answered quickly. "I cleaned up my room and I cleaned the kitchen before I left. 'Nise said they gonna clean the other stuff."

"They did?" his mother asked.

"They say they *gonna.*"

"What did you do today?" I asked.

"Ahhh, nothing much."

"Like what?"

"I went shopping and got that stuff." He pointed in the direction of the kitchen but at nothing in particular.

"That didn't take all day," I teased gently. "What else did you do?"

"Nothing much."

"What do you usually do during the day?"

"Work part time," he told me.

"Where?"

"At the Probation Office."

"Did you do that today?"

"No."

"How many days a week are you there?"

"Several days out of the week," he answered in a firm voice tinged with resentment at the interrogation.

"What type of work do you do there?"

"Huh?"

I repeated the question.

"I do a lot of things. I answer the telephone. I, I mail in reports. I call up their clients and I file the mail in the boxes, and that's about it."

"Do you enjoy it?"

"It's temporary."

"What would you like to do?"

"Security."

"Oh, yeah?"

"At first I really wanted to be a policeman, but I changed my mind."

"Why?"

"'Cause I can't carry a gun. I am a Christian now, and God said thou shalt not kill. If I kill someone, then I would break one of the commandments. Isn't that right, Momma?" he shouted, though she'd only gone the ten feet to the kitchen to refill her coffee cup.

"Security guards carry guns, don't they?"

"I'm going to be unknown," he explained.

"You mean, like under cover?"

"Right."

His whole life changed, he told me, when he got saved. "I used to do a lot of things, like going out, going to clubs and drinking. I stopped hanging around my old friends I used to be with. A lot of them turn their back on me ever since I told them I got saved through the Holy Ghost. They told me, 'I give you two more weeks before you go out and sin again.' But I kept going to church. And when I see them a month later and told them I'm still saved through the Holy Ghost, they were shocked. They told me they not my friends anymore. And I told them I don't care. Jesus my friend."

"You have new friends now?"

He hesitated. "A few."

"Are you pretty much a loner?"

He laughed and shook his head. "With Jesus inside of me, I don't feel alone." Suddenly he gushed, "I forgot to tell you this. I won the usher-of-the-month award at church three or four months ago." He rushed out the room to get the plaque.

"Yes," his mother said as she put on another gospel tape, "he be there all the time. I think he missed one time since he's been going to church three or four months."

The Reverend Al Green started singing.

"I used to keep a list of two hundred records I wanted to buy — from the fifties, the sixties, the Coasters, the Platters, Al Green, Diana Ross. Then I got saved," she told me.

"Me too," Richard said, showing me his award.

I said, "Saved a lot of money, huh?"

"You got that right," he told me. "I gave all my rock 'n' roll records away."

"I've been looking for a recording of 'Fix Me Jesus.' Do you have one?" I asked.

"I have 'Jesus Will Fix It,'" he answered eagerly.

"No. I've been looking for the version used in 'Revelation', the Alvin Ailey dance." They looked at me blankly, and I was instantly ashamed that I might have embarrassed them with the unfamiliar reference.

"I don't have a very large collection," Latasha's grandmother said apologetically.

Shay came home and said hi to me with soft annoyance in her voice, her eyes never making contact with mine. My presence rubbed at the unhealed wound she carried from her cousin's death, and she wanted all reminders of it banished. She looked at her grandmother. "M'dear, they won't cash my check without an ID, I don't have one." She'd been given a summer clerical job at Danny Bakewell's Brotherhood Crusade office.

"I guess your mother will have to cash it for you." Suddenly buoyant, her grandmother asked, "Shay, whose record is that?"

"Tasha's," she answered, a conditioned, instant response whose only reward was the fleeting joy the song's association conjured up for her grandmother. Then, to the music, the child walked back to the room she shared with her mother and Ronnie. *Everything is gonna be all right . . . He's coming back for the true and good, just like he said he would.*

Ruth said, "I'd be ironing or something and I'd have on 'Jesus Will Fix It,' and she'd come and switch it to 'Everything Is Going to Be All Right.'"

We sat for a long time with little conversation, listening to the music. Then she volunteered quietly, "I know I'm going have to move from here. I come home from work and I be okay. But then some of Tasha's friends come over and it gets to me." She started trembling. "Sometimes I pass her friends' houses or the center, that Algin Sutton Recreation Center where the kids play, and it's having an effect on me. I just passed by one of her girlfriend's house the other day and started crying. And I realized I was crying because they are still alive and she's" — her voice cracked — "not . . . She was more my daughter than granddaughter. Soon Ja Du has her daughter to laugh with. I hear her daughter is going to college, and she's there with her mother and everything and I'm left without a granddaughter and it hurts, very bad; it hurts. She was my joy; now I don't have that. There must be *hate* in their culture to shoot somebody like that. I admit Black folks have killed too, but a pistol is not the answer . . . If I really hated I could start a lot of things going, I could have a vendetta going on . . . *You"* — the word came out a painful squeak — "start thinking about *violent* things when you start hating." I sat stonily, but felt the prick of recognition. "I'm just glad I accepted Christ in my life. Oh, Lord, I feel that he has blessed me . . . Sometimes Tasha and me" — she started rocking gently, her voice quivering with misplaced inflections, and I felt her suppress a volcanic force that sent veinlike fissures through her words — "we . . . g-go, to the store, you know, *down*-town. I got her some dresses, a cou . . . ple of dresses, and I said, 'Tasha . . . take-these-two-dresses-right-here'" — she said it in a rush, as if there was no other way to get the words out. "And Tasha said, 'No, M'dear. You don't have to buy but one. You don't have a whole lot of money.' And I said, 'We got to get them for church.' And that's like the last time we were together, alone," she said quietly, having capped the volcano for now, "just the two of us.

"We stopped in for some pictures, too. Woolworth, you know, four pictures out of the machine for a dollar. Two of them were nice, but she didn't know how to pose. When the red light come on, you had to pose. I think she was off target. But on the third one, she got on target. We laughed about that and she say, 'M'dear, I didn't know what to do.' But she got it together," her grandmother said proudly. "Two come out real nice, but she gave them away to somebody. I wish I had more pictures of her. I don't like the one they got on the buttons and flyers. She looked much nicer than that."

It was dark now. Neither Joshua nor Veronica had come home yet.

"I know Veronica and Joshua are at the recreation center — Joshua loves his basketball. But I told them I'd like for them to come home from school first, then go out."

We heard footsteps, then a man's voice at the open front door. "How you all doin' this evening." It was Brother David, the member of the Justice Committee who'd helped to disturb the peace of the Biltmore ballroom. We greeted each other. "I hope I'm not interrupting anything," he said.

Ruth just smiled. "How you doing, David?"

"I'm just fine, Ms. Ruth." He picked up a book on the coffee table, *Psychology of Winning,* and fingered a set of tapes called *Positive Self-Image.* "What is this? Some subliminal programs?"

"Ah, no, not subliminal. This tells you about your self-image, things like that. I got my real estate tapes there too, and my goals tapes. I got sales tapes. It tells you about no money down. This man said all you gonna have is rent receipts if you don't buy." And she pulled out a batch of rent receipts from a folder holding the tapes. They made a rustling sound as she waved them in the air. "He's right, that's all I got, and I don't want that for the rest of my life."

Ronnie came home and sat down without speaking. I'd been coming to the house off and on for weeks, and after a few heartbeats asked her, "Did you tell me hello?" She said nothing, looked at me shyly, her left eye larger than the other and strangely immobile, then reached for me with open arms and hugged me. David had left and Ruth was in the kitchen.

"Ronnie, you need to let me do something to your hair," her grandmother said. Sections of the child's hair stood in peaks at different angles from her head. Her grandmother surveyed it and said, "I'll wash it a little later for you and press it, hear?"

I never saw Joshua that night. He seemed to live at the Algin Sutton Recreation Center. On the occasions I did see him, the boy, who looked as if he'd be an even smoother, more beautiful ebony as a man, and had already inspired women to say they could eat him with a spoon — was silent, with question marks in his soft eyes, in my presence.

I picked Ruth up from work the next day, and we spent the early evening talking in her living room again. "I got these shoes on sale at Payless, but they got to go back," Richard said. "They don't fit."

"On sale for what?" his mother wanted to know.

"It's in there in the bag." Richard told her.

She pulled out the sales slip. "Fourteen ninety-nine."

"They usually cost seventeen ninety-nine," Richard said.

"I remember the time I used to buy shoes for a dollar ninety-nine cents."

"When was that?" I asked her.

"Oh, Lord, when I was a young girl, like a teenager."

Ronnie ran into the living room. "M'dear, can I have some ice cream?" The truck was outside playing its siren song.

"Didn't I give you a dollar?" Richard asked her.

"No, you didn't. Fifty cents."

"Uh-oh," Ruth said, "You want some money? Oh-Lord, better go in there and get them books and learn some words."

"M'dear," Ronnie whined, "give me fifty cents."

Richard threw in, "That's what my mother used to do to us sometimes. When we wanted money she'd say, 'Ah, go get the math book; go get the spelling book.'"

Ruth nodded. "Yes, I'd give two cents a word. Then give them a bonus word worth a dime. I'd give them a lot of words so they could accumulate. But you know, they'd leave it just as if I didn't say anything. I guess they didn't want that ice cream that bad. Or maybe they wanted it at the time, but they didn't want to do what it took to get the money to buy it."

Veronica's face was hanging near the floor now. "I want ice cream," she whined.

"I know you want ice cream, darling. M'dear know. M'dear know," she told her tenderly. Veronica went over to the sofa and tried to crawl into her grandmother's lap. "They get to the place where they run over me if I don't make them earn that money." She told Veronica to get up. "Oh, Lord, I sat on this couch so long I can hardly get up. Got to circulate," she said, hoisting herself up.

"Richard," she called, "would you go to the store for me?" She was going to make some more spaghetti and meatballs. She went into the warmer kitchen area, but it could have been hotter. The perennially shaded apartment was one of the cooler unair-conditioned places in town that day. *101 degrees in Woodland Hills . . . 98 at Riverside . . . 102 at San Bernadino, 98 at Palmdale . . . but 87 at Santa Monica*, the TV weatherman informed us.

"Okay, Mama," Richard answered. It was a short drive to the Boys supermarket but a long walk in the heat.

Pouting, Veronica rubbed up against her grandmother. "Here." Ruth handed her fifty cents. "Go get you some ice cream. But when you come back you have to study some words."

"You gave in," I said lightly.

"No-no. She's gonna do the words. But it'll take Richard a while, and I know she's a little hungry. In the meantime, I'm going to write down her little spelling words and then I'm gonna *subtract* that money from it."

The next day I was alone with Joshua in the living room, waiting for his grandmother, as he strained in the bare light to do his homework, a workbook full of words he had to define. He'd gotten right all the ones he'd done. I praised him. He looked at me shyly, said nothing, but smiled, ever so faintly.

We'd been riding together a few minutes when she asked me, "Did you go to college?"

"Yes, m'am."

"Four years?"

"Yes."

"Did you do more than that?"

"Yes."

"Oh, my. You have a Ph.D.?" Ruth asked.

"No, a master's."

"That's really nice and everything. It's best if you want to advance to go to college?"

"It can help."

"If you get a Ph.D. you'd be called doctor," she said with admiration.

"I don't really need a doctorate. But I do enjoy learning," I said as we sat under a freeway overpass, waiting for the light to change. I was concentrating on the traffic, concerned that she'd be late for work. I had been late picking her up, and she wasn't ready when I arrived. She'd noticed a spot on the blouse she'd put on that morning and decided to change her whole outfit — that, and six people competing for one bathroom, caused her uncustomary tardiness. She was always attractively dressed — usually a pretty blouse, like the white one she wore that morning with a portrait collar, and a full floral print skirt. And she carried herself with a simple dignity.

"I enjoy learning about things too. On television, I like watching public TV, learning about different cultures," she told me. And then she shared with me that she'd gone to college for two years. "I actually went four years, but I say two because I have two years' worth of credits. What happened was I was under a lot of pressure at the time. It was pretty rough for me and everything."

She'd been on her own since she was seventeen. What she said next, the redundancy of it in the lives of poor people, made it too painfully familiar for jaded observation. She had become pregnant and dropped out of school. Having children, taking care of them. Then, taking care of her children's children. That's the reason Denise followed her to L.A.; she couldn't handle trying to work and raising Shay alone.

"I've had little jobs off and on. In East Saint Louis, I went to Lincoln Adult Evening School to get my high school diploma. When I started college and everything, you had to pay your rent, your bills. Oh, God," she said more bemused than self-pitying, "raising children by myself. Sometimes I had to buy food and just not go to college. When I was in school, I sometimes only had a quarter. It cost a quarter to take the bus to school and back. I had to decide which way I was going to ride and which way I was going to walk." Most times, she decided to save the quarter for the ride back home, "'cause I knew I'd be so tired."

We pulled into the parking lot behind the welfare office and she got out. She had to be at her desk by seven-thirty, and it was a little past that. "Thank you so much. I really do appreciate this," she said.

"Have a good day. I'll be back at four-thirty."

"I'm telling you," she said, as she buckled her seat belt for the ride home, "I got to get me some kind of business of my own."

"Was there a problem because you were late?"

They were strict about time, she said, but there was no problem. "They add up the minutes you're late, and if it reaches a certain point, then you get a reprimand."

Until Latasha died, she'd not missed a day's work. "If you be on time and don't miss any days, everything's okay. You gonna do the work when you get there. So as long as you take responsibility for those two things and just make up your mind to work five days a week and enjoy yourself on Saturday and Sunday, things will be fine.

"But ownership of your own is better than anything. I want some nice property, something people would enjoy living in, for myself as well as other people."

She fell silent while I concentrated on navigating the rush-hour traffic. I'd noticed there weren't many places to eat, except greasy spoons, around her Gage Avenue office. "Where do you have lunch during the week?"

"Well, today we had Mexican food — a place across the street from my job. I guess it was a hot tamale and some beans and slaw and some rice. They didn't have any hamburgers, or I would have had that. The food tasted okay, but I guess there's nothing like my kind of food."

"Burgers?" I said with a laugh.

"I like hamburgers, but I like collard greens and cabbage and things like that. I can't understand Richard. At home, in East Saint Louis, he ate ham shanks and cornbread and collard greens and potato salad. Since he got here, he's been eating so much junk food. I would rather have me some good greens, a piece of corn-bread, and potato salad — something like that — any day."

I asked what she thought about her visit to a Nation of Islam mosque with Denise the previous Sunday. Denise had been invited to let the members know how they could aid the Justice Committee's efforts.

"They read out of a different bible, the Koran. And they were talking about the Black man should get out and do something for himself. And the Black man should take control and Blacks should get off their behinds rather than wait for people to do something for them." She was nodding. "I believe that too. We been oppressed long enough, they say. But you know what really astonished me?"

"No, what?"

"They believe Muhammad is a savior just as we believe Jesus is the savior. And you know, I thought about that. Muhammad did not come down here and die for me on the cross. And it come to my mind that Muhammad did not rise on the third day for me to have eternal life. They believe in the resurrection, but in the mind. Do something for yourself. That's what I think too. But Allah, God? Muhammad a savior? That would be a conflict for me."

As we neared the apartment, I asked her if she'd had a chance to get counseling for the children.

"Denise called the Victims' Assistance Program and they arranged for a Saturday counseling session, but I had to take Veronica to the doctor."

"What was the matter with her?"

"Ah, well." She hesitated, then said, "She had to go to the eye doctor."

"I noticed something the matter with her left eye. What happened? Is that a birth defect?"

"No, no, no. Tasha hit her in the eye with a fork."

Coolly, I asked her, "What happened?"

"She didn't mean to do it," her grandmother said defensively.

"She kinda got mad with her, got upset, and threw the fork at her. It went right in her eye and put her eye out. But when that happened Tasha told me, 'M'dear, I'm so sorry. I wish it hada been me.' She was all upset after that. She didn't know Veronica's eye was going to be put out."

"Does she have any vision out of that eye?"

"She can't see but out of one eye."

CHAPTER 6

RICHARD raised his arm and gave a dismissive flip of his wrist in the direction of the Dus. "I used to work for those people," he grumbled. Soon Ja Du, her husband, Billy Hong Ki Du, and their oldest son, Joseph, sat nearby with their attorney on a bench in a fifteenth-floor corridor of the Compton Superior Courthouse.

"When?" I asked.

"Last year. During the summer. In June."

"June of 1990?"

He nodded. "When I was there, only an aunt named Martha, and the son, named Joe, and the father, Billy, worked there. Mrs. Du wasn't there. They fired me because I wouldn't work for free."

"What do you mean?"

"They fired me because I refused to work overtime." Another family member, he explained, left, and the Dus hired a replacement. "But that person didn't come in until twelve o'clock, so they asked me if I would work overtime for them and I said no. And he said, 'You supposed to work for free, do what Black people are supposed to do.'"

"Now wait a minute. Who said this to you?"

"Billy Du," he answered emphatically. "And I looked at him, stamped my foot, and said, 'No, I'm not working for free.' And he said, 'Fine, go home.' So I went home, and two hours later the son, Joe, called. He said, 'Why didn't you stay there like my father told you to?' I said, 'He told me he's not going to pay me for working overtime.' He said, 'Well, Richard, you're fired.' And I said, 'Fine,' and hung up on him."

I asked Latasha's uncle if he'd had any other problems with the Dus. "They treated me nice most times," he told me. "Although every move I make he would watch me, even in the bathroom. He thinks I take tissue. That really upsets me."

"Who was this now?"

"Mr. Du, the husband. I never take anything," he went on. "I ask for what I want. And if he said no, fine. I'm not going to steal or take nothing if he asks me — I mean, unless I ask him," he corrected, "or her or whoever in the store at the time," he went on, struggling to be precise. "I cannot make him or her give me an orange juice or soda or whatever I want. I would have my own money on me, but sometimes, once in a while, they should give me something free or a discount, since I work for them. But otherwise they treated me okay. But they were really terrible to the customers, never smiling or saying thank you. I would do that when I bagged the groceries."

I seized his declarative mood to probe him about a rumor. "Are you feeling better? Have you completely recovered from your stab wound?"

"Ah, ah, yes, I'm okay," he answered.

"It happened shortly after Latasha was killed, around where you lived?"

"Yeah, uh-huh."

"How did it happen?"

"I'll-I'll-I'll tell you about that later."

"Where were you stabbed?"

"Roxanne!" he suddenly shouted, spotting the deputy district attorney prosecuting the Du case. "Hi, Roxanne!" he yelled to her across the corridor.

"How are you?" she responded, straining to be polite and dignified while hollering in a courthouse.

"I'm much better now, I promise," he boomed.

"Promise?" she called out at half his volume.

"I not gonna act up no more," he assured her.

There had been an outburst by Richard in the courtroom. He and everyone else involved with the Du case had been frustrated by the delays and round of pretrial hearings. In May, a grand jury indicted Du for first-degree murder. The D.A. had sought the indictment to avoid a preliminary hearing and expedite the trial. But the defense kept stalling. It was five months since Latasha's death.

On this particular August morning, a phalanx of sheriff's deputies and bailiffs blocked the Harlins family's view of the proceedings. And in the competition for front-row-center seats that occurred with each court date, the Du family and their supporters beat them this time. There was a sense of defeat among the Harlinses even before the actual trial began. And during a short recess, Richard angrily demanded that the officers move, then snapped at reporters when asked what the uproar was about. "No comment!" he shouted, as the rest of his family, their friends, the Dus, and their advocates shuffled out the courtroom, each side jostling the other and muttering insults.

Just before he revealed his short tenure with the Dus, I found Latasha's uncle standing outside the courtroom during the recess, talking to a family friend. He stamped his foot. "Sometimes it gets to me. I want to grab them by the neck and just start choking."

"They want to provoke you into disrupting the court so they can say they don't want us here anymore. All the time we have been in there they've never stood five or six abreast in front of us before. But you have to remain calm," Malkah told him, gently touching his shoulder with a graceful hand that sported intricately painted four-inch-long nails.

She was another member of the Latasha Harlins Justice Committee. Unknown to the family before she read about Latasha's death, she'd become, in just a few months, Denise Harlins's closest confidante and press liaison for the committee. The older woman, who was about the same age as Ruth Harlins — and seemed to play the role of both big sister and cool mama to Denise — went variously by the names Gina Rae and Queen Malkah.

"Why they need all those security people?" Richard asked her.

"Because," she answered in a motherly tone, "we're *bad* people." Richard cackled. And as if telling him the details of an incredible fairy tale, the one-time exotic dancer widened her eyes in mock alarm and explained, "We just scare folks and everybody shakes in their boots when we come to court." I expected her to whip out cookies and milk next.

"Yeah," he agreed, "they think we're bad and gonna start some mess."

"Right. They started it, and we ain't done a thing."

The seething hostility displayed that August morning had characterized these courthouse encounters since Soon Ja Du was arraigned in Compton Municipal Court on March 26 and charged with first-degree murder. She faced thirty years to life in prison. She pleaded innocent. More than a hundred members of the Valley Central Presbyterian Church, where Du was a deaconess, packed the courtroom that day. The outnumbered Harlins family sat in the front row, center aisle, businesslike in their dress and demeanor.

Security was heavy. Four bailiffs were posted in the courtroom. Two deputies stood off to the side in a holding cell, while two others observed the proceedings from a corner. When Du appeared in the courtroom, a group of middle-aged Korean immigrant women let loose an anguished cry.

Once the privileged child of the only doctor in a Korean farming village, she hobbled to her seat, her hands cuffed behind her back, her neck seemingly unable to support her bobbing head. Her face was puffy, her right eye badly bruised and swollen. Her breathing seemed labored, and she sounded as if she were weeping. Two Black male deputies flanked her, gingerly holding her by the elbows, easing her into a chair. She laid her head on the defense table, then slumped in her chair, a bent figure in a prison-issue navy smock, orange uniform, and crisp, white Reebok hightops — the laces removed as a standard jailhouse precaution against suicide.

As intended, Du's appearance aroused all but the Harlins faction's sympathies. To my eyes she definitely looked as if she'd gone through the ringer twice. Certainly, when she traded her homeland for the uncertainties of America, a first-degree murder charge was not among them. She stepped on United States soil in 1976, the same year Latasha was born, lured by the hope that her three children would thrive outside Korea's oppressively competitive school system. But the housewife and former Seoul University literature major was confronted with a shockingly diverse culture in America, a minimal grasp of English, and, for the first time in her life, was forced to work for wages. She found work as a couch assembler, then became a crocheter in a women's garment factory. When her husband, whose limited English kept him from rising beyond repairman at a Radio Shack store, bought his first market, the strain on her was too much. Working fourteen-hour days, she suffered from chronic migraine headaches and was hospitalized for several weeks after falling into what her family described as a coma.

My *Times* colleague John Lee, a Korean American, said that the sluggish drawl of Du's native North Chung Chang province was the butt of national jokes, but that her family enjoyed a position among the town's elite. I tried to imagine what her native village was like. The human interactions there could not have been very different for her father and his patients than for my Guyanese grandfather and the poor Georgia Blacks and Whites whose babies he delivered and who paid his fees in chickens.

I thought, too, about the calcified bitterness of my dethroned immigrant grandmother, who, till her delusional last breath, demanded an accounting of the silver.

I was not just the product of a community of willing Black

immigrants who both gained and lost status, however. While I felt an empathy for Du, harsher thoughts resonated with me as well. I remembered a woman named Jan Ford Atkins, a member of OMNI, the group planning to boycott several Korean immigrant businesses. There was an intensity about her when she spoke, but it was the cool, blue heat of a flame. She argued that the language barrier and cultural differences were not the essential problems between Black customers and Korean merchants. Not when you have Korean business people yelling racial epithets. "It's something Korean merchants don't want to correct. Even if their problem stems from a lack of fluency in English, I don't feel that we should have to learn their rude ways and accept it because they are here." Then, in a flat, bitter tone that conjured up the centuries-old anguish of a people, she told me, "I don't know what it's like to go into a foreign country and be free. I just know how it is to be raised the way I am here. I don't know how it is to take a culture somewhere and have to adjust because my culture was taken away. So there's a lot that I don't understand when it comes to the Koreans."

Du sat slumped through most of the hearing, apparently tranquilized. Her doctors would later say that the defendant was severely depressed and suffering from paranoid episodes since her incarceration. Doctors at Martin Luther King, Jr., Medical Center, where she'd been brought after the shooting, told police she faked unconsciousness, opening her eyes and looking around her hospital room when she thought herself unobserved.

She had been imprisoned without bail at the Sybil Brand Correctional Facility for Women the night of the shooting, then made a brief court appearance on March 19, represented by her first attorney, a Korean American named Tyson Park. He was granted a delay so that a Korean translator could be obtained and the forty-nine-year-old merchant examined for injuries.

Within a week, Lloyd had taken over the case. At the March 26 arraignment, he described Du as a housewife who posed no threat to society and had never been arrested for anything in her life. He pleaded she be released on a reduced bail set between $25,000 and $50,000.

The District Attorney's Office argued against it. "In this case," contended the young deputy D.A., Roxanne Carvajal, "she apparently killed a fifteen-year-old for no reason."

Lloyd implored the court. "I don't think there is any question she will appear in court. She can hardly stand or sit here in the seat. She is badly in need of medical care," he beseeched, choking back tears.

Carvajal pressed that the crime with which the merchant was charged was too serious to justify the granting of bail.

Lloyd renewed his appeal, this time on purely humanitarian grounds. "She is sick," he boomed, his voice ringing with moral outrage.

"We consider her to be a flight risk because she is from Korea and has ties to Korea," Carvajal rejoined.

Finally, Judge Morris B. Jones ruled that Du was entitled to bail on condition that she surrender her passport and stay away from her store. Billy Hong Ki Du fell to the floor, weeping. Her bail was set at $250,000. A Black man leaped to his feet. "How much did they pay you?" he yelled at Lloyd. Then he muttered under his breath, "You're a disgrace."

Korean Americans in the crowd burst into applause when the arraignment was over, and Lloyd spun around, telling them, "We'll have none of that."

Everyone wanted to know how Lloyd came to represent Du. One rumor circulating among downtown bureaucrats was that Mayor Bradley had called in a favor from his friend and former law partner. The symbol of a prominent Black attorney with well-known ties to His Honor defending the Korean immigrant merchant might defuse the ethnically polarized emotions surrounding the case. Further, it could be a potent antidote to the false image of Blacks and Koreans perpetually at war with each other, some contended. It might suggest, as well, that "responsible" Black people still held the moral high ground at a time when legitimate Black rage, inappropriately expressed, gave credence to the myth portraying the Black masses as menaces to middle class culture generally. Too, it might be an indicator of where the mayor's own sympathies lay. He had developed downtown Los Angeles at the expense of the city's poorer neighborhoods, and his pro-business inclinations had been rewarded with political contributions from a variety of Asian American businessmen.

Lloyd maintained that no Byzantine political machinations lay behind his selection. Joseph Du simply called him. "I defend people who are charged with crime," Lloyd told reporters. "I have received criticism from Blacks for taking this case. But I am in the business of practicing law."

The counselor had well-developed contacts with Korean Americans. He had owned a building on Western Avenue, in the heart of Koreatown, before selling it to Koreans, who turned it into the Korean Community Center. He'd defended many Korean Americans over the years, visited Korea, and, he reminded reporters, even rode in the Koreatown parade.

Lloyd also told reporters that, despite police claims to the contrary, Du (a) shot in self-defense after being attacked, (b) fired the gun accidentally, and (c) did not shoot Latasha in the back of the head.

On May 22, in Compton Superior Court, a judge told all the attorneys involved in the case to shut up.

"Is the family name Soon or Du?"

"Du, Your Honor," answered Lloyd.

"This case will be tried in court, not in the media," said Judge Robert D. Mackey. "There has been a tremendous amount of discussion in the press about this case, and it will cease."

"Is that the judge?" Malkah asked as she eased into her seat before the proceedings began that day. Mackey, a light-complexioned Black man wearing a pale yellow shirt, brown pants, and a brown leather pouch strapped around his waist, stood talking to Lloyd. "That'll make you sick to the stomach," assessed Malkah, surveying the judge.

"As long as he knows his job," someone else in the Harlins contingent told her.

"Well, I guess you won't see it with his legal robe on."

Later, at a meeting of the Latasha Harlins Justice Committee, an African American woman — a long way from skillet and a lot closer to the judge's golden hue — would rub her face with an index finger signifying Mackey's light skin was a problem. Colorism had managed to insinuate itself here, too. Several others on the ad hoc committee nodded in agreement.

The judge was already suspect by virtue of his profession — dead-up in the establishment — he was part of the city's Black bourgeoisie; and, as a light-skinned member of it, had allegiances that must be monitored. As proof of his sensibilities, some committee members argued that he seemed to grant every motion Lloyd offered. But then, using a peremptory challenge, Lloyd made a motion for another judge.

"Mrs. Doe."

"It's pronounced Dew, Your Honor," Lloyd said.

On July 29, the case was transferred to Lois Anderson-Smaltz, a White woman recently appointed to the bench by the new governor, Pete Wilson. "Motion denied." Denise liked those words. Lloyd had requested a continuance — his third.

"What's new and different?" the judged demanded. Nothing, she answered for him.

"I'm not ready." Without preliminary hearing transcripts, police reports, and the actual videotape of the shooting, Lloyd was helpless to do anything but ask for another continuance. He explained that he had just returned from vacation and was now too busy handling another case to give his complete attention to the Du trial until August 16.

That wasn't the prosecution's fault, argued Carvajal. The district attorney had filed a discovery motion on June 13, informing the defense of all the evidence that would be presented at trial.

"You're a sole practitioner?" the judge asked Lloyd.

"Yes, Your Honor. It would take another six months for another lawyer to prepare."

He was irresponsible in not ensuring his client a speedy trial, the judge scolded. Then, through an interpreter, she told Du she had to understand that it was her responsibility to hire an attorney who could bring her case to trial. "You can't avoid a trial by hiring a lawyer who is not ready. I will not continue this case to August sixteen."

Angrily, Lloyd said that he had never, in his long, illustrious career, received such a reprimand. Then he sputtered, "I am prepared to give Mrs. Du her money back."

The judge advised Du that any other attorney she might consider hiring should be ready to go to trial or she'd better retain other counsel.

But no courtroom could be found until August 12, so Lloyd got a delay anyway. When the day came, I spotted him sitting at one end of the court corridor with his client and her family.

At the other end, the Harlinses and their supporters congregated, among them several members of the Fruit of Islam, the Nation of Islam's security force, from Muhammad's Mosque 27 in South-Central. They assumed their characteristically impeccable and imperious stance. Near them, in front of the door to Anderson-Smaltz's courtroom, a line of young African American men dressed in Black stood at militarylike preparedness.

I walked over to Lloyd and the Dus, greeted them, and shook Mrs. Du's hand. I'd been trying to set up an interview with the family through Lloyd. My relationship with the Dus and their attorney was cordial at the time, and Lloyd kept assuring me that such a meeting would be arranged. I kept pushing, but I knew it was unlikely. In this case, more than the obvious tribal boundaries had been set.

There was the inevitable wariness: the Harlinses and their supporters were suspicious of the Korean-language press and much of the White-controlled media. The Du contingent was leery of Black reporters from both the African American and White-owned media. But the Dus also felt betrayed by the city's Korean immigrant community as a whole. Soon Ja Du's behavior had brought shame on her people, some said, and certainly had made it difficult for Korean Americans to do business in the Black community. "I am angry with her family," announced Yang Il Kim, president of the Korean American Grocers' Association at a public forum in L.A. a month after the shooting. "They never apologized to the Korean community at all." A multiethnic coalition of Blacks, Asians, and Latinos denounced the killing as the worst sort of violence perpetrated on a customer by a merchant.

Yet Korean Americans knew the strain on the lives of merchants in the ghetto. Even if they were a generation or more removed from that experience themselves, they knew of it from their parents, their uncles, aunts, cousins, friends. So there was a deep empathy for Soon Ja Du as well, perhaps best typified by those who thought she was stressed out, unstable, and had no business working in a situation known to be perilous.

That many Koreans shook their heads and thought his wife crazy was not the united front that Billy Hong Ki Du wanted, one insider told me. He's kind of "thuggish," the person said. One night, the former Korean army major and Tae Kwon Du expert summoned family members and friends to a meeting at his tract home in the San Fernando Valley. He expected a sizable contribution from them for his wife's defense, he told them. And he expressed outrage at the lack of support she was receiving from other Korean Americans.

I walked toward the middle of the divided courthouse corridor to speak to a reporter from the Korea Times. As I did, Billy Du cornered me, put his arm around my shoulders in a gesture of surprising familiarity, and pulled me toward him in a huddle. "He's trouble. Don't listen to him," he instructed, motioning with his head toward Richard, whom he'd seen me speaking to minutes earlier.

"He told me that you demanded that he work for free one time. Did you?"

"No-no-no."

"He said you told him he should work for free because that's what Black people are supposed to do, work for free. Did you say that?"

"I never said work for free. Richard would not work after I paid him $150. Don't listen; he's trouble."

I reminded him that I would like to interview him at length. "When this is all over," he assured me, and backed away.

He was a strikingly handsome middle-aged man, with a lean body, angular face, and thick, almost white hair. He might have been considered elegantly debonair were it not for the hint of Las Vegas–style, ring-a-ding-ding, sixties swagger: a bit of Sammy, a bit of Sinatra. I recalled the daughter of a prosperous Korean American merchant telling me that she'd had lunch with him once. He was a family acquaintance, and what she remembered most about the lunch, besides his man-about-town attitude, was his cellular phone. He loved showing it off. "My mother felt a lot of sympathy for Mrs. Du when she read about the shooting," the young woman said. She remembered her mother commenting that Mrs. Du worked very hard while Billy Du liked to distance himself from the day-to-day drudgery of a merchant's life.

If Billy Hong Ki Du had a bit of the Vegas playboy style, his oldest son, Joseph, seemed like a nigger with an attitude. He had the same sullen, chip-on-the-shoulder demeanor I'd seen on put-upon men of color in every ghetto I'd ever lived in or passed through. I watched him walk over to Denise and speak.

"What did he say to you?"

She sucked her teeth. "He said it was an accident. His mother didn't mean to shoot Latasha." I went to the other end of the corridor to speak to him. I asked him to verify what Denise had told me.

"Why don't you ask her," he said grimly.

"I'm really not trying to bug you. I just want to make sure what she told me is correct."

Wearily, he muttered, "Just too many people involved."

He had been more talkative at his mother's March arraignment.

That day, his sister, Sandy, a student at Biola College studying for the ministry, waved her hands wildly at reporters and told them from a distance, "I'm not going to talk with any reporters. They came over to our house in the middle of the night and scared the hell out of us." His younger brother, Mike, a married engineer, seemed to have been kept carefully under wraps by the family. He was in court sporadically and carefully avoided the media. But on the day of the arraignment, Joseph volunteered to reporters, "My mother is made a scapegoat of Korean-Black tensions. She was merely trying to protect herself. Why is it they never publicize all the Koreans who were killed?" His father, spotting the exchange with reporters, shouted, "Joseph!" He held his son in a stern gaze and admonished, "Be quiet."

And so, for the most part, he had been, except for the deafening inner pulse of a festering bitterness unheard by others but, like pus dripping from a man's every pore, hardly unnoticed.

Koreans speak of *han,* a bitterness so deep in their culture that it seems genetic. It was nurtured, some said, to ensure its transmission, its permanence. It so thoroughly defined the Korean collective unconscious that *han,* one writer penned, "is where the heart is." Such bitterness required little self-cultivation in the life of Joseph Du.

He had arrived in America at the same age Latasha left it, fifteen. Sandy and Mike Du arrived at a younger, more malleable age than their brother, and some speculated that this made their adjustment to a new culture far less traumatic.

A male adolescent from a homogeneous Confucian society — albeit a modern and urban one — Joseph Du had to contend with raging hormones, as well as a foreign geography, culture, and language. And as the eldest, he had to assume adult responsibilities sooner than the others: fourteen-hour workdays in the family's stores and a walking bull's-eye for gang terrorists.

Even as the *People v. Du* made its tortuous path through the legal system, three alleged gang members were about to be prosecuted by the district attorney for assaulting Joseph and robbing the Dus' store. It was because of gang intimidation that his mother was in the Empire Market the Saturday she shot Latasha, the family said. She wanted to relieve her son, who had begged his father to sell the store.

"Joseph Du broke his ass trying to make it with the people in that neighborhood," said Matthew Mahoney, a detective with the Los Angeles Police Department's antiterrorist unit. "He hired them, tried to get along with them, and they took advantage of him."

But other Korean American merchants in the South-Central neighborhood cast a more jaundiced eye on the thirty-year-old son of Soon Ja Du.

"Joseph is making his own problems. He never smiles. He never makes friends with the Black community. He is known to be quite rude," said one store owner who didn't want to be identified.

"The gang problem is not that bad," another merchant claimed. People steal from him all the time but they always come back the next day to pay, the liquor store owner declared.

Another shopkeeper theorized, "Gang members seldom steal, because they have money, unlike some people in the neighborhood."

But Joseph Du angrily told reporters that gang members are a big threat to Korean American businesses. "All Koreans in South-Central Los Angeles are just constantly harassed. Yet they do nothing. You know how a thug is good at finding a vulnerable victim? Gangs are good at finding helpless communities."

Still, many fellow Korean immigrant merchants insisted that the Dus were to blame for their problems with the gangs. "They don't know how to deal with the Black community," one asserted. "Why do they do business without trying to learn about them?" he asked.

"It's very easy to make friends with Black people, because they're very sweet people at heart," yet another shopkeeper told the *Korea Times*. "If you take the initiative, they always follow. They smile back. They talk to you. I don't see why the Dus can't do that."

Their responses seemed self-censored amalgams of truth and fear. The merchants may have feared retaliation from some elements in the African American community if they criticized Blacks. The Du store had been picketed, shut down indefinitely, and firebombed. The words that had been plastered across the door on butcher paper were now painted on the store: C L O S E D FOR MURDER & DISRESPECT OF BLACK PEOPLE.

A week after Latasha's death, a Black customer who read about the shooting walked into a market, shouted ethnic slurs at the Korean American woman who owned the store, then punched her in the face and left without paying for a candy bar.

The same day, three Black men attempted to rob a Korean American owner of a stereo shop in L.A. but were thwarted when a Black store owner next door came to his rescue.

Two days later, thirty-five people began picketing outside the Watts Market, believing that the owner, Chung Lee, was married to a relative of Soon Ja Du. Ironically, Lee was known as a model merchant. And he was the co-chair of the Black Korean Alliance. Initiated by the county's Human Relations Commission, the BKA had been formed to develop mutual understanding between the two communities following the murder of four Korean American merchants by Blacks in Los Angeles in the spring of 1986.

Within a week of Latasha's death, Brotherhood Crusade president Danny Bakewell served notice that the BC would draft a list of businesses rude to customers and use picket lines and acts of civil disobedience to force them to close.

Then on June 4, a retired Black boxer named Lee Arthur

Mitchell walked into Chung's Liquor Market in the 7900 block of South Western Avenue in South-Central L.A. and was shot to death. Mitchell, who was unarmed, allegedly tried to buy a wine cooler but was turned away when he offered to pay less than the cost of the drink. He offered a piece of jewelry to make up the twenty-five-cent difference. When the store owner's wife refused Mitchell a second time, he reached into his coat pocket and motioned as if holding a concealed weapon, police said. When the forty-two-year-old man went behind the counter and allegedly tried to remove money from the cash register, store owner Tae Sam Park tried to stop him. They scuffled. Park pulled a pistol from under the counter. He fired repeatedly, striking Mitchell five times.

Park suffered three broken ribs during the struggle with Mitchell, a popular neighborhood resident who'd been working as a boxing trainer.

An autopsy showed traces of cocaine in Mitchell's blood, and police ruled the case a justifiable homicide. The store's surveillance camera was broken at the time. There was no videotape of the incident.

Mitchell's family and friends protested the police findings and branded them a whitewash. Bakewell and the Reverend Edgar Boyd, whose Bethel African Methodist Episcopal Church stands across the street from the market, launched a ninety-day boycott of the store. The church had been trying to rid the area of liquor stores for a long time, especially those which sold drug paraphernalia — as did Park's, Boyd charged.

In the aftermath of the Mitchell shooting, Bakewell said he was determined to shut down Chung's Market and, attenuating his rhetoric, paralyze *any* business in the city treating Black customers unfairly. He'd been accused of singling out Korean immigrants, so he had broadened his attack. For, as anyone who lived in the Black community knew, it wasn't just some Korean American merchants who treated customers rudely.

"By all means," asserted the former director of the Southern

Christian Leadership Conference in L.A., Mark Ridley Thomas, "if any Korean American merchant is treating customers unfairly, employ every nonviolent means of direct action to put that particular business out of business." But the same standards should apply to everyone, said Ridley Thomas, now a Los Angeles City Council member. "I have lived in the African American community all my life. I know only too well what the level of service is to African Americans by African Americans, and that those merchants are not called to accountability." Undoubtedly, there was a double standard.

"I've found that most of the sentiments aimed toward merchants who are from other parts of the world are born of the frustrations African Americans experience generally," he added. "It may or may not have to do directly with the particular merchant. It has more to do with the history of exclusion around economic opportunity for African Americans. And that is compounded by the long-standing xenophobia that characterizes most Americans, irrespective of ethnicity."

On Memorial Day weekend, just before the Mitchell shooting, two more Korean American merchants were killed, Jung Woo Oh and Myung Yul Na. By late August, there had been a total of four shootings involving Blacks and Koreans since Latasha — about a death a month. And four Korean-owned stores had been firebombed.

Pleas from the Black Korean Alliance and others to view the Harlins killing, and the violent encounters between Korean immigrant merchants and Blacks generally, as business disputes without *racial* overtones were viewed skeptically. The BKA issued a statement on June 11 that attacked the media for consistently focusing on interethnic tensions and emphasizing them out of the context of the overall high rate of crime in poverty-ridden communities. This, charged the BKA, whose implied targets were the *Los Angeles Times,* in particular, and the broadcast media generally, "is misleading and socially irresponsible. It has the effect of actually creating and fanning the flames of ethnic discord in the inner city communities."

In part, this was a matter of blaming the messenger. But the media did consistently portray the tensions as fundamentally *racial* and cultural in origin.

Stories that sought to explain the complicated economic and psychological issues that underlay the tensions were few and far between. And one with my byline in the *Los Angeles Times,* explicitly challenging the notion that these tensions were purely racial or cultural, was slapped with the headline CULTURAL CONFLICT.

Most editors just didn't get it.

"Like who?" the editor wanted to know. My *Times* colleague John Lee was trying to tell the thirty-something White male editor that Black and Korean tensions were often reported out of context. Other immigrant groups have had this problem, not just Koreans. Hence the "like who" demand. The editor, John recalled, insisted that "this is an issue of Blacks and Koreans." When Lee mentioned that Jewish immigrants had been in similar conflicts with Blacks, the editor said, "That's only one other group. Who else?" This was not a low-level editor writing for an inconsequential rag but one of those vertical blurs who'd been pushed to the top and who displayed an ignorance of United States history all too common in newsrooms.

Lee was on deadline and didn't have time to tell him that Blacks have been living in northern urban enclaves en masse only since the great migrations from the South that occurred between 1915 and 1960. Until the urban rebellions of the sixties, Jews — historically excluded from other occupations because of anti-Semitism — were the money lenders, pawnbrokers, and merchants in Black ghettoes, the early middlemen. Even with a thirty-something editor, one would have thought it common knowledge that Jews were the ones run out and burned out during the fire last time.

But few, certainly not in the mainstream media, were willing to articulate a view that simultaneously denounced the violence, placed it in the context of the nihilism sweeping America, and admit *race* was the subtext of these conflagrations, as, even more fundamentally, was class. Or say that, like the East Indians in Africa, the Chinese in Southeast Asia, Armenians in Turkey, and the oppressed Jewish diaspora around the globe, Korean immigrants were playing the role of middlemen — between manufacturer and consumer, employer and employee, owner and renter. And like middlemen minorities throughout the world, they were a buffer for elites in an economically unjust system, bearing the brunt of the poor's hostility because they were the ones dealing with them daily. In other words, said the scholar Edna Bonacich, an expert on middleman minorities, "this has much to do with the way capitalism works."

And no critique of capitalism was going to be offered by the Black Korean Alliance, which was loaded with Korean grocers and Black would-be entrepreneurs looking for a deal. "Really," one African American BKA member told me, "I'm just there to network with some of the Koreans 'cause some joint ventures could come out of it."

In her confused and diffuse bitterness, Denise Harlins had made evident a visceral class alienation that transcended color as we sat in the Pacific Dining Car: *These politicians riding around in their limos and Cadillacs while Mama and me have to take the bus. I think there is a conspiracy going on over our heads and everybody is going to end up getting rich and the family is going to end up in the slum house, just the way it usually is set up.*

And the mayor made matters worse, playing to such perceptions when he made his first direct public pronouncement on the tensions in front of the Korean-owned Champion Liquor Deli, gutted by a firebomb on August 7, five months after Latasha was killed.

His smooth, waxen face glistening in the midday summer heat, the mayor stood in front of the fire-gutted market, surrounded by Korean American businessmen, Black clergymen, BKA members — some of whom represented various civil rights groups — reporters, and neighborhood residents. The shooting of Latasha Harlins, he acknowledged, "has unleashed a flood of grievances, tensions, and misconceptions that both communities, have, over time, gathered about each other. These tragedies must stop, and I am here today to demand that some members of the African American and Korean American communities stop engaging in actions that are detrimental to both groups."

The arson fire at the bombed-out store behind him was believed to be the act of a gang member who had a feud with the store's owner, Tae Suk Kim. It was unrelated, the mayor told the crowd, to the Bakewell-orchestrated boycott going on at Chung's Market on 79 Street.

He thought the 79 Street boycott detrimental to mediation efforts, but said his comments were not directed at "any peaceful organized efforts." But failure to condemn this rash of firebombings can "serve to escalate violent attacks against Korean storekeepers in South-Central. Our residents must not acquiesce to the forces of violence and brutality in an effort to gain economic leverage. I will not tolerate retaliatory action against any legitimate business in this city, and I promise to devote the resources necessary to prosecute those who would participate in such destructive activity."

Korean American businessmen wanted him to denounce the boycott, as New York's mayor David Dinkins had (too late, many New Yorkers charged) after Blacks launched an eighteen-month boycott of two Korean-owned markets in Brooklyn. They didn't understand that Blacks were not monolithic. They felt Blacks should speak with one voice. He was the mayor, he was Black, he should be that voice.

"Don't do it," many of the mayor's staff cautioned him. "It'll send the wrong message to the Black community — that you care more about private property than the death of a child." But the mayor told them he knew his people and he knew what he must do.

His people were pissed.

A reporter called out, "What have you told the merchants here about the attitude that people have condemned in this area with respect to how they treat their customers?"

"That issue was raised this morning," he said, at a meeting he'd convened with Black and Korean American leaders, police, and a mediator from the U.S. Justice Department. "It's very much part of our strategy," he said vaguely; then offered the familiar lines: "We have to get better mutual understanding of the differences in the cultures of these two racial groups. And we have to stress that courtesy in a market is something that is expected and demanded."

"We are told that this merchant, here, has been chasing young people out of the store," another reporter yelled.

"I'm not aware of that," Bradley answered. "I don't know anything about that."

Asked by another reporter if Black and Korean relations were "stabilizing" or going downhill, Bradley spoke of the national phenomenon of intraminority group tensions.

"As you know, the first major incident of this kind started in Brooklyn many months ago. What we are trying to do here is avoid hardening of attitudes so that we don't have situations such as that. We are not critical of ourselves or some other city, we are simply looking to the future now. What can we do to prevent this from happening again? I'm determined to do that."

Bradley thanked the crowd and began to walk to his car as a woman called out, "Excuse me, excuse me. I live in this community. Can I ask a question?" Her name was Desira Ruggles. "I'm a teacher," said the woman, who pursued Bradley as he listened but continued to his car without making eye contact. "I live around the corner. I know you talk a lot about the fact of respect in the wake of the Latasha Harlins murder and the Lee Arthur Mitchell murder. We can talk about respect — that's one thing — but when it comes down to actual deeds, that's where it's coming up short. And I'm just wondering how you think the average person in the street is going to deal with this situation."

"We will not tolerate —" the mayor started.

"'Cause you're talking about —"

"We do not tolerate —"

"Because who you're talking about is the elite," she said, pursuing him.

"We do not tolerate —"

"We're talking about the people who live in this community," she pressed.

"We do not tolerate crime committed by —"

"Right down —"

". . . whatever racial —"

". . . the street at the Empire Liquor Store. Latasha Harlins, fifteen years old, was murdered . . .

". . . group," the mayor said. "And the lady is being prosecuted; that's the point I am making."

"I'm just curious. Have you been down there, have you talked with the common people?" she asked, reporters following them. "The people who have to use these facilities?"

"The case of Latasha Harlins —"

"That's who I'm concerned about —"

"That matter is being handled in the courts," the mayor said patiently.

". . . and the Lee Arthur Mitchell case too."

"The district attorney —"

"No, no," she persisted. "When it comes to the fact that I, as a member of this community, have to go into these stores, that's a different thing." It's not just respect; it's life and death, she said.

"The police and the district attorney in the Mitchell case said that there is no basis for prosecution," the mayor told her.

"Well, that's what they said. That's not what the people in the community are saying."

"All we can do is go by the evidence they found," he told her without rancor, but also as if he were an elegant, disengaged automaton. Then he got into his car.

Reporters besieged the woman. "I am a teacher in this community," she repeated. "I know how the people are treated. I have never been treated badly by this particular merchant, but I know people in the neighborhood who have. I have been in other stores and followed as though I am a thief. I have been spoken to in a rude manner." The mayor is meeting with the elite, she said, while the people who have no place else to shop are getting abused and killed.

The Dus' store stood some thirty blocks south of Champion Liquor, encompassing a neighborhood of struggling working-class families in neat homes, modest apartments, as well as squalor. In the blocks that defined that census tract where Latasha lived and the Dus worked, the per capita income was $5463, compared with $16,149 for Los Angeles County and $14,420 for the nation as a whole.

Denise often spoke resentfully of the beautiful home filled with black lacquer in which the Dus lived — one she and members of the Latasha Harlins Justice Committee picketed — and the pleasant neighborhood that surrounded it.

But in Mission Hills, the San Fernando Valley suburb where the Dus resided, the per capita income was $13,076, more than twice that of the residents of Latasha's neighborhood, though hardly an indicator of the "filthy rich." The Dus' census tract included 2545 residents. The 271 Asians who lived in the neighborhood — which was mostly Latino and White — earned $20,557 per person. The smattering of Blacks who lived there — thirty-two — had per capita incomes of $36,713.

Latasha's neighborhood was twice as densely populated, with 5710 residents. Blacks there had incomes of $6659 per person.

The 114 Asians the census counted in the area earned $6158 per person. The 708 people identified as White living there made $4098 per person, just a little more than the 2665 Latino residents, who had per capita incomes of $3885.

No court could or should be expected to reconcile the disparities that characterized the two neighborhoods, but in many respects, that is what the *People* v. *Du* was about.

Joseph Du, stocky and brooding, snuffed out a cigarette and dragged himself toward the courtroom of Lois Anderson-Smaltz.

This is a political trial, the judge declared on August 26, and, reversing her earlier ruling, granted the defense's motion to move the trial out of the mostly Black city of Compton.

"The potential for bias," said Anderson-Smaltz, "lies in the process of coming to court and being influenced by the various contingents. There is a high level of tension due to the serious nature of the facts in this case. My concern is that there will be a great deal of pressure from the local community in the Compton area on the witnesses, the jurors, the court staff."

Illustrating her concern, the judge said a Korean interpreter refused to come to the courthouse, fearing she'd be attacked if she traveled through Compton. "It's not that an impartial jury could not be impaneled; it's more the pressure that surrounds this particular courthouse in Compton."

The case would be tried somewhere in Los Angeles County, but the judge didn't know where or when. There wasn't an empty courtroom to be found.

Larry Aubry winced and sucked in air in the hall outside Anderson-Smaltz's courtroom. "I thought that judge was way out in left field," said Aubry, a former mayor of Inglewood, newspaper columnist, and consultant to the County Human Relations Commission. He surveyed the tense crowd milling in the hallway. "I'm just observing the scene, as they say." He was the commission's African American liaison to the Black Korean Alliance. "I'm surprised that Carvajal didn't object to the change. I thought that was pretty outrageous — that Compton is too dangerous a place to hold the trial. This is a courthouse people come to all the time."

A few feet away, a crowd of reporters stuck microphones and cameras in Ruth Harlins's face. "When we first started coming to the court, there was an enormous amount of Koreans there and nobody said anything. But now that we have more support, they want to move the trial."

Neither the Harlinses, the Dus, nor the majority of their supporters are from Compton, that city's mayor, Walter Tucker III, told reporters. "I'm highly disappointed in the ruling and I question the reasoning. The intensity around this case will follow the trial wherever it goes. If it ends up *not* in an African American community, I'm sure the courtroom there will also be filled with controversy."

CHAPTER 7

THE BIG RING on his right hand bore ivory and seemed to await a kiss. "I have $200,000 right now," he said bombastically; "nickels and dimes sent to the Brotherhood Crusade by mothers and sisters." He could use that at the drop of a hat to buy out a Korean merchant. But this was the plan. "I had a deadline, some time in 1992," to open a chain of mom-and-pop stores in the Black community. But the momentum built by Latasha's death and Mitchell's meant he might accelerate his timetable. "The people are ready; the time is ripe. But don't print that yet; I don't want to tip my hands to the Koreans," Danny Bakewell instructed. I hadn't agreed to anything being off the record and just listened.

It was a day in late June of 1991. A young woman, a college student working in his office for the summer, took notes during the interview. We sat in his spacious office at the Brotherhood Crusade headquarters, a three-story property surrounded by abandoned factories and parallel to a railroad crossing. It was usually well maintained inside and out, but on weekends it became a pit stop for homeless people nestled in its doorway and junkyard dogs — one gnawing at the maggot-riddled carcass of an unrecognizable creature one Sunday afternoon when I drove by.

Bakewell usually reached the place in a chauffeur-driven Lincoln Town Car, coming from his spacious home in the San Gabriel Hills above Pasadena, or the home he and his wife, a

former city attorney, owned in Santa Barbara, or, north of there, from their 375-acre ranch in Lompoc.

The former high school football star had straight, close-cut salt-and-pepper hair, sported a beard, and favored elegant double-breasted suits and shirts with *Danny* stitched on the French cuffs. His striking figure was frequently seen next to Louis Farrakhan when the Nation of Islam leader spoke in L.A. and would be seen flanking him on the podium at the momentous Million Man March. On this day, a suit of gray pinstripes adorned the New Orleans native's back. But he could dress down when the occasion demanded.

Wearing dark glasses and a silk T-shirt under his jacket, he strutted one Saturday into a packed Black church meeting, took the podium, and told the crowd that people whine, "Danny, you ought to dialogue with the Koh-*ree*-ans." He slurred the word. "I am already having a dialogue. I am having a dialogue with my people." Then, peppering his comments with "niggers" this and "niggers" that, he told the mostly Black crowd he could turn hundreds of "niggers" out to picket and protest in a snap. A Black man in the audience rolled his eyes in disgust, leaned over, and said, "I don't care who it is; I don't appreciate anybody standing up in public and calling me a nigger." Expressions on other faces suggested he was not alone. But the three hundred who filled the pews of Bethel African Methodist Episcopal Church for a town hall–style meeting were largely his supporters. They applauded his pugnacious manner and rhetoric, a style that owed as much to thirties-era, Hollywood-gangster flicks as it did to Stokely and H. Rap.

He was forty-five and shuttled between boardrooms and street demonstrations. His Black militant cant obscured, for some, his fundamental philosophy: capitalism. He was a wealthy businessman with ties to the political establishment, including Tom Bradley. During his nineteen years as the crusade's president, he'd turned it into one of the nation's most prestigious Black charities. "He's got double barrels," a former business partner said. "He's got this broad political support and then he's got this street support, too. Folks in South-Central think he walks on water." A Danny Bakewell by any other name might be called a *don, padrone* — shit, to give the water-treader his due, he'd have to be called the Pope of South-Central.

He enjoyed being admired and, observing my designer threads and commenting on my stylish haircut, signaled his admiration for women. Appropriate to the man, I fixed my face in rapt attention and, for a first-time meeting, found him remarkably candid.

"Yeah, in each of these stores," he went on, "Mom and Pop Incorporated would be on the walls and some signs" — probably in the Black liberation colors of red, black, and green, proclaiming, "Dignity, Respect, et cetera," he tossed off with the sincerity of a used-car salesman. "And we'd give some coffee to the homeless. Fruit and vegetables to welfare mothers and their children — but this is a money-making venture. Fifty percent of the Mom and Pop profits would go back into the business. Fifty percent to the Brotherhood Crusade."

He'd received no salary as president of the crusade the last four years of his tenure, but all that went to the crusade enhanced Danny Bakewell's political reach and his economic portfolio, some claimed. Carl Galloway, a Black doctor who unsuccessfully sought a city cable franchise in which Bakewell was an investor, was one of them. "Danny is a person to whom you can say, 'You guys are extortionists,' and he'll say, 'No, this is for the Brotherhood.' You'll say, 'This is a rip-off.' And he'll say, 'This is just to bring Blacks together.'"

The store Bakewell had his eye on now was Chung's Liquor, the market where Lee Arthur Mitchell had been shot on June 2. Since then, in the eyes of Denise, Bakewell seemed to abandon the Harlinses' cause in favor of the Mitchell family's and the shutting down of Chung's Liquor. Why, I asked, given the police findings of justifiable homicide in the Mitchell case, did that incident seem to merit so much more of his attention?

"We *closed* that down," he said of the Dus' market with a slight jerk of his body, then relaxed, like a satisfied political gunslinger reholstering his weapon.

Besides, the Du store was not "in the best location." It's big, he explained, and "we may not get the best deal trying to buy that store. Chung's Market is perfectly situated. It's the right size and we could get it for $200,000, probably less." Regardless of who buys it, "I'm going to put him out of business. Nobody's doing business with him" since the boycott started. Koreans are being imported from "all over the city" to keep him from folding.

It was true, a group called the Korean American Emergency Task Force was pumping $6000 a week into the store to keep it open. And that couldn't last. "That's good," he pronounced. "Now they know I can put *any one* of them out of business."

But this, he revealed, "is just the tip of the iceberg. We are organizing something I call the Honor Committee. I don't know if I should talk about this." I turned off my tape recorder but encouraged him to continue. "It will consist of thirty organizations and churches. Each church or organization will commit to no more than twelve days a year. If I got thirty organizations committing to twelve days a year [picketing a designated site], that means you out of business. That means, your number comes up, you're gone. You're history. You can't survive that. I only need to do that once or twice and I will have absolute, major control of this community."

He'd already built the Brotherhood Crusade into one of the nation's most prestigious Black charities, doling out millions, over the years, to mostly Black charitable, educational, civil rights, health, and social service organizations. To do so, he'd won hardfought battles to convince more than a dozen corporations and local governments — including the city and county of Los Angeles — to permit their employees to contribute to the Brotherhood Crusade through payroll deductions. In 1990, the BC collected donations totaling $1.5 million.

At the same time, Bakewell had amassed a small real estate

empire, ranging from run-down apartments in South-Central Los Angeles to shopping centers in Pasadena and Compton, as well as his ranch and two houses.

For several years, he was the president of a municipal securities firm with elegant offices on the top floor of the Wells Fargo Building overlooking downtown Los Angeles. While the bold Bakewell lacked a license to sell securities, his political connections proved valuable to a firm competing for government bonds.

The same ties benefited his real estate ventures. Friendly council members in Compton granted him exclusive rights to develop two shopping center sites and committed city funds to the project, while Bakewell initially contributed little of his own money. Los Angeles city officials helped him obtain a stake in a controversial cable television franchise, with no down payment, according to another investor.

The late Los Angeles councilman Gilbert Lindsay helped him become a partner in a major downtown development, First Street North. One of Bakewell's biggest fans, Lindsay once said he wanted to create a Black millionaire — and Bakewell was a prime candidate.

"Clearly he has grown in stature [as a community activist] and clearly that has been converted into business prosperity," said a former aide to Lindsay and to Bradley, Bob Gray, who made an unsuccessful bid for the City Council in a campaign Bakewell helped finance. "But there is nothing illegal about that. And as far as I know, there is nothing unethical about that."

As the Pope himself put it, "I can do well and do good at the same time." But the populist rhetoric in the service of personal gain simply painted Danny as demagogue to others. He was too complicated to be simply that, I thought, but he was that, too.

While he lobbied for government support of a shopping center in an ethnically mixed neighborhood near the University of Southern California, Bakewell mobilized a busload of Black people, many of whom did not live near the project, to denounce White opponents. Bakewell was an investor in the shopping center — a fact he did not hide — and eventually won approval for it.

His leadership of the Korean American store boycott, as well as his efforts to oust the Los Angeles police chief Daryl Gates after the King beating, had antagonized some mainstream politicians. But it was the boycott issue that strained his friendship with Tom Bradley. Moreover, the president of the Los Angeles County Human Relations Commission, complaining that Bakewell had been inflaming ethnic tension with his hot rhetoric and confrontational style, suggested that the county reconsider permitting employees to contribute to the Brotherhood Crusade through payroll deductions.

But if anything, his supporters said, Bakewell was calming tensions by giving people an outlet for their rage. "He symbolizes a kind of strength that a lot of people in our community are looking for," said Maxine Waters, the popular Democratic congresswoman from Los Angeles. "Our community feels betrayed oftentimes by political leadership, feeling that so-called leaders are too soft, too accommodating to everybody else's interests. They want a strong voice; they want heroes."

A people without land but a nation within a nation, as Du Bois put it, hungry for respect, tired of being symbols of powerless morality thwarted by immoral power — Danny was the hero who knew the words and music to the psychic blues and played it superbly.

And he got here from where? I asked.

"I came here in 1967, basically looking for a job."

"Couldn't get one in New Orleans?"

"Couldn't get a job." He'd dropped into the University of Arizona on a football scholarship and dropped out after a semester. "I was lovesick," he explained. He'd married his childhood sweetheart, Aline, in 1964, the same year he graduated from high school. "Twenty-five years later, we're still married."

"So love made you leave Arizona?"

"There was a lot of that. But I didn't like the environment, a very racist environment. My father told me if I go west, there's integration; you don't worry about color. That was 1965, the height of the civil rights movement. Things were changing, and parents would talk to you with an eye to what they would like the world to look like, as opposed to what it was."

He went back to New Orleans, searching. "I didn't know what I wanted to be, but I knew I needed out of New Orleans. I got involved in the movement."

There were a lot of movements, lots of organizations, in the seventies, I told him. I had joined the Congress of Afrikan People, perhaps the most progressive of the Pan-Africanist, cultural nationalists of the day, headed by the activist and writer Amiri Baraka, a.k.a. Leroi Jones. "Baraka named me Itabari; my mother chose my last name. What movement were you part of?"

"I segued from involvement in the integrationist movement to the nationalist movement. When I hit Los Angeles I moved more fervently into the nationalist movement." After the Watts uprising and the murder of Martin Luther King, things were "turning to a very hard-core kind of dialogue." In other words, the focus was on what "Black people needed as opposed to what everybody needed, very selfish in terms of our aims and goals. Positive reinforcement. We recognized it didn't matter so much what other people thought of us as it did what we thought of ourselves. We had to do a lot more introspection."

But he could not sustain himself, a wife, a son, and the two daughters that were to come on introspection. "I did jobs around. I did waiter work, which is what I knew how to do and did in New Orleans. I worked at the Friars Club, saw all the big shots, worked in some of the grandest hotels. But then I started working in the community with an organization called Neighborhood Adult Participation Project." It was the leading antipoverty job-training program of the era in Los Angeles. "We'd take a person on welfare and put him in the social welfare department for the county." In turn they would "sensitize the bureaucrats who were dealing with welfare recipients to what they were really thinking. So it was a time when you were trying to bring together community and the establishment."

Really, he said, it was an era of social change in which institutions didn't know "whether to do flips or go blind." Two thirds into the century they were trying to get their arms around a changing environment much like the one confronting the nation today. "Black people were coming into play sitting down with White people and telling them to go to hell, I don't owe you anything. A whole mindset that was just new to White people. For whatever reason, the University of Southern California in Los Angeles made me an offer." He went there as the first Black trainee in their personnel department. "They wouldn't hire me as a professional personnel representative because I didn't have a degree."

The job, he said, was a good fit. "I was really sensitive to and plugged into the whole employment program because I had been so *ostracized* myself on the employment level." His words pricked. They were without his usual dramatic overkill, spoken with the wincing softness of one whose bare feet moved through cobwebbed rooms littered with the shards of a young man's shattered pride. "I had never really been able to get a good job. NAPP was an okay job on the community level. But I always felt I had something to offer. This whole college thing was smothering me. The whole employment thing was tied to a level of education that most Black people didn't have, and it was a convenient way to send you on your way. Yet many of the jobs that we were recruiting for at UCLA just didn't take a college education to do. UCLA eventually hired me as professional personnel rep. I earned my stripes."

In the meantime, he became "enamored of the Nation of Islam. I was just enamored with the issue of self-help. I was just awestruck by the fact that Black people have to stop talking about what we want to do and do it. And I felt of all the organizations around, the Nation of Islam, under the Honorable Elijah Muhammad, was doing more for Black people. Even if you don't agree with everything, it was like, you have to make a commitment."

And to a Roman Catholic youth who had attended parochial schools all his life, the "organized, disciplined way the Nation forced you to live," was reasonable, comforting. He stayed in the Nation from 1968 until Elijah Muhammad's death, in 1975.

"Was his death the reason you left?"

Actually, it was "just a good sort of escape period for me when Elijah Muhammad died." Unlike most members of the Nation, he maintained outside interests. Most brothers who join the Nation "fall out of the rest of life. They are not involved in any other organizations." He managed to juggle both worlds. That was hard at first, he admitted, because he was ready to proselytize at the drop of a bean pie.

"I mean, I was a bow-tie-walking, newspaper-pushing Muslim for a while. I even took my son on paper pushes. But I had to learn I couldn't push Islam down people's throats."

To be honest, he said, he'd been compelled to join the Nation largely because he wanted his son to attend its schools. "They said you had to take your children out if you weren't a Muslim." So he did the expedient thing.

"It's hard to call myself a practicing Muslim. I don't study as I should. Still, I consider that my way of life. I don't smoke. I don't drink. I don't do those kinds of things. One of the greatest things I learned from the Nation is a great appreciation for Black women," he said earnestly, "and how to pay honor and homage to them." That reinforced his natural instincts, he added. "I have a great identity with and appreciation for my wife, and of course, my daughters. They're sixteen and seventeen. I know honestly that I have never wanted for my wife, any woman I have ever had, or sisters, or mother, what I want for my daughters. And it was at that point that I realized I was a chauvinist."

"So, you're not macho anymore?"

"No," he said with a soft laugh. "I'm realistic. We all grow up."

I wondered about his childhood in New Orleans. He was an exceptionally light-complexioned African American man whose hometown was infamous for its pathological color hierarchy, and much of my work at this time was focused on colorism, multiethnic identity and, specifically, the antagonism between a new generation of so-called multiracial people of partial African descent and the traditionally defined Black American population, which saw *multiracial* people as seeking a separate status from Blacks to gain preferred treatment in American life.

"I'd guess you'd say my parents were poor folks, average working poor folks." His father was a bricklayer and his mother a factory worker before she divorced her husband, went to business school, and became a secretary for a labor union in the sixties. Their house was a shotgun number in the Treme section of New Orleans, a Black part of town that in its heyday was home to many of the city's jazz musicians.

"I was talking to a friend about this not long ago — I never felt poor, because we always had something to eat. And I went to Catholic schools, always. In high school, I had a football scholarship and worked in the cafeteria [to help with tuition]. So we never had much money, but private school was always paid for."

He visits home now and realizes that "New Orleans has a lot to offer. But as a kid, I just wanted to get out. Black New Orleans was enamored by the White New Orleans. The mentality was to just be satisfied. Which I guess was the mentality of the times for Black people. And the color consciousness that was taken to the extremes in New Orleans, didn't just exist there, I later learned."

In New Orleans people ran that "whole Creole thing and it was something that I totally rejected. I just hated that. My family, my grandparents certainly, I think, took a sort of pride in being Creole. But we never isolated ourselves. I was never told" — he stopped and seemed to mentally flip the pages of a family album. "My grandparents were very dark, for example, on both sides of my family. But generally, my family is light-skinned. My great-grandfather on my father's side was very dark. My great-grandmother on my mother's side was very dark." And he has spent some time, he admitted, trying to find that "point of penetration," where White blood entered the Bakewell clan.

Point of penetration, I thought to myself. He said this as if it were the exceptional New World experience, or as if the experience of humankind had not been endless migrating and mixing. But I knew I was thinking in academic terms in a country dedicated to antebellum notions of identity, myths challenged by the reality people lived and had lived daily. I said nothing. Besides, he had been influenced by one of the most intellectually backward, on this score, nationalist organizations that ever arose in compensatory response to White Supremacy. Not unlike the Nazis, Nation of Islam mythology viewed miscegenated blood as a cesspool, but empathized with Blacks who were obviously "mixed" by saying they knew it wasn't their fault but the evil doings of devil-White-men-rapists.

"My great-grandfather's father, " he went on, "was a very, very successful White man in New Orleans who had this baby with this Black woman." He never acknowledged the child, but "my great-grandfather looked like anybody's White man."

On his father's side of the family, "they all came out very African, French, and Indian."

But no distinctions were made within his family. And outside it — he was a jock, "but I was one of the brightest guys on the football team. I hung out with the guys. All that sort of got me over." But there was "this psychological thing. You're sort of close to looking like the enemy, so you are always challenged more. You always have to prove yourself. But I did so much of that at such an elementary level that when people come up to me now — Well, not so much now. But in my earlier days of activism, they'd ask, 'Aren't you uncomfortable saying we Black people this and we Black people that?' I said no. Feeling comfortable in one's skin comes when you get a certain self-worth."

"Was joining the Nation of Islam a way of affirming your identity?"

"Not consciously," he said. "But it certainly could have been. Because I remember my grandmother — she was a very dark woman — and my grandmother's thing was: 'Don't marry nobody who looks like me.'"

"Yeah," I told him, "I had relatives who'd say 'stay out of Africa.'" He threw his hands up slightly and shrugged his shoulders in grim acknowledgment.

"So in terms of what I see of Black people in America, when you go back, even the darkest among us were always trying to get their families closer to looking like White folks. Not so much because they wanted them to look like White folks, but they knew they would be given greater opportunity."

One of his grandfathers felt he had done his children a great service because none of them looked like him. "They were all caramel brown or light, whereas he was dark. So if he didn't do anything else for them, the fact that he had chosen a woman to 'get them out of Africa' was a major contribution to the rest of history for his family line."

He reflected quickly. "You know, I might be light-skinned by California standards, but in New Orleans, at best, I might be *yallah*," he slurred. They might say even "brown-skinned." When they talk light in New Orleans "they talking newspaper White." Whites in New Orleans, unlike most Whites outside the South, were as attuned as Black people to the finely calibrated hues that constituted "Black." "If the police pulled you over, they knew who a nigger was and who White folks was. You could be standing side by side and they'd split you off, no matter how light you might look to a Northerner."

Those experiences, in a strange way, "were real positives." There was no mistake about who he was. "I had," he said with conviction, "a secure sense of self and competence, even though the self and sense was not as a Black man or African American. It was as a Negro. But I had a great sense of identity with my people."

Then, underscoring why he was a water-treader of biblical

proportions, he explained: "One of the things that gives me the cutting edge over anybody else" in the Black community is that "I don't make any pretense about what I stand for. I stand for the preservation and enhancement of the quality of life for Black people. Period. If anybody gets in the way of that, I'm not for that. I'm for eliminating them. Because my mission is to bring home the bacon for Black people. It's not to bring home the bacon for Mexicans or Koreans or the other people. That's not to say that I start out in an adversarial position with them. We all learn how to work together and so forth. But I cannot *not* stand up for Latasha Harlins because somebody gives me some philosophy that Koreans were once enslaved and we kind of are the same people and all of that. That's secondary to my mission. And Black people, I have found, will not turn me out because of that advocacy."

He returned to the Lee Arthur Mitchell case. "We did not move on that situation until we got the briefing from the police department. And I will say to this moment that the police report does not add up in any way, shape, or form to justifiable homicide. It just doesn't sound like someone who went to rob somebody and needed to be killed."

Why?

"Number one," he elaborated, "the man went to the scene on a bicycle. Number two, he did not have a gun. Number three, the police said the argument ensued over an item that cost a dollar-thirty, and he supposedly couldn't pay for it." Yet, according to the police, "there was a dollar and ten cents on the counter and he had forty cents in his pocket."

Tae Sam Park, the owner, was in the back of the store, he said. His wife and a store clerk were standing at the front counter. Mitchell supposedly had his hand in his pocket, as if he were packing a gun. Park came to the front and started to argue with him, both stood in front of the counter. They fought. Park went behind the counter. Picked up his gun.

Then, according to Bakewell's interpretation of the police findings — and the version accepted in much of South-Central — Park told Mitchell to "stick 'em up."

"If somebody is challenging the safety of my family, or me, but particularly my wife or children, I'm not saying 'stick 'em up.' I'm going to shoot your ass the moment I got the drop on you." Further, Bakewell reasoned, "there is just this preponderance of evidence that doesn't corroborate what Park told the police."

For instance, the police said that when the clerk and Park's wife ran out of the store, the police were right there. "They didn't have a chance to come back and get their story together." It turns out not to be true, claimed Bakewell. They went across the street, called the police, came back, went into the store, then came out again, according to witnesses. And the surveillance camera in the store, all of a sudden, wasn't working. "But I was told by a police officer that the last frame on the store's videotape had the woman dressed the same way she was dressed that day, but the camera supposedly was not working for a week."

"So what?"

"I understand from a police standpoint — my wife is a lawyer — there are only three witnesses — the two owners and the clerk — and all of them are Korean and that's all they got to go on. All this hocus-pocus, about what she wore, when they made the call, when they came back and out again, doesn't mean much in a court of law. So far as they're concerned, this is justifiable homicide."

But, assuming his pontifical tone, he said he told the police: " 'I understand you got to do what you got to do, and we got to do what we got to do.' And my position is that's the kind of relationship we should have with the police. We're not going to get in your way and we're not going to break the law, but we are not going to sit back idly and accept what you tell us. 'Cause, remember, that's the same thing the Korean said over there about Latasha."

Soon Ja Du said Latasha "was trying to rob her. It's only because we got 'em on tape that we can prove that's a lie. And there are people who will tell you that Latasha Harlins was a little bitch. That she was running the streets. None of that matters. I talked to one reporter who said Mitchell used cocaine. And I told him, 'Are you then going to start shooting senators and IBM executives and Congress people?' Because dope is a problem in our society."

Of course, it was not just a matter of Lee Arthur Mitchell's lifestyle. An autopsy report had revealed cocaine in his system, which the body metabolizes quickly. That traces of cocaine were found might indicate that he'd used the drug recently enough to account for his alleged irrational behavior: faking a gun, trying to pay for a beer with jewelry when he actually had the change, riding a bike to a spontaneous, rather than planned, commission of a felony.

Bakewell dismissed all this with "I am not here to defend Lee Arthur Mitchell in terms of his lifestyle. I am here to defend a community who sends people in those stores day in and day out. And I am saying that if you operate a business in our community, you have to have a greater degree of respect and accept a greater degree of responsibility for being able to do business with us — and not kill us at the drop of a hat. I don't think there is any basis for Lee Arthur Mitchell to have been shot five times in the chest and not have a gun."

They've drawn their guns any number of times, Bakewell said of Tae Sam Park and his employees. "It was just the first time they killed anybody. But that wasn't the only problem," he declared.

These merchants "prey on all our weak points. We set [Park] up; we had a brother go in there and buy a pipe from him for eight dollars." Park kept drug paraphernalia under the counter. "They sell gang paraphernalia, too, blue rags and red rags — colors of the Crips and Bloods, L.A.'s two infamous street gangs. They are cultivating an economy which is disruptive to our community. Any Black merchant doing that is worthy of the same treatment," he threw in, "need to put their asses out too. This is not so much about Koreans as it is about Koreans who are exploiting the community. If they were in the community and had a whole different attitude, we wouldn't have to concentrate on putting them out of business. We could concentrate on going into business."

And what prevented Blacks from going into business wasn't just red-lining by White-controlled banks, he readily acknowledged. "The reason we don't own most of the stores in our own community is because we have been out-positioned. Maybe we're going through a phase that every ethnic group goes through. I don't know. But the reality, which even Black people seem to forget, is that pre–civil rights, we owned all the businesses in our community."

That's not true, I said. But we did own many, especially those which provided personal services, like beauty and barber shops, out of necessity.

"What the immigrants are doing is out of necessity too," he responded. "We were not immigrants, but we were as much outsiders as the immigrants are." And, he said, reflecting some of my own thoughts, we remain outsiders and need to act as if we were immigrants.

Of course, whatever their background, immigrants are a special kind of people. They have a drive that sets them apart from those they decide to leave behind and those they encounter in a new homeland. African Americans recognized this and, mostly in private, sometimes in public, spoke admiringly of Asian, African, Russian, Caribbean, Latino, and Arab immigrants who came to their neighborhood and were willing to put in the long hours it took to make a mom-and-pop operation work and often to risk their lives in troubled neighborhoods. And they admitted that most African Americans were not willing to do that. The reasons have been subject to debate for years.

While some scholars claim that, since Black immigrants have, comparatively, excelled in the United States while African Americans have not, in terms of educational attainment and income,

White racism is no longer an impediment to Black success. I don't think so.

Racism continues to limit opportunities for both the native-born Black and the Black immigrant, but the psychic complications that arise from the African American's experience of White domination in the U.S. are different. A significant impediment for African Americans is the profound psychological effect of exclusion and marginalization here that does not usually exist for Blacks in societies where they are the majority; and the higher level of self-esteem they bring with them as a result. There is a tremendous sense of confidence that comes from seeing people like yourself achieve, even fail — as humans are wont to do — in the daily give-and-take of life. There is the rhythm of normality, the beat of a healthy heart from feeling that you belong. White people know this. The ones I know who go to Japan come back complaining about how ethnocentric the culture is, how out of place they felt. I remember, especially, the tall White woman — an anthropological anomaly in Japan — who suffered through childbirth on a delivery table that could not accommodate her head and shoulders.

Further, there is the experience of my own family: their education in the former British colonies was better than what most African Americans had any hope of receiving when my maternal grandparents came here just after World War I. And my cousins who emigrated from Guyana in the 1960s, had had a high school education that surpassed what most Americans get in the first two years of college; not to mention what is taught in the deficient, degrading institutions that pass for schools in most inner cities. This educational disadvantage speaks to the structural inequalities that keep many African Americans from excelling.

Too, knowing, as they do, that the currency that financed the nation's wealth was our ancestors' sweat and blood, African Americans are loath to act as if they just got off the boat and start from the bottom. That attitude was going to have to change, I felt. This was a touchy area between native-born Blacks and Black immigrants, the latter frequently inclined to lord their relative success over African Americans whose struggle to extend democracy in the face of brutal oppression had made their achievements, as well as those of other minorities, possible. Nonetheless, larger numbers of African Americans were going to have to consider the example of the Caribbean Americans and Africans who were faring better than they.

I focused fully on Bakewell again, nodding in agreement; then heard him say, "Take Katy." Uh-oh. A Farrakhan inflection had entered his voice and I knew that a Nation of Islam–style parable was coming.

"We created a marketplace of our own, and here come Dr. King and the whole Civil Rights movement. We went past Katy's Kitchen to try and go down to Walgreen's and eat hamburgers with the White folks. We were going to *make them* take our money." Katy survived, but business went down dramatically.

Now here's Katy's son. Katy was able to send him to college, and she would like to turn the business over to him. But he doesn't want to be stuck in a hole-in-the-wall restaurant. Besides, he tells her, "I'm an investment banker. Straight out of school I can start making $40,000." Then his uncle Bubba jumps in and says he can make $100,000 with the family business. "Yeah, but it don't look right," Junior tells him. "I can't wear my suit."

"So," said Bakewell, "we've been displaced. Mentally we're displaced. Consequently, the Koreans come and Katy wants out of the business. She's old and on Social Security. Life is different now — all the gangs. At one time she could stand up to all that. But she's tired. Her son says sell the business. Move to New York. We'll get you a place. She sells. The Koreans get a deal. Katy didn't really know how much the business was worth. They take it over and it's up and running, making beaucoup money, and they're making it off of us."

Putting Katy on the hook until another interview, he summed

up: "They've taken over businesses that we once had and the generation that owned them has moved away. The generation that may be professionals now are not living in the community anymore. They're not affected by the change in the old neighborhood. But the reality is that only ten percent moved away. Ninety percent are still affected by it and they have very, very bad experiences with these merchants."

Analyzing what he alleged was a macho attitude among these merchants, Bakewell added, "What I think the Koreans have said to each other is this. 'The way you deal with these niggers is you have to be firm. You have to send a message.' The same thing our mothers used to tell us when we were on the block: 'Look, you fight with one of them, you beat 'em. You send a message and they not goin' mess with you anymore.'"

I'd been told that the Korean American merchants had been offered, but had rejected, some hanging-tough tactics. The Korean American Emergency Task Force, established in response to the boycott of Chung's Market, got a call, a member of the group said, from several Jewish merchants who had owned stores in Black neighborhoods before the Watts rebellion. "'We've had to deal with these Blacks before,' they told them. 'If you want help withstanding the boycott, let us know.'" The offer was debated and ultimately declined, the insider said. Few in South-Central would be surprised at hearing such a story. And it took no great skill to fan the Black-people-against-the-world-sensibility that lived like flora in the guts of African Americans. And this, of course, is what Bakewell did. I respected his take-no-prisoners stance. It was the demagoguery, in the service of self-interest with the trickle-down capitalist philosophy attached — it didn't work under Reagan — that made him an elevated poverty pimp. Still, I liked him — no, appreciated him, the way one appreciates something complex, possibly dangerous, and very entertaining.

"Everybody else is making a big living here; I don't know why we can't," he said. "That's why I am hell bent on developing some successes. We have to re-educate our people. We have to get them re-enthused about our ability to be successful. And we have to show them that it doesn't hurt and it isn't dangerous — no more dangerous than going to your mother's house, which nine times out of ten is still in the neighborhood you grew up in, and is right down the block from where these gang shootings take place."

But it was dangerous. And he knew it. His father, Frank Bakewell, had left New Orleans to run a series of small businesses in Los Angeles in the early 1980s. One night, robbers entered the check-cashing business he operated in a shopping center his son owned and shot him dead.

The son never mentioned this. Life is tough. Things happen.

His mother, Marybell, said her boy Danny always had a knack for business. "He used to tell me, 'You know, Mother, if I had money, I'd buy a place and sell a place and buy a place.'"

The Pope's plan for South-Central: "You will see a physical change in the economic complexion of this community." No contractors will be allowed to build in the Black community unless they hire African Americans. You will not see grocery stores or a MacDonald's not owned or staffed by Black people. There are existing Black businesses, he said, "that believe they could do more business, but they need a loan. Well, if I get my honor committee to visit the bank, I can put them out of business too. See, this just ain't about the Koreans. There's a bank called Great Western on the corner of Vernon and Crenshaw [the heart of South-Central]. They do more business with Black people than all of the Black savings-and-loans put together. And I venture to say they give less in loans to the community than all of the Black savings-and-loans put together. We can go to that bank, put pressure on them. But they've got to know that we are a potent folk as well as a needed ally. That's what I am about."

Bakewell was filling a leadership vacuum in the city, and what, I asked him, did that say about Los Angeles' Black elected officials.

"It is easy to just, well, it's almost like you just get complacent.

It takes a lot of effort to do what I am doing." He'd suddenly become quite politic. The statement was notable for its failure to mention Bradley, one of his patrons. "It's not that I need any accolades or deserve any. It is what I consider to be part of my responsibility. But it is different from just coming to work, having a meeting, preserving the status quo. You have to go out there on the picket line, keep folks together. It's a lot of shit. That's what it takes. And to some extent, those of us in leadership have fallen victim to the same thing that those of us who don't want to take over mom's business have fallen into. This is the nineties. We don't picket, we don't do that type of thing, putting people out of business."

Then, his voice heavy with contempt, he told me about a call from the local chapter of the NAACP. "This brother called on the Latasha Harlins thing and whined, 'What you doin'? You gonna put those people out of business. Why you do that? We tryin' to create some Korean-Black dialogue.'"

Indignant, the people's prelate told him, "Who is it that's going to defend Black people? That could have been my daughter, your daughter, your son murdered in that store. We cry for everybody. Who is it that cries for us?"

CHAPTER 8

ON SEPTEMBER 24, 1991, in Department 106 of the Los Angeles Superior Court, jury selection began in the case of the *People of the State of California* v. *Soon Ja Du*. Experienced judges who had been offered the controversial case refused it. "Let Mikey eat it" was one of the wisecracks floating through the courthouse among reporters. "He'll eat anything." Indeed, when Joyce A. Karlin — Joy, to her friends — was offered the case, she welcomed it. "I thought it would be a challenge," she said.

On September 30, a tall, dark-suited, middle-aged man with broad shoulders strode through the courthouse corridors. A neon-bright, orange- and lime-colored backpack swung incongruously from his hand. It was a well-used bag, one I could imagine a young child dragging along the ground as he walked home from school, or toeing absentmindedly as it lay on the pavement while she waited at a bus stop with friends. It bore a large, white-faced, black-rimmed, battery-operated clock frozen at 1:30. It might have held Crayolas as bright as the electric colors of the bag itself and sheaves of loose-leaf paper marked A+ in red. Latasha, after all, was once an honor student, news accounts frequently reminded us. But the bag contained a yellow toothbrush, a tube of Zact toothpaste, a pink-lidded jar of Moon Drops dry skin cream, a pair of dark blue pants, a blue paisley-patterned blouse, and soiled black panties.

The bag's contents signaled to police that she was a runaway. The Harlinses insisted she wasn't. She'd simply spent the night before she died with her best friend, they said. A girl named Marcolette.

One day during the trial, Marcolette appeared outside the courtroom, surrounded by the Harlins family. She was sixteen and pregnant. I got her address and phone number; then she seemed to disappear. Her telephone was disconnected. She was not at the address she'd given me. Eventually, I'd find her and learn, among other things, that she'd never seen Latasha the night they were supposed to be together.

When she met me at the door, her hair was neatly pulled back in a French braid, making more gaunt her long face, with its sharply pointed chin. She had a smooth, Hershey-bar-colored body, over which she wore a long white shirt, trimmed with lace, and dark leggings. Like Latasha, she ran track and remained slim, even now, in the ninth month of her pregnancy. If Latasha looked as much like Marcolette Wideman as people said, then Ruth Harlins was right. No picture of her grandchild ever did the dead girl justice.

Though she was only a year older, she thought of Latasha as a little sister, Marcolette told me as her two-year-old son, Christopher, bounced around the living room. It was hard to tell how many lived in the apartment besides Marcolette, her son, and her mother. But there was a lot of traffic in the messy apartment, which stood just blocks away from the equally modest but well-kept flat Ruth Harlins tried to maintain.

Christopher was the child she had been carrying when I last saw her in the courthouse. He was a handsome boy with heavy-lidded, almond-shaped eyes that gave his round brown face an Asiatic cast.

"Was Latasha running away the night before she died?"

"She wasn't running away," Marcolette said. That particular night, she just wanted to be with the guy she was seeing, she told me.

I asked Marcolette what she knew about a man who lived

across the street from Latasha, the one I heard she was supposedly dating. "Ron?" she asked.

"I'm not sure of his name." Actually, I never knew it. "How old was he?"

"Older," she said.

"What did he look like?"

Marcolette blew air through her teeth and made a gentle hissing sound. "It was too long ago. He moved out of the neighborhood. I know he was short, about Latasha's height. He had a curl and was brown-skinned."

But there was another man Latasha was seeing, she told me. A man named Jerry Foster, who worked at the Algin Sutton Recreation Center in the park just a few blocks from Latasha's home. I remembered Ruth Harlins waiting long after dark for Latasha's brother and sister to come home from the center. At one point, Latasha was seeing Jerry and Ron at the same time, Marcolette claimed. Denise had told me about Foster, too. She'd suggested that he had had an improper relationship with her niece.

"Did you know Jerry, too?"

"Ah-huh." She answered like she knew him well.

"When did you two get tight?"

"Me and Tasha?"

"No. You and Jerry."

"I was going with him before Tasha," she told me. But the girls met him at the same time, because they both hung out at the recreation center where he worked.

"So Jerry was your man first."

"Yeah."

"Were you and Latasha competing for him?"

"No," Marcolette assured me. "Like, he was talking to me first, then we broke up and he started talking to Tasha, then I start talking to someone else. And it went like *that,*" she told me, as she shrugged her shoulders and her voice rose in a girlish squeal at the end of the sentence. "After Latasha died," said the teenager, "we got back together again. He loved me a little bit but not more than he loved Latasha."

Foster, she said, is Christopher's father.

"Does he know that?"

"Yeah, he knows it. He denies it. But everybody on the block knows it's his kid," she said. "They tell him the boy looks just like him. He has a lot of kids who look just like him." Much later she told me that Foster's name is on the birth certificate.

Christopher's "aunties," Foster's sisters, she explained, visit guys on Marcolette's block and play with Christopher out on the street sometimes. But that's the extent of the child's contact with the Foster clan.

"Oh," she slowly recalled, "he did help me out a little bit once."

"Did he give you money?" I asked.

"No, he just bought a box of diapers."

"That's not a lot of help," I said.

"I know," she answered, "but I don't care anymore." Steve, the father of her next baby, is helping her now.

"How old is he?"

"Thirty," she said.

"What does your mother say about the fathers of your children?"

"She just say, 'They too old.'"

It was late evening when I walked into the Algin Sutton Recreation Center. Jerry Foster was sitting on the edge of the stage in the gym, overseeing a basketball game. He squinted at me as I approached. It was the first and last time he looked directly in my face.

Denise Harlins claimed he had roughed her up in the gym a few months before Latasha's death, when she publicly accused him of pursuing her underage niece.

Foster looked up, down, then sideways, and said, "What happened, the actual thing was, I was running a basketball league in the gym. This was an adult league, so this was at night. And at that time, she didn't like Latasha hanging out at the park at night, and Latasha was up at the gym watching the game. Denise, first of all, came in drunk."

"She told me she'd had a beer but wasn't, in her words, 'sloppy drunk,'" I told him.

"Oh, she was drunk, trust me," Fostered said. Since she was disrupting the game, he "escorted" her out. "I pushed her out of the gym. I didn't manhandle her or beat her up or anything."

He and Latasha "were really, really, really close," he admitted, but Denise "thought it was more than it was." Foster, who told me he was twenty-nine, looked older. He had a light beard at his chin, almond-shaped eyes, and an Asiatic cast to his round, pleasant face. He looked as if he'd spit out Marcolette's son.

"Latasha didn't like her aunt," Foster claimed. "She really loved her grandmother deeply." But the friction with Denise provoked Latasha to "leave the house for two or three days, then come back, and leave again after the next battle with her aunt."

So, in general, she was running away from home for short periods of time, he claimed. But the night before she died he is sure she wasn't trying to escape from home; she was just hanging out with friends.

"How can you be so certain?"

"I know for a fact that she was over her friend's house."

"Which one?"

"I don't know which friend she was over, but I know she was over one of her friend's house because they were all at the park that evening before she died. And they said the next day they were all going to the mall or something. I don't know what happened after that." I moved off the subject for the moment and asked him about Latasha's brother, with whom I knew he was close. Away from the basketball court, the boy seemed nearly as spectral a figure as his sister — sad, quiet, ghostly in the shadows of his grandmother's living room.

Joshua took it really hard when his sister was killed. He hated Koreans and didn't understand, said Foster, that all Koreans were not the enemy. While he didn't claim to be of Asian descent, Joshua's mentor told me he was born in Japan and had lived there the first year of his life, while his father was in the military. This, apparently, was to let me know he had a more sophisticated view of ethnic relations than other folks in the hood. He informed me, as well, that he studied recreation and physical education at the University of Southern California. "Got my B.S.," he told me, like a man who thinks his shit don't stink. "I played professional football in Montreal, Canada — that's the Canadian league. I played there for two years until I messed up my leg. Ruptured my Achilles tendon," he explained, lifting his left leg.

I asked him if counseling might help Latasha's brother. "Naw, unless it's someone like me. He doesn't trust many people. I take him everywhere with me." Thanks to his influence, "Joshua's attitude has improved. But he still doesn't trust too many people since his sister died."

"What about getting him out of the neighborhood?" I suggested. It can't help that he lives around the corner from the store in which his sister was killed. Foster dismissed that notion, too.

"A supposedly better neighborhood is not going to do much good for Joshua. South-Central is in him now."

Some people thought that the worst of South-Central was in Latasha and that she was a little bitch, I told him.

"She was just street savvy," he defended. "They take her being tough out of context. She had street sense. In South-Central, you better have street sense."

The recreation center has a day camp, he told me, and Latasha's maturity and compassion were evident when she worked there with kids, three, four, and five years old. On those days "we would talk for hours," he remembered. "She could converse like a woman with a college-level education," he assured me. "She didn't apply herself in school," he went on. "But if she'd applied herself, there wasn't anything she couldn't do."

"Did she ever share her plans for the future with you?"

She wanted to be a lawyer, he knew. She never got over her mother's death or the fact that the woman who was convicted of killing her was released after only five years in jail. As a lawyer, she thought she could protect her family as well as her community. "I had gotten her several applications to go to USC. And she was talking to a couple of advisers at USC I hooked her up with. She really wanted to get herself geared to go back to school and go to USC."

"If you were so close and such an important adult figure to her, why," I wanted to know, "couldn't you convince her that playing hooky wasn't going to get her into college?"

"It was just those outside elements," he insisted. "Her real boyfriend was the one who kept her from going to school. His name was Ron," he volunteered.

"Now this Ron was much older than Latasha, right?"

"Yeah, he was like twenty-two or twenty-three."

"But your relationship with her was platonic, brother-sister?"

"Brother-sister," Foster assured me.

"You never had a sexual relationship with Latasha?" I asked.

"Never, oh, no. Never with Latasha. Never."

"I'm not going to let you assassinate my niece's character," Denise fumed. "You're trying to make her look like she was some kind of slut, supposedly sleeping with these men. I am sick and tired of having to defend my niece's reputation, my entire family's. People who didn't know Latasha have been ripping her apart from the start. It began with the police when they said she was a runaway; Latasha was never no runaway. Then Charles Lloyd tried to portray her as some kind of gang member to the media. Why would you listen to anybody like Jerry Foster? Who is he? Or Marcolette. Latasha's not here to defend herself, and I am sick of it!"

"You led me to both of them, Denise," I reminded her. "*You* accused Foster of pursuing your niece."

"And as for him talking about me and Latasha, what does he know? What do you know? I was trying to guide her, the way I would my own child. I was being a parent to her, and parents and children have differences. That don't mean Latasha hated me.

"I'm still trying to do something in the wake of my niece's death," she went on, "like start a foundation in Latasha's name for teenage girls" or a residential facility for unwed teenage mothers. "How are these claims about my niece going to look when I'm trying to do all this?"

"If they're true, it's going to look like Latasha was human. It will look like she was prone to the same sexual pressures that many teens face from peers, and worse — sexual exploitation by older men. These are the very girls you would want your foundation to help in Latasha's name."

People would not see it that way, she said. "They'll try to use this to keep me from helping anybody else. I'm going to need money to start such a program. A foundation can't run off of your heart and love."

"I told you from the start, Denise, I was not out to sanctify Latasha."

"You didn't know my niece," she railed. "Only her family knows who she really was." And it was a struggle to find that out from them, I reminded her.

"We told you what we wanted you to know."

"Precisely."

I telephoned Marcolette, and she laughed when I told her that Jerry Foster denied ever having had a sexual relationship with Latasha.

How was it possible for him to have had a sexual relationship with her or Latasha and not have anybody see them? "Where did you two get together?" I knew Foster sometimes stayed at his mother's house in L.A. and that she worked during the day. He also had a place in Lancaster, a satellite of L.A. about fifty miles north of the city going toward the Mojave Desert.

"Well, once we was up over his . . ." She was distracted and her voice trailed off.

"His what? Where his mother lives?" I asked.

"Yes."

"So the only time you got together sexually was at his mother's house?"

I heard her sigh. "Can't say right now."

"Oh, there's a crowd around?" I asked.

"Yes."

"Was it at the Algin Sutton Center?"

"Uh-uh."

"In the back seat of a car?"

"Uh-uh."

"In a hotel?" I asked.

Marcolette said, "Yes."

I told Marcolette that Foster claimed not to know where Latasha was the night before she died.

Her only response was, "The day after the funeral, he told me: 'I'm the one who dropped her at the store. She wanted to get some juice. She had the change in her pocket.'" Then he left her to go to work at the park a few blocks away. It was about 9:40 A.M.

The keeper of the backpack was the chief investigator for the prosecution, Detective Jerry Johnson. The strapping White cop had told me months before that he had a son, and if Soon Ja Du had grabbed him the way she grabbed Latasha, his boy would have slugged her, too. Kids frequently put things in backpacks, thoroughly intending to pay for them, he said. "But these kids just don't think."

I watched him place the backpack on the prosecutor's table. In an evidence room of the courthouse, I'd eventually sift through the contents of the bag, lingering on the jar of Moon Drops. Latasha was fifteen. Did she have dry skin? There were so many things prematurely old about her. But neither trivial intimacies nor substantive truths about the girl would emerge inside the courtroom. The essence of this woman-child would remain un-known, her existence merely symbolized in the courtroom by a white Styrofoam head, topped with a black, UCLA Bruins cap, and a metal rod rammed through it all. The rod followed the trajectory of the bullet that killed her, entering the back of her head, piercing the elastic band of the Bruins cap, exiting the right side of her skull, high above her temple. Perhaps that emblem — and her blurred image on the grainy black-and-white videotape — is all there should have been. Her character was not supposed to be on trial. She was not the one charged with first-degree murder.

CHAPTER 9

". . . 911 emergency."

"Yeah, this is Empire Liquor Market . . ." The man's voice was breathless, panic-stricken. His accent was thick. *". . . we got a holdup. My wife, shoot-a . . ."*

"Listen, listen, let me get a person out there. You're at 9127 South Figueroa?"

"Yes."

"Okay, hold on, just one second, okay? Let me get the policeman and then I'm going to come back and talk to you."

"Okay." He panted.

"How many people robbed you?" the dispatcher, a woman, asked with practiced control.

"Only one, one, people."

"Was he Black, White, or Hispanic?"

"Huh?"

"Was he Black, White, or Hispanic?"

"Ah, he is a Black."

"Okay. This Black man, what was he wearing?"

"Black woman," he told her.

"And did she have a gun or a knife?"

"No, nothing."

"What is it, what is it —"

"She want to take out my money," the man said.

"She took the money out of your cash register?"

"Yeah . . . my wife . . . she got gun . . ."

*The man started yelling frantically at someone in the store,
"No-no-no. Go! . . . Hello, hello . . ."*

"Sir, which direction was she going?"

*"Ah," he groaned, "I don't know . . . I was outside. There was a
gun noise and I come in. So, my wife —"*

"Your wife didn't see her?"

"Yeah."

"Okay, sir. Is anybody hurt?"

"Yeah-yeah, hurt."

"Who's hurt there?"

"The . . . woman. My wife shot her."

"Your wife shot the lady?"

"Yes."

"Ohhhh. Hold on."

*"Yeah-yeah-yeah," the man told a policeman entering the
store, "it was a robbery, it was robbery . . ."*

In the mute surveillance videotape of the shooting, Billy Hong
Ki Du is seen running into the Empire Market and picking up
the phone. He places the call to the 911 operator. The young
children who witnessed the fight have run out, and the man
with the doo-rag tied around his head has been waved away
by Du and shambles out the door, muttering to himself. A policeman enters, spots the body, and takes the phone from Du.
The cop searches the rear of the store, and another officer enters. Both policemen rush outside, passing Latasha's unchecked
body.

Subject to Rashomon-like interpretations, the film was the key
piece of evidence around which Prosecutor Carvajal presented
a clear, systematic case against Soon Ja Du for the killing of
Latasha Harlins. The presentation was notable for its lack of
passion. It was the same evidence that Lloyd and his White co-
counsel, Richard Leonard, used to make the plausible case
confusingly argued by attorneys who seemed ill-prepared — that

Du (a) shot Latasha in self-defense and (b) the shooting was accidental. Further, they would try to make the jury doubt that Latasha had been shot in the back of the head at all.

The prosecution's first witness was Jarrod, a frail and frightened-looking little boy in mustard-colored overalls and a brown polo shirt.

Interrogating the nine-year-old, the svelte prosecutor in high heels, dark blue suit, and brown hair brushing her shoulders spoke with the sweet firmness of a novitiate in *The Sound of Music*. But she was no novice. The thirty-seven-year-old assistant D.A. had been prosecuting cases for twelve years. Yet there was a tentativeness about her, a lack of authority, that dismayed the Harlins family. I wondered if she'd rise to the authority of a Mother Superior before the trial's end.

"I want to take you back to the beginning of this year, back in March. Did something happen when you went to the Empire Liquor store with your sister?"

"Yes."

"What happened?"

"Well, me and my sister went to the store to get my mother some hair gel. This — and this girl walked into the store, and she went straight to the juice section. And then she didn't go nowhere else and came straight up to the counter and was going to pay for it, the juice, and she had it in her backpack where you could see it. And the Oriental lady started pulling her shirt — her sweater — and telling her, 'That's my orange juice,' and kept pulling it. And the girl says she was going to pay for it. And the girl was telling her to let her go, but she wouldn't."

"And then what happened?" Carvajal asked.

"Then she was calling her bitches," Jarrod answered.

"Who was calling her a bitch?"

"The Oriental lady."

"And what was the girl saying?" Carvajal asked.

"'Let me go. Let me go.' And she — she —"

"What happened then?"

"And then the Oriental lady brung the stool from behind the counter and threw it, but she missed. And she put the orange juice back on the table, and then the Oriental lady moved it. And as she was walking away she shot her."

"Okay. Jarrod, you keep saying the Oriental lady. Is that someone who is here in the court today?"

"Yes," he told Carvajal and pointed to Du.

"Jarrod, did you see whether or not Latasha had any money?"

"Yes."

"Where was the money?"

"In her hand," he said.

"When she went up to the front and told the lady that she was going to pay for the orange juice, did she show her the money?"

"Yes."

"I want you to tell me what you heard — what words you heard Latasha say."

"She said she was going to pay for it and 'Let me go.' And that's all I can think of right now."

"Do you know if Latasha used any bad words?"

"She didn't use no bad words," the child said.

"Did you hear Latasha call the lady a bitch?"

"No," he said again.

"You don't remember that?" Carvajal asked.

"No," he answered.

"Okay. Now, what I'm going to do is play the tape for you. All right? And what I want you to do when I'm playing the tape is tell us what you heard both people on the tape say. Do you understand?" He told her he did. But there was a problem with the tape player, and during a ten-minute recess the courtroom buzzed as the stern-faced spectators nudged and shuffled their way into the corridor.

A female bailiff prodded Richard Harlins along. He turned on her: "Don't push on me."

She looked at him evenly. "That was a freebie, okay?"

The new judge's first words to the spectators was a warning: she would not tolerate any of the disruptions that had marred previous court proceedings in this case.

I introduced myself to Karlin before the trial started and asked if she'd consent to an interview when the case was over. Naturally, she was noncommittal.

On the bench, her petite form, topped with curly blond hair, made her look like a kid sitting on a stack of phonebooks. At one point, newspaper articles about her suggested she was a Latina, because she was born in Venezuela. But no, one of her former co-workers in the U.S. Attorney's office assured me, "she's as American as apple pie."

She grew up in the Chicago suburb of Highland Park. Her father, Myron Karlin, once president of Warner Brothers International, was a film distributor with MGM when she was born in Caracas in 1950. When I assessed her face to face — the tight string of pearls around her neck, the gracious but aloof manner — she reminded me of a Junior League matron.

When I thought about the palpably angry, motley crew of African Americans that packed the courtroom each day — elegantly suited but clench-jawed Black professionals, laborers in soiled work clothes, Muslim brothers and sisters in uniform, and the always present, microphone-ready ex-stripper with the four-inch claws speaking for the Harlinses — and how this judge might perceive them and Latasha's community, I felt I'd eaten bad fish.

I knew a few judges, some of them in my own family, and was not unfamiliar with judicial demeanor, so I noted my visceral prejudice against Karlin and tried to shake the Junior League image.

On a trip to Chicago, for instance, I visited David Schippers, the attorney who had hired Karlin straight out of Loyola Law School (which she entered at nineteen). She waited tables to pay her way through law school, he said admiringly. She's no spoiled rich girl, he assured me.

But that sick feeling took hold each time I surveyed the disciplined dozens of Korean Americans from Du's church who attended court each day. Who in this bunch — if anyone — would Karlin invite to her daddy's home in Beverly Hills or the one she shared with her husband, U.S. Attorney William Fahey, in the virtually all-White community of Manhattan Beach?

Du trembled at the defense table. The recess only delayed what she knew would be numerous replays of the death scene. Her daughter tried to give her a drink of juice, and a bailiff stopped her.

"She can have water, can't she?" Lloyd snapped.

"Yeah," the bailiff answered.

Sandy Du caressed her mother's distraught face. It was her face, too, its features and its anguish. She gave her mother the water. Jarrod swiveled in a nearby chair, his chin buried in his chest as he bit the top of his overalls. Du began to sob and her daughter with her.

The trial resumed. The jury stared intensely at the television monitor as Jarrod put words to the silent film. The young narrator stood next to the television set. "Jarrod, I'm going to play the tape again," Carvajal told him, "and what I want you to do is tell me if —"

"That's me," he blurted, seeing himself on the screen, then repeated his earlier testimony. Carvajal finished with him and turned him over to Lloyd. If the relatively young prosecutor was noteworthy for her seeming diffidence, the veteran Lloyd was remarkable for the nerves rattling in his voice. While he could become impassioned, there was nothing smooth about his style.

"Jarrod, how many times did you see Mrs. Du, the lady you called the Oriental lady — that's Mrs. Du sitting right here. Okay? How many times did you see the young woman hit Mrs. Du?"

"Once," Jarrod said, contradicting his earlier testimony.

"May I move this, Your Honor?" Lloyd said, pointing to the large monitor on a cart. "Of course," he said pushing it, "a younger person should do it, not an old man like myself. Now," he asked again, "how many times did you see the young woman hit Mrs. Du?"

"Twice," the boy answered this time.

"Did you ever see her knock Mrs. Du down?"

"No."

Lloyd played the videotape again. "Now, where did you see the young woman hit Mrs. Du?"

"In the eye."

"How many times?"

"Once."

"Did you see her or — or where else did she hit her?"

"Nowhere else."

"She hit her one time?" Lloyd pressed.

"Yes."

"That's all?" Lloyd asked.

"Yes," the child repeated.

"Did you hear Mrs. Du yelling?" Jarrod said he did.

"She started yelling when she grabbed the girl's sweater, didn't she?" Lloyd asked.

"Yes," Jarrod answered.

"And she was yelling when the girl hit her in the eye, wasn't she?"

"Yes."

"And she was yelling when she was trying to take this gun out of something — strike that. Did you see Mrs. Du — have you ever seen this before — did you ever see this?" Lloyd held up a brown holster.

Jarrod said, "No."

"Did you see Mrs. Du fumbling with a gun?"

"Do you know what 'fumbling' means, Jarrod?" the judge asked.

"No."

"All right," said Lloyd. "Jarrod, did you see Mrs. Du when she — when she came up with the gun?"

"Yes."

"Was the gun shaking in her hand?"

"No."

"It wasn't shaking in her hand at all?"

"No."

"How long was the gun in Mrs. Du's hand before you heard a shot?"

"One minute," the child told him in error. From the time Latasha walked to the counter until she dropped dead on the floor was about thirty-five seconds.

"All right," said Lloyd. "Did you hear the young woman call Mrs. Du a bitch?"

"No."

The boy had been interviewed by police on videotape hours after the shooting. Lloyd asked him if he remembered telling the police then that Latasha had called Du a bitch.

"I don't remember," he said.

"Now, Jarrod, did you see what happened to the orange juice?"

"Yes. The girl put it on the counter, and she shoved it away."

"It was a short woman, wasn't it," asked Lloyd, referring to Du.

"Yes."

"This young woman was taller than Mrs. Du, wasn't she?" Lloyd asked.

"Yes."

Latasha was five feet six inches tall and weighed one hundred and fifty-two pounds. Du was a very sturdy, middle-aged woman about five feet, four inches tall, not the frail old lady the defense constantly suggested.

"Now, Jarrod," Lloyd asked, "you never did see Mrs. Du strike the young woman, did you?"

"No."

"Do you know what it means to strike someone?" the judge asked. He said he did.

"You never did see her hit her, did you?" Lloyd asked again.

"No."

Then Lloyd demanded, "Which hand was the young woman holding the money in?"

"In her right hand."

"Which hand did she hit the woman in the face with?"

"Her left."

"The young woman struck Mrs. Du in the face with her left hand?" Lloyd asked again. "May we play the tape one more time?" he asked the court. Latasha had slugged Du with her right fist. Afterward, Lloyd asked the boy, "Do you know your right hand from your left hand, Jarrod?"

"Yes."

"Would you show me your left hand?"

The boy raised his hand.

"For the record, he's raising his right hand," said Lloyd. The child's face drooped with shame. "Did she ever hit her with a right hand or the other hand?"

The flustered boy said, "Yes."

Jarrod's sister, a thirteen-year-old girl with square gold hoops hanging from her ears and a self-assured manner, took the witness stand. She was not easily intimidated, and corroborated most of her brother's story. Carvajal asked if she knew Latasha.

"No," she said, then described Latasha's movements as she walked from the back of the store. "She had put the orange juice in her backpack, and it was sticking out clearly so you can see." Half of it was sticking out of the left side of the bag, Alana testified. And she had paper money in her hand, "about two to three dollars." The girl said she believed Latasha was ready to pay for the juice because she was holding the money toward the counter.

"What happened then?" Carvajal asked her.

"She walked to the counter and the clerk was asking her was she trying to steal her orange juice."

"Now, is that the first thing that you heard the clerk say to the Black girl?"

"Yes," Alana told her.

"What exactly did you hear her saying?"

"She said, 'Are you trying to steal my orange juice?'"

"And what did the girl say?"

"No."

"What happened then?"

"The Oriental lady kept asking her was she trying to steal her orange juice over and over, and the Black girl said, 'No.' So the clerk grabbed her by her sweater, and they was fighting for a minute. So then, the Black girl socked her, and then they was scuffling for the backpack, and the clerk got it and threw it behind the counter, and the orange juice fell in front of the counter so . . ."

"Then what happened?"

"The clerk threw the stool at the girl, and she moved back, and when she went to go pick the orange juice up and give it to her, the Oriental lady snatched it behind the counter, and then as the girl was walking toward the door, she shot her."

"You said that they were scuffling, kind of fighting?"

"Yeah."

"Did you hear them exchange words?"

"Yes."

"What did you hear?"

"They was calling each other bitches."

"Now, are you saying that the clerk was calling the Black girl a bitch?"

Contradicting her brother, Alana said, "The Black girl called the clerk a bitch first and then the Oriental lady told her, 'Bitch, are you trying to steal my orange juice?' And the Black girl just kept cursing back and forth."

"What do you mean when you say cursing?"

"They was just saying bitch."

"Is that the only bad word you heard?"

"Yes."

"How many times did you hear the clerk call the Black girl a bitch?"

"Once," she answered.

"Did the Black girl ever tell the clerk that she was trying to pay for her orange juice?"

"Yes."

"When did she do that?"

"When the Oriental lady started grabbing on her."

"So it was at the very beginning?" asked Carvajal.

"Yes."

"When she said 'I'm trying to pay for it,' could you see at that point where the money was?"

"Yes. It was in her hand. At first she was trying to put it on the counter, but then the Oriental lady started grabbing her. So she wasn't doing nothing with it. It was still in her hand."

"Did you see the clerk get a gun?" Carvajal asked.

"Yes."

"And where did she get this gun?"

"Under — under the — under the shelf on a little board."

"And when you saw this gun, was it in something or was it just a gun?"

"It was in a gun pouch," Alana told her.

"Where were you when you first saw the gun?"

"I was still at the counter."

"Did you see when she got the gun out of the holster?"

"Yes."

"Did it appear to be easy to get the gun out the holster, or did she have to kind of work at it a little bit?"

"She had to work at it."

"Now, the holster has a snap. Do you know if the clerk had

to unsnap this before she took the gun out or not? Only if you could tell."

"I couldn't tell."

"When the clerk had the gun out of the holster, what was the Black girl doing?"

"She was trying to walk out the store," Alana said.

"Was she saying anything to the lady at that point?"

"No."

"When the girl got shot, when you heard the gun go off, which direction was the girl facing?"

"Toward the door."

Carvajal asked whether she had ever spoken to Mrs. Du before, and the girl said no. But she had been in the store many times before.

"Have you ever heard her speak?" Carvajal asked.

"Yes."

"Have you ever heard her speak in English?"

"Yes."

"Have you ever heard other people speak to her in English?"

"Yes."

"When she spoke in English, did you understand what she was saying?"

"Yes."

Lloyd approached the witness. "Good afternoon, Miss Hall," he said gallantly.

"Good afternoon," she responded with equal dignity.

The videotape was replayed. "Is that you standing at the counter, Miss Hall?" asked Lloyd.

"Yes."

"In looking at that tape, did you ever see Mrs. Du hit the young woman at all?"

"Yes, with the stool."

"Oh, she hit her with the stool?" Lloyd asked incredulously.

"Yes," the girl said.

"Do you recall testifying at the grand jury?" She told him she did. "And didn't you tell them that she threw the stool but you think the girl got out of the way?"

In a sure, insistent tone she answered, "I said she probably got out of the way, but the stool still hit her on the leg."

"But you didn't say that to the grand jury, did you?"

"Say what?"

"You didn't say that she hit her with the stool, did you?"

"No."

"All right. Did you ever see the young woman knock Mrs. Du down?"

"Yes."

"How many times?"

"About twice," she said.

"How many times did you see her hit Mrs. Du?"

"Four times."

"And where did she hit her?"

"In the face."

"You didn't tell the police at that time that she hit her in the face four times, did you?"

"No," Alana told him.

"Now, the young woman called Mrs. Du a bitch before Mrs. Du had ever used the word, isn't that right?"

"Yes."

"And as a matter of fact, Mrs. Du never did use the word *bitch,* did she?"

"Yes, she did."

"Did you hear the girl say to Mrs. Du, four or five times, 'I'm going to kill you'?"

"No."

"At some point when you were in that store, you and your brother moved away from the counter, didn't you?"

"Yes."

"And you moved away from the counter because they began to fight; isn't that right?"

"Yes."

"And first you moved over just a short distance, and then you ran farther away; isn't that correct?"

"I didn't run farther away. I moved back."

"You moved back. And you moved back because you heard the girl say, 'I'm going to kill you,' didn't you?"

"No." She had never heard Latasha threaten Du's life, she insisted. She moved because the fight scared her and because "they always have problems at that liquor store."

Police officers testified that they found two dollars lying on the floor next to Latasha's corpse; and retrieved the .38-caliber Smith & Wesson that killed her, as well as a carbine rifle and ammunition stashed behind the counter.

As Denise Harlins approached the witness stand, Lloyd leaned over to talk to Sandy Du. "It's going well," he assured her.

Harlins's testimony for the prosecution was brief. She identified her niece as the person in a police photograph whose head lay in a pool of blood. And the backpack, she said, belonged to her daughter, Shay. Latasha had borrowed it.

Lloyd stood, a heavy gold bracelet on his right wrist gleaming under the courtroom lights. "There will be no questions." Of the ten witnesses the prosecution would call, Denise Harlins was the only one who knew Latasha.

The trial moved swiftly. At the end of the first day of testimony, a Monday, Karlin conferred with the attorneys and said, "It looks like we'll be instructing the jury Wednesday."

Outside the courtroom, Lloyd told reporters this was the most difficult case he'd ever handled. Not because of the facts in the case. It was a very simple case; the video said it all. It was self-defense, he told them, as he had told the jury in his opening statement. Du was viciously assaulted by Latasha Harlins, he asserted, but the merchant "never intended to kill Miss Harlins."

Meanwhile, Du's controversial case remained overshadowed

by a nation in the grip of the peep show on patriarchy playing on television across America: the all-male Senate Judiciary Committee hearings on the nomination of Clarence Thomas to the Supreme Court and the monkey wrench thrown into the proceedings by Anita Faye Hill. Law Professor Hill, accusing him of sexual harassment, was, despite Thomas's claims to the contrary, the one psychologically stripped and strung up for a high-tech testosterone lashing.

And as one pack of reporters followed the Dus and Harlinses through the courthouse, others surrounded the star of another high-profile case pushing Latasha's into the national background: Charles H. Keating, Jr., accused of defrauding thousands of small investors of $250 million in the Lincoln Savings and Loan scandal. That case would be tried before a law-and-order judge, like Karlin, who would become associated with the most sensational murder trial in modern United States history, Judge Lance Ito. While reporters chased the Dus through the sun-drenched rear lobby of the courthouse one afternoon, Lincoln's sixty-seven-year-old owner — gaunt, towering, and glassy-eyed — lumbered in shackles past Billy Hong Ki Du, who spoke frantically into his ever-present walkie-talkie, checking with the family's many bodyguards.

Undoubtedly, in L.A. and beyond, a squabble, even a deadly one between members of two minority communities, was the entr'acte as the nation waited for the other shoe to drop in the King beating. (I know I couldn't convince *Essence* magazine, with its Black target audience, that the Black-Korean issue portended great violence. In fact, East Coast publications generally did not comprehend the significance of relations between the country's emerging new majority: colored people, already the majority in Los Angeles. In the East, discussions of "diversity" — ethnic relations as a whole — were cast in the old Black-White mold. Despite my gripes about the paper, what I could write about the subject saw the light of day in the *Los Angeles Times* in the years leading up to Latasha's death.) The White cops charged with excessive force would come to trial soon. But the irregular "Black-Korean" war, subsumed by that antebellum-style whipping of King caught on new-fangled technology, inched closer to Sa-I-Gu as the Black boycott of Chung's Market reached day 106. Bakewell swore to keep the pickets parading for at least ninety days, and would not stop until the Koreans cried uncle.

CHAPTER 10

"Owwwwww!" The Koreans weren't crying uncle yet, but I was. "Owwwwww!" I was hacking my way through the Du trial — a lingering cough from the lung infection. And now there was something else for me to contend with. My body always revolted when I was stressed out.

"We're bleeding a *little* more than usual," the doctor explained, continuing to snip away.

"I thought," I said through clenched teeth, "the cervix wasn't supposed to have any nerves."

"Oh" — *snip . . . snip* — "it's just that I'm pulling you a *bit* more than usual." I'd lived in doctors' offices as a child and knew too well the lukewarm tone of a clinician distracted by the procedure at hand. Though she'd been recommended by a friend and was well regarded professionally, I was not reassured.

Long ago I'd had a precancerous condition that required the removal of a section of my cervix. A recent Pap smear had come back abnormal, and this was my second biopsy of the month. The doctor hadn't taken a large enough sample the first time, so the pathologist's report was inconclusive. "We'll have to dilate you," the doctor explained, and sent me home wearing a twig that looked as if it had been around since Cleopatra's gig. Walking around with a piece of a tree stuck in you was not the most pleasant sensation, and I arrived for the second biopsy tense and in mild pain.

"Ow . . . ow . . . ow . . ."

"Okay, now try to relax," the doctor said. Despite a certain kind of haughtiness that my cultural radar recognized as African American princess airs, this doctor certainly made me more comfortable than the gynecologist I'd dropped months before in Los Angeles for, among other crimes, consistently misreading, skyward, my low pain threshold. Still, I wanted to smack this one about now. Her nurse, a White woman in her fifties with a gentle manner, patted my arm.

"Don't worry," the nurse told me sweetly. "If you bleed too much, I'll give you some of my blood." Then I caught her look furtively at the doctor, down at me, then smile wide and tight with chipmunk cheeks and a closed mouth stretched to a slit. The mouth opened and the voice that issued out was distant and musing as she launched, from the primitive recesses of her mind: "But you know what they say about getting one drop of Black blood. One drop makes you Black. Uh-huh," she underscored for herself. Then spinning out this wild non sequitur with gathering speed she announced as one word, "*Iheardthatallmylife.* Uh-huh, all my life in New Orleans, that's what they said. One drop does it to you. *Isn'tthatridiculous?* But that's what I heard all . . ."

"Owwwwww!"

"You okay?" the nurse inquired with a smile, then ran on, "All my life, that's what they said."

My muscles tightened. I felt a twitch in my left eyelid. I looked past the stirrups to the bent head of my physician. I wanted to kick it. Where did she get this lunatic from? I could imagine the nurse's ethnically tailored tales to others: "How you doin', Mrs. Grossman? Just relax. Most of the procedure is familiar to you. The doctor will insert the speculum to examine you — but it'll be nothing like what I heard those Nazis did to Jewish women during the Holocaust, so just take it easy . . ."

In the city whose pre-riot tourist propaganda would have us believe it was the sophisticated metropolis synonymous with those end of millennium buzzwords *diversity* and *multiculturalism*, I now had to endure forced enrollment in the Little Dab'll Do Ya School of Genetics.

"Don't worry," I snapped at the nurse. "You can't turn Black by osmosis."

In my mental universe, the encounter with the nurse from the Big Easy was part of the web of *racial* farce and contradictions in our national life that left me howling with either laughter or contempt. The incident was a tank of fuel added to the psychic propane driving my work at the time. And each scene like it compelled me to find a forum for dissenters like Velina Hasu Houston, the *multiracial* activist with whom I disagreed in fundamental ways, but respected.

Not long before the doctor's visit, I'd sat in a Santa Monica café with Velina, a writer whose life and art were devoted to refuting the little-dab'll-do-ya notion that clung, leech-like, to the nurse's psyche, sucking out reason. The dark diminutive woman would tell me repeatedly, in conversations that ranged over several years, "I am Japanese, African American, and Native American. That is my biological truth."

As the Du case progressed, I would write about color conflict among Blacks and the related issue of *multiracial* identity for a book called *Lure and Loathing: Race, Identity, and the Ambivalence of Assimilation,* a collection of essays that explored W.E.B. Du Bois's classic statement about the double consciousness that defines Blacks in America. With Velina in mind, my contribution to that work would be called "Sushi & Grits."

Her eyes scanned me skeptically as salty air blew through the door of the tiny café and mixed with the aroma of ground coffee. A playwright whose work navigated the cultural and psychological terrain of Amerasian life, she did not trust me to explore the territory she inhabited. Though it was she who sought me out initially because I'd written sympathetically of the issues *multiracial* Americans face, she feared that I too would "rape" her. That's what Black people have been doing to her all her life, she claimed, committing political and psychological rape on her person. And I'd do it by writing in a way that distorts the reality of

Americans like her who assert their "biological truth" and seek an identity separate from Blacks.

That's when she launched into her tirade, accusing the African American community of trying to annex anyone with "one drop of African blood." Yet, she said, making a point I felt African Americans had to face, when *multiracial* people want to voice their unique concerns — political support for Amerasian refugees, many of whom have African American fathers, funding for works of art that present the complex cultural views of, for instance, a Black Korean American — they are told to shut up and just carry out the political agenda of Blacks.

"They are saying, 'Come join us.' But it's not because of some great brother or sister love — it's political. To me, that's a totally unethical way of saying that you want people to be a member of your community." That's when she pronounced that, as far as she was concerned, "all slavery is over — whether it's physical slavery on the plantation or political slavery that gives one group, like African Americans, the audacity to say that they own people because they have one drop of African blood." Because if that's true, she steamed on, then they own Samoa and they own Guam and they own Fiji and they own Tonga and they own Hawaii. And if the statistics that say "one out of five European American families has Black blood are true, then we're living in an African American nation and we need to have a revolution" and get rid of all this oppression. But the one-drop theory is not true, "and it's audacious, greedy, and ridiculous" for African Americans to say that it is.

Something Baroque played too loudly in the café as I strained to listen to Velina's ahistorical and apolitical diatribe. The warm Pacific Coast day belied the approach of winter, much as Velina's body, delicate but voluptuously wrought, belied the dragon within. She wore a prickly, weighted, long-trained cape of pain that she swirled and lashed mightily, flogging enemies real and perceived.

It was, of course, White slave owners in the antebellum South who designed the little-dab'll-do-ya rule. They wanted to ensure that Blacks of mixed heritage — often the issue of White masters who had raped enslaved Black women — had no special claim to freedom because their fathers were free. They inherited the status of their slave mothers and were categorized with presumably pure Blacks to ensure the perpetuation of the slave population. In the postbellum era, the alleged inferiority of African blood — no matter how little of it one possessed — was used to rationalize the continued social and political subordination of Blacks.

A seeming legal anachronism, the conviction that any known or perceived African ancestry makes one Black remains unchallenged by our highest court. As late as 1986, the U.S. Supreme Court refused to review a lower court's ruling that a Louisiana woman, whose great-great-great-great-grandmother had been the mistress of a French planter, was Black. (Given her Big Easy origins, perhaps I was a little harsh on my blood buddy the nurse.)

Facing this reality, African Americans wisely made a political virtue out of a necessity, asserting that we should not let our heterogeneous ancestry divide and render us politically dysfunctional, as many argue is the case with Brazil's color-stratified African heritage population.

The United States did attempt to document degrees of *racial* mixture by using *mulatto, quadroon,* and *octoroon* census classifications during the latter half of the nineteenth century through the census of 1920. But after 1920, these categories were jettisoned in favor of the binary notion of *race* that was the social and political reality of the nation — as a landmark case of the nineteenth century documented. *Plessy* v. *Ferguson,* the U.S. Supreme Court case that established the doctrine of "separate but equal" in 1896, contained the argument that not only was segregation wrong but that plaintiff Homer Plessy, by virtue of his European ancestry (he was seven-eighths White, to be precise), had been unjustly denied access to railroad accommodations offered

Whites. Upholding the one-drop rule, the Court said forget it, stamped him Negro, and sent him toward the caboose with all the other "Blacks."

This U.S. caste system forged a *racial* consciousness that valorized rejection of invidious color distinctions within the group.

The novelist and long-time executive secretary of the NAACP, Walter White, who died in 1955, attested to this collective sentiment when he wrote: "I am a Negro. My skin is white, my eyes are blue, my hair is blond. The traits of my race are nowhere visible upon me . . . [But] I am not white. There is nothing in my mind and heart which tempts me to think I am. I am one of the two in the color of my skin; I am the other in my spirit and my heart."

This honored embrace of an initially imposed *monoracial* identity has also been a psychological balm, one used to efface the brutal history of rape and concubinage associated with Black identity in the Americas. Certainly not the reason for the pervasive Native American ancestry among New World Blacks or many of the unions between Africans and Europeans in colonial America or their descendants today, rape stands as a historical impediment to our collective embrace of a miscegenated identity. The political denial of that complex ancestry has, in part, been the calculated decision of generations of Black leaders, and the visceral one of the *race,* to avoid the pain, confusion, and dilution of the politically galvanizing rage that might occur if an oppressed people acknowledged that Ma or Pa is "the enemy."

But Velina was dismissive of the historical record. "I understand that these racial categories are created and perpetuated by the dominant White society." But it's ludicrous that African Americans continue to accept them. "Are they also going to accept the fact that the dominant White society says African Americans are stupid? Or that all African American men have large penises? Or that African American people are lazy and slow? Or that all African American men rape?" Because all this language, all these definitions of what an African is in this country, and the stereotypes about African American culture "come out of the same pocket." So if they are going to accept this definition of an African American being based on the one-drop-of-blood theory, then they are going to have to accept all the rest, too. "They are saying we will allow the dominant White society to tell us who and what we are. I am not going to do that."

Personal struggles over "mixed-race" identity in the United States are not new, of course. They are the stuff of literature, films, and pulp fiction. That the concerns Velina raises are becoming part of what could be a politically explosive national debate relates to a profound demographic shift in the country not seen since the massive waves of immigration in the late nineteenth century.

Thirty years of increased immigration from Latin America, Asia, and the Caribbean has added eighteen million people of color to the crucible of American life, one in which *race* and class antagonisms contest the promise of democracy.

Whites account for 74 percent of the population now. But this massive immigration, and the higher birthrate among Latinos and Blacks, has contributed to new non-White majorities in major urban centers and may, demographers predict, lead to a new national majority by 2060, if not sooner: people of color. Latinos are a significant part of this demographic darkening. The percentage of Blacks, the largest minority group now, accounts for almost 13 percent of the population but is shrinking relative to the growth of Latinos. A panethnic group with varying degrees of African, Native American, and European ancestry, Latinos now number twenty-five million (10 percent of the population) and are predicted to be the nation's largest minority by the year 2010. Some 3.5 million Japanese, Chinese, Filipinos, Koreans, Laotian, Hmong, and Vietnamese are among the new immigrants; as are thousands of dark-skinned East Indians, Pakistanis, and Bangladeshis. The increased immigration and intermarriage among all groups account for the rising *multiracial* population.

High on the political agenda of many now-vocal and organized *multiracial* Americans and their families is the demand for a new U.S. Census category that would specifically identify citizens of mixed ancestry. Whether such a category would be labeled *biracial, multiracial, multiethnic,* or something else, as well as how it would be defined, is the subject of ongoing debates.

AMEA, the Association of Multiethnic Americans, a national affiliation of groups advocating the interests of individuals of mixed ancestry and their families, as well as Project RACE (Re-Classify All Children Equally), are the most vocal and organized advocates of such a category, and they prefer the term *multiracial.*

The size of the multiethnic population is subject to debate, too. The 1990 census showed that two million children were born to people who said they were married to or living with someone of a different *race.* But that two million figure grossly underrepresents the *multiracial* population, say advocates of the new category. The exact figures are unknown, because the census currently requires people either to identify with one of four officially recognized "racial" groups or to check "other" when filling out data for the Census Bureau.

Since 1977, those four *racial* categories — American Indian or Alaska Native, Asian or Pacific Islander, Black, and White — have been set for the entire federal government by the Office of Management and Budget's Statistical Policy Directive 15. Directive 15 also recognizes ethnicity — but for one group only — Hispanics, with Hispanic Origin and Not of Hispanic Origin categories. In 1990, 9.8 million people refused to identify with a single *race* on the federal census and indicated "other." The Census Bureau estimates that most of those who did were Hispanics, for whom the concept of a *monoracial* identity often seems alien.

This emerging population of multiethnics is narrowly defined by the most vocal advocates of a new *racial* category — parents of *multiracial* children. Many of these parents were married after the U.S. Supreme Court struck down the last of the nation's antimiscegenation laws in 1967. That decision, *Loving* v. *Commonwealth of Virginia,* invalidated the laws in several states which had made *interracial* marriage a crime. These couples see their offspring as the first generation of "legitimate" *multiracial* children born to *interracial* couples whose marriages — without state exceptions — have the sanction of law.

More often than in the past, these couples assert, their children are raised in homes with both parents present, parents who impart their varied cultural traditions and social perceptions to these children. This distinguishes their kids culturally and psychologically, they often claim, from earlier generations of *mixed-race* children who were frequently abandoned by one parent and raised with a *single-race* identity. Therefore, only their kids — the first generation offspring of *interracial* couples — should be considered *multiracial*.

But not everyone agrees. The ranks of this new generation of *multiracial* Americans is bolstered by an older one, people who were never socially allowed to define themselves as such, but have been emboldened to do so now by the activism of their younger cohorts and their parents. Further expanding the ranks of those demanding a *multiracial* census category are the kin of *interracial* couples — grandparents, siblings, cousins — who have helped form support groups for families like theirs across the nation.

A combination of forces — pressure from this emerging critical mass, congressional hearings in 1993 exploring the need for such a category, and recommendations from the National Research Council that the government find better ways to measure the increasing ethnic complexity of its people — compelled the OMB to test a multiple-ancestry question for the mid-decennial census in 1995. Early in the process, the OMB would not tell the public how the question was constructed and the terms defined. But responses to the question in field tests will determine its inclusion on the 2000 census. That decision must be made by the fall of 1997.

Because the parameters of the new *racial* category were unknown at the start, its advocates think the test question was designed to fail. The government, the scholars, researchers, civil rights organizations, and many other special interest groups that have a stake in the way the government collects and tabulates *race* and ethnic data assert the importance of maintaining continuity in these categories so that data remain compatible over time. Any change to the categories of tabulation could threaten that. Advocates of a *multiracial* category believe this intransigence results from both bureaucratic inertia and a desire among politically motivated groups to maintain the *racial* status quo.

Though thwarted for years by the federal bureaucracy, these activists have gained ground at the local level. The lobbying efforts of Georgia-based Project RACE made that state the first to require a *multiracial* designation on all government and private documents requesting *racial* information. Enacted in 1994, the legislation was sponsored by the Georgia state senator Ralph David Abernathy III, son of the late civil rights leader, who declared that the recognition of *racially* mixed Americans is long overdue and is the next "human rights frontier."

While it was, ironically, a state of the Old Confederacy that first passed the most sweeping legislation acknowledging *multiracial* citizens on all state forms in the post-Loving era, Indiana and Michigan followed suit. The Ohio legislature in 1992 and the Illinois state legislature in 1993 required school districts to provide a *multiracial* category on all forms requesting the *racial* identification of students. And by the spring of 1996, many other states were considering similar legislation. Among them were California, Massachusetts, New Jersey, New York, Oklahoma, Oregon, Pennsylvania, Texas, and Wisconsin. In Maryland, a *multiracial* bill passed the legislature but was vetoed by the governor. It is the strategy of Project RACE and its supporters, like AMEA, to get enacted so many state laws recognizing *multiracial* Americans that acceptance of the category at the federal level becomes a *fait accompli.*

The momentum at the state level has been growing because of the demands of parents of *multiracial* children who have been subjected to — and in most states continue to be subjected to —

eyeballing. That is, visual inspection by school authorities who arbitrarily determine the child's *race* if she refuses to check one of the assigned *monoracial* categories.

In one such case, a kindergarten child in Maryland sat captive while a school secretary marched in and announced to the entire class that she'd come to decide the girl's *race*. In Georgia, when another child tried to explain to her teacher that she was "biracial," the teacher scolded, "You'd better go home and figure out who you are — you can't be both." In a North Carolina classroom a teacher told one teenager, "You're so light, are you sure your mother knows who your father is?"

Such incidents, multiplied a thousandfold across the nation, are stoking demands that a *multiracial* category be included on the federal census and used uniformly by all government agencies. This official acknowledgment, and the social recognition and political representation likely to follow, are essential to the self-esteem and self-interest of *multiracial* people and their families, advocates argue. But the factors that make such a category so necessary for *multiracial* activists are the same reasons that representatives of minority groups often oppose the *multiracial* designation.

Any tinkering with the census is going to be politically touchy, since the creation or destruction of congressional districts, and hence the careers of politicians, is tied to the population shifts it documents. But the specific concern raised by a proposed *multiracial* category is that it would siphon numbers from so-called parent populations, something especially threatening to minority groups whose political power might be diminished. This prospect is most alarming to Blacks because of the stigma attached to African heritage in the United States.

Given the myriad ancestries of African Americans, Black civil rights organizations fear that their members will abandon in droves the perceived tugboat of Blacks for the exotic *multiracial* cruiseship.

More broadly, OMB Statistical Policy Directive 15 is appropriately viewed as part of the judicial, legislative, and administrative machinery that has been constructed over the past thirty years to combat and eradicate *racial* discrimination. The census count, tied to legal and programmatic responsibilities embedded in current law, is used to monitor and enforce a panoply of civil rights protections based on the tabulation of citizens by mutually exclusive single-*race* categories. Most significant among these protections is the Voting Rights Act of 1965, won, after generations of struggle, at the cost of life and limb. But the data compiled under this policy have been indispensable, as well, in monitoring and enforcing public school desegregation plans; federal and private sector affirmative action plans; the Fair Housing Act; gauging the access of minorities to home mortgage loans under the Home Mortgage Disclosure Act; monitoring the enforcement of the Equal Credit Opportunity Act; and assessing environmental degradation in communities of color.

Those hostile to a *multiracial* category contend that its consequent disaggregation of groups could make the collection of useful data on *race* difficult if not impossible.

In 1993, Ohio Democrat Thomas Sawyer chaired a series of hearings on proposals to modify ethnic and *racial* questions on the 2000 census. The now defunct Congressional Subcommittee on Census, Statistics, and Postal Personnel met its demise with the Republican takeover of the House of Representatives in 1994. Before its death, though, it considered an array of issues: Arab Americans, for example, are lumped with White Americans but say they are discriminated against as an ethnic minority and want their own category. (I know that my husband, an Egyptian-born Arab, is clueless about the concept of *race* in America, and though he looks it, refuses to be identified as White.) Native Hawaiians wanted to be placed in the Native American category rather than in the Asian or Pacific Islander designation, which suggests they are immigrants, not aboriginal people. Some Latinos suggested that their group be viewed as a *race* rather than as an ethnic category — a regressive proposal, I think. But the issue that drew the most attention was the *multiracial* proposal.

There are a number of competing purposes that make it very difficult to come to a clear answer for or against the creation of a *multiracial* category, Sawyer told me. Using a favorite phrase, the forty-seven-year-old former schoolteacher noted that all the *racial* categories reflect the "temporal bias" of changing ages. And those categories now reflect competing goals. "The legal ones tied to constitutional civil rights protections. The question of personal and group identity, that is a complex and evolving set of notions." And then the need, which falls somewhere between the two, for understanding demographic change in the country as it occurs. And while it may not have a clear scientific or anthropological basis, "these categories become the terms by which we understand who we are — accurate or not."

And even if we continue — as we undoubtedly will — to judge ourselves primarily through perceived social reality, rather than scientific or anthropological ones, the census does not reflect a significant shift in the "temporal bias" of our age.

"The country is changing at a very rapid rate now, and the categories have not changed for the last twenty years. The census numbers may be precise," Sawyer concluded, "but they are precisely wrong. They do not reflect the reality of who people think they are."

Who people think they are, as the one-drop rule proves, is often imposed by external forces. By the enactment of discriminatory laws, ranging from restrictive immigration to imprisonment of certain citizens to prohibitions against access to certain jobs and education, the United States government historically racialized persons and created a racial consciousness. To a great extent, were the government to acknowledge *multiracial* Americans, it would foster a sense of community where, at best, an embryonic group identity now exists.

There is a presumption among Blacks that such a community — socialized outside the burdens of a rigid racial caste — would be hostile to the political agenda of the current population of African Americans. (Who knows what African Americans will think if and when we are born into a future society less bound by *race*?) The mere desire to disaggregate — the heresy of refuting the one-drop rule — seems sufficient proof of hostility to African Americans. But the latter is not a monolithic group that agrees on everything. And there is no proof that most *multiracial* Americans, as people of color, would automatically be politically more conservative, for instance, than Blacks or Latinos are as a whole. The creation of a *multiracial* category would certainly alter the current *racial* alignments. Whether that bodes good or ill politically, from the vantage point of Blacks and other minorities, is unknown.

Sadly, however, by the early nineties I had interviewed scores of multiethnic Americans of partial African descent who, because of mutually unresolved identity problems, saw Blacks as the enemy. I knew from my own preoccupations as a writer that the strongest advocates of any position were usually motivated by some sense of outrage over a wrong done them or a loved one. The activists may not have represented more mute voices in the *multiracial* community as a whole, but the talk from the loudest voices did not bode well.

"Why should I identify with the Black community," one woman spewed, when every day of her life she saw her mother beg for Black acceptance but be shunned and psychologically battered because she looked White. The woman speaking was a typical African American, the product of generations of ethnic mixing, married to an Asian American, I later learned. I overheard her comments while a crowd milled in a courtyard outside a room where MASC, Multiracial Americans of Southern California, was holding its annual conference, called Kaleidoscope. It was the late eighties. It was a support group for *multiracial* individuals and families and the first organization of its kind I'd encountered.

That woman's venomous tone was echoed throughout the conference by several *interracially* married Blacks toward the African American community and in conversations I had with multiethnics of partial African descent to whom MASC led me.

When, for a conference I helped to organize, I asked this woman to explain her reasons for supporting a *multiracial* census category on camera, she agreed. But only if her identity was concealed. And so she sat in the shadows, her face obliterated by the dark, venting her contempt for Blacks, and admitting, finally, that she hated being thought of as a Negro. This self-loathing, this desire to distance oneself from a stigmatized Black identity, was nothing new and it was, variously, the subtext, pretext, and context of many of the conversations I had with multiethnic Americans of African heritage.

But I did not believe this to be the case with Velina. She proudly asserted — correctly or not — that she was totally a woman of color. She presumed her African American and Native American father had no European ancestry. She had no connection to the legacy of brutal sexual coercion between Whites and Blacks. As I would learn, her alienation from African Americans was rooted in a very specific set of experiences.

She got along, she told me, with Black people who allowed her to be who she is. She called them "Black liberals," and saw me as one. I despised the label. It reinforced a sense of separation. I was a tolerant outsider.

But to look in Velina's face, or that of the woman who spoke in the shadows, was to behold a sister, a cousin, an aunt — for surely they looked no different from my kin, either by direct lineage or the broad bonds of culture and history — and yet see writ a contempt and fear that propelled me to the margins of a distant galaxy, the place their eyes informed me I belonged. And I felt myself calling "sister" to them hollowly, into the void, an irritating echo heard and unanswered. That there were potentially millions like them and millions more being born to people like them who viewed me, might view all like me in the future, at the preferred distance of light years chilled my salty tears. And it frightened me politically.

Maintaining unity among people of African descent, without walking in lockstep, was an absolute necessity in a nation as historically hostile to Black empowerment as this one. It was a political conviction as well as an emotional yearning. Given my personal history, however, I believed my African ancestry was the tonal center of my existence, but one always ready and willing to be riffed upon. I had subconsciously, then consciously — prodded more and more by people like Velina — begun to construct an individual and group identity liberated from the ethos of the plantation. One that had more than enough room for the Velinas of the world — without making the price of admission the death of their non-Black selves.

While Velina's Black-bashing rhetoric — all too common among *multiracials* who knew little about the Black side of their heritage — was painfully ahistorical to my ears, this point was not: relegating the one-drop rule to history's trash heap. And were African Americans ever given the psychological and political space to think with a modicum of consistency outside the distress of oppression, we would, I hope, see that the path out of the *racial* prisons of our mutual creation lies in a rejection *not only* of the little-dab'll-do-ya theory but ultimately a rejection of *all racial* categories.

But we are not going to be given that space. We shall have to forge it. Attempting to create a forum where this and related issues will be put on the front burner for American journalists, I organized a symposium for the National Association of Black Journalists, called "Blacks in a Newly Multicultural America." It was less than a year before Latasha was killed and Rodney King jacked up. And with the missionary zeal typical of me at the time, I was intent on making Black journalists, and the many other editors and writers who attended the annual conference, address the political, economic, and cultural relationships between Blacks and new immigrant groups, as well as the substance of Black identity at the millennium. My overarching concern, the subtext for my efforts then and now, was to confront the internal as well as external forces that undermined the power of Black people to organize in their own best interests, to reach out and form progressive coalitions with other people of color and progressive Whites.

At the conference, a panel of writers, scholars, and political activists confronted, for the first time, some of them said, what it meant for a person of African ancestry in the United States to define herself primarily as *multiracial*. Velina was among the panelists. Asserting her biological truth and calling for a new *multiracial* census designation, she inevitably became the lightning rod for the 1990 convention.

Responding to her, Charles Stewart, a Democratic Party activist, directed the hundreds of journalists and editors gathered in the room: "If you consider yourself Black for political reasons, raise your hand." The overwhelming majority raised their hands, and Stewart, surveying the predominantly African American crowd, noted, "When I asked how many people here believe that they are of pure African descent, without any mixture, nobody raised a hand." The point, he said, is this: "If you advocate a category that includes people who are *multiracial* to the detriment of their Black identification, you will replicate what you saw — an empty room. We cannot afford to have an empty room. We cannot afford to have a *race* empty of Black people — not so long as we are struggling against discrimination based on our identification as Black people." This was the Black Party line and was greeted with much head-nodding approval.

Asserting one's biological truth was met with scattered hissing. And Velina had to escape sharp elbows aimed at her by several angry members of the crowd who followed her from the ballroom, where the symposium was held, to a packed smaller workshop, where the discussion of *multiracial* identity continued. Once there, arms ready to slam her crossed against torsos twisted away from her in objection. And here and there, a head turned so that a glare could be shot over contorted shoulders just to underscore the point.

"Those people were vicious, hostile," Velina said with a shudder afterward. "These are supposedly yuppie African Americans. These are journalists. These are not lower income people without education. These are educated African Americans hissing at me. Hissing. That was frightening. And being subjected to that was like a political rape and a racial rape."

There were several kind voices in the room, Velina recalled. One Black woman rose, faced the crowd, and said, "Shame on you, shame on any of us for being the gene patrol and trying to tell people who they are."

Those voices were few and far between, Velina lamented. "I was sitting on a panel with bright people and as far as I was concerned they had a brick in their heads. [That experience] really set me back, because if these educated African Americans are going to be so hostile and abusive toward me, especially in a public arena, then what hope is there [to build bridges between us]. I really thought I should have worn a crash helmet."

I had to admit that I was shocked at the visceral hostility that leaped at her — though I shouldn't have been, given all I'd written about colorism in the preceding years.

CHAPTER 11

L URKING EVERYWHERE but seeming to come out of nowhere, color talk in the African American community was often
a casually employed rhetorical weapon of first resort. Recount-
ing her childhood in Ohio during the seventies, an acquaintance named Gwen recalled the time a young girl in her neighborhood got mad at Gwen's light-skinned mother and launched
a tirade that began and ended with "You high-yella bitch." A
child herself then, Gwen said the incident seemed inconsequential, though not isolated. But we both noted, as the eighties
progressed, an escalation of such rhetoric, increasingly employed in the context of a threat and an implicit expression of
a deepening class alienation among Blacks sometimes reflected
in color.

"You talk like a fuckin' White girl," the anonymous brother
informed my voice mail system at the *Los Angeles Times* well into
the nineteen-nineties. "You need to change that message. I seen
you on TV, and I got a leash for yella bitches like you."

He stalked her. Somewhere along 125 Street he'd spotted her and
would not give up pursuit, winding his way through dense human traffic as she approached Lenox, then Seventh, then Eighth
Avenue. All along the way she saw crowds stopping to look behind her, but she was not a rubberneck and kept steppin'. She
didn't stop even as screamed curses rose above her head and
the din of sidewalk merchants hawking cheap purses and rich
African cloth, even as accusations yelled yards away from her

indifferent back competed with the blare of car horns and police sirens that were always part of the commotion on Harlem's
main thoroughfare. Unmistakably, something was going on behind her back, she knew; too many people walking toward her
had stopped to stare by now. But there were so many dramas
played out on the city's sidewalks daily, she thought it safest
to mind her own business. It was a beautiful summer day and
she just wanted to catch some rays. But when she did finally
pause, to look in a store window, she saw the reflection of a dark
man, maybe in his sixties, jumping up and down, flailing his arms
and yelling obscenely. "Most of it was gibberish," Gwen said. But
she clearly heard him scream: "You think you're better than I
am . . . I know what your mama was up to." The light brown–
skinned woman fled into the store to escape the man, who continued his harangue from the sidewalk. About fifteen minutes later,
she emerged, saw him nowhere, and made her getaway.

Gwen was a designer of jewelry and an East Coast braiding-
parlor acquaintance. More than in the usual beauty shop, the
long hours, sometimes days, it took to braid a head meant one
could catch up on the episodes of life's drama one was too busy to
witness firsthand — all while enjoying, if one were wise to these
marathon sessions, a fine, picnic-style lunch. "Was that a rare
occurrence?" I asked, offering her a banana from my bag of
provisions. She refused but accepted a slice of homemade chocolate cake and a plastic champagne flute filled with black cherry
seltzer water.

"It was unusual that a complete stranger would attack me
because I am somewhat light." When she was growing up in
Ohio, the town adjacent to hers was full of *interracial* families,
she told me, many of them comfortably middle class. "People
often assumed that if you were light, you came from one of those
families. And there was some resentment among darker African
Americans that you were better off than they were if you were
light." She didn't come from that town. Both her parents were
very light-complexioned African Americans who "owned their

own modest house, but little else — except a car. We really didn't have much."

She said she never thought of herself as exceptional in any way — not even particularly light. "I just didn't think a lot, if at all, about color." But her New York experiences made her increasingly conscious that at least some Black people perceived her as exceptional.

There was a street preacher in the Brooklyn neighborhood she moved to from Ohio. "She used to stop me every day to say hello. She always called me sister. And it was a nice warm feeling when we spoke." But one day the preacher accused Gwen of ignoring her.

"I saw a sister who looks like you walk by me for several days now and not speak a word," the preacher told her accusingly.

Gwen assured her repeatedly, "It wasn't me."

"Oh, she must look like you then," the preacher relented. "You know, what we call an understanding."

Gwen, a woman in her early thirties who wore her hair in long dark dreds, eventually saw the woman the preacher was talking about: a bleached blonde with short-cropped hair. Other than being generically light, they weren't even the same complexion.

"That really upset me, that she and her circle thought something about me was wrong. Though I was excused because it was not my fault that, to some, I would look like a racially mixed person." Of course, she is a *racially* mixed person — a New World Black.

Easily written off as street crazies, perhaps, the street preacher and the irate stalker were not the only Blacks who viewed her as a sister with a proviso. She said that was made abundantly clear when she came to New York to work as an intern at a museum in the late eighties.

"I was introduced to another intern, a very dark woman from Trinidad. I extended my hand to shake hers, and she literally rolled her eyes at me" while offering a limp extremity.

When there was an error in their first paycheck, the woman

walked over to Gwen and told her, "'I guess you should go in there and flash your high-yella skin and big brown eyes.' Meaning I could get it fixed and she couldn't. Or suggesting I should ask them to correct it for both of us. I finally told her, 'Don't start that shit. I don't know what your problem is, but don't even start it.'"

Having these encounters in the workplace "really undermines collegiality," Gwen understated, "so I just tried to ignore her. But her stuff got so blatant we almost had fistfights."

One day, the woman ordered lunch and was eating it at her desk in a cubicle they both shared. "She had this salad with a piece of lemon on the side. She picked it up," Gwen said, "and started rubbing the lemon all over her arms and face and purring, 'Isn't this beautiful?' talking about her skin. And I said, 'Yes, it is.' She seemed really surprised that I didn't say anything different. But that didn't stop her." She wore her hair in dreds too, but said Gwen shouldn't be allowed to. Dreds were for real Blacks, like her. "And she would leave notes around the office addressed to me that read: 'God don't like ugly.'"

With snowy hair topping his drooping head, and in a sad voice, the White copy editor who'd handled my story on colorism solemnly told me, "What a shame, Black people being racist toward their own." Then he walked away forlornly, shaking his head. I shook my head, too. Some people just didn't want to get it.

America is a documented pigmentocracy. One particularly influential study, published in 1990, showed that the social and economic gap between light- and dark-skinned African Americans is as significant as "one of the greatest socioeconomic cleavages in America," the chasm between the income and status of all Blacks and Whites. A dark-skinned Black earned seventy cents for every dollar a light complexioned African American made. A light-skinned African American, however, earned only fifty-eight cents for every dollar a White American made. But most telling, said the study's authors, Michael Hughes and Bradley R. Hertel, professors of social psychology at Virginia Polytechnic Institute and the State University of Virginia, were the percentages for Blacks and Whites who were employed in professional and managerial occupations — high-status jobs. Almost 29 percent of all Whites held such jobs, while Blacks held only about 15 percent. That is nearly a two-to-one ratio. Ironically, the same ratio held true for light-skinned Blacks, 27 percent of whom held such jobs, compared with dark-skinned Blacks, 15 percent of whom were employed in these positions.

Significantly, when Hughes and Hertel compared their findings with studies done between 1950 and 1980 on the relationship between skin color and socioeconomic status, they concluded that nothing had changed appreciably. The effect of "skin color on life chances of Black Americans was not eliminated by the civil rights and Black pride movements."

Understandably, African Americans are loath to acknowledge such disparities, even though we aren't to blame for them. It undermines the image of ethnic solidarity.

"It's absurd for any Black person to be talking about [color distinctions among African Americans] without talking about White supremacy," insisted the psychiatrist Frances Cress Welsing, whom I quoted in the article. The controversial author of "The Cress Theory of Color Confrontation and Racism (White Supremacy)," which traces the roots of White racism to a fear of genetic annihilation of the planet's White minority, screamed at me: "It is White people that keep saying and imposing that if you look like an African you should be at the bottom of the choice spectrum."

That's what Hughes and Hertel, both White social psychologists, concluded from their study, too.

African Americans still want to deny the problem, however. One of the brightest, and funniest, people I know, the essayist Stanley Crouch, claimed: "Hysterically overstated. If that were really true, most Afro-Americans I know couldn't even have

Christmas dinner, 'cause they'd have too wide a range of people in the family. I mean the light-skinned ones would have to meet on Avenue L for light, and the dark-skinned ones would have to meet on Avenue D for dark." Four years later I asked Crouch if he still felt the same way. More so than ever, he told me, this time adding earnestly that of course he used to "hate" light-skinned people, but he got over that.

While all Blacks suffer discrimination in America, the darker one's skin, the more one's humanity is ignored. "You know the Links?" asked E. B. Attah, a Nigerian-born sociologist, referring to the elite Black social-service organization. "Well, I had a member of the Links showing me pictures of different chapters," said the scholar, who has taught at Atlanta University. "When she encountered a dark-skinned woman in a picture, she'd say: 'How did *she* get in there?' I'm very dark-skinned, and anybody in this country who is dark-skinned can tell you about encountering situations of lighter-skinned people devaluing you as a human being because of your darkness."

A packed lunch at my side for the duration, I sat this day in a left-coast braiding parlor when two men walked into the L.A. shop and waited for a friend. "Did you see the guy Pam brought to the party last night?" one asked the other.

"I was too busy jammin'. What did he look like?"

The other man chuckled derisively. "If you'd seen him, you'd remember. The nigger looked like eleven fifty-nine."

My mouth dropped and I lifted my bent head. "You mean a shade shya midnight?"

The guy laughed. "You got it, sister."

In a wholly *racialized* and color-struck nation, the demands of *multiracial* Americans for special recognition seem acid on ancient and contemporary wounds in the Black community. And among the rawest of those wounds stem from internecine battles over color. The pain and rage, however, are no less real for *multiracial* Americans like Velina. And though she often sees me as the enemy, I have always viewed her as a spirited but wounded sister.

CHAPTER 12

"MY GRANDFATHER committed suicide in 1953." There were many reasons, Velina Hasu Houston told me. Her mother's father was a wealthy landowner. During the United States occupation of Japan, his property was confiscated as part of U.S. resettlement policies that democratically divided and distributed land to peasants who had been tenants of major landowners. "So my grandfather lost most of his land. It had been in his family for centuries, and for him to be the patriarch and let it slip out of his hands was a major shame." But the greater shame was the loss of the war. "A lot of the older Japanese, especially the men, were shocked. They didn't think that they could be defeated. Then there was the fact that my mother had fallen in love with an American. Any American."

This American was a military policeman. One day, while he was riding through the city of Kobe in his jeep, his helmet suddenly fell off. The music of teenage girls giggling as they walked home floated toward him when he stopped the jeep to pick it up. Like many daughters of wealthy families from the countryside during wartime, these girls had been sent to dressmaking school in the big cities of Japan to keep them safe and out of the uniform factories. One of the girls, stepping from her crowd of friends, reached the helmet first, handed it to the officer, and for the first time looked into the face of a man the color of soy sauce. His eyes were so warm and gentle and loving, she was not scared at all, she would tell her daughter one day.

Several years would pass and many letters exchanged between

the seventeen-year-old girl and the thirty-year-old soldier after their first meeting. Thirty days after her grandfather committed suicide, Velina lost her grandmother to cancer. It was then, Velina said, that her mother felt free to marry the man she loved and eventually leave Japan. With her parents and an older sister, two-year-old Velina left Tokyo and arrived in Kansas in 1960. It was there that her life as an Amerasian in the United States began. And, she said, "it was awful."

She lived in Junction City, Kansas, the town outside Fort Riley where her father was stationed — and not by happenstance. After World War II it was Army policy to send GIs who returned to the States with Japanese wives to certain Mid- and Southwest locations, like Fort Riley, isolating them from Japanese American population centers on the West Coast.

Innocent and hopeful in the land of the melting pot myth, these GI wives and their families would inspire Houston's trilogy, *Asa Ga Kimishita (Morning Has Broken)*, *American Dreams*, and *Tea*, tracing the journey of a Japanese woman who leaves her ancestral homeland to wed an African American soldier, and the cultural obstacles she faces along the way in Japan, New York, and Kansas.

Tea, the work that put Houston on the map as a playwright, opens at the flashpoint of cross-cultural despair. One of the women, a war bride named Himiko, commits suicide after shooting her abusive husband. In a sea of Great Plains coffee-klatches, five other war brides gather in Himiko's home for a ceremonial tea and the urgent need to share their experiences.

An earlier play, *Father, I Must Have Rice*, in which a woman who calls herself Japanese African weds a Japanese American, humorously explores the sensitive, festering character of the bride's African American father, who, deep down, wants his child to marry "Black." At one point in the wedding the father complains, "Rice bags are racially insulting. You don't see Blacks throwing watermelon seeds at Black weddings."

Of her own father, Velina's memories are vague, comforting,

rose-colored flashes: *Kind . . . sensitive . . . and loved children, my mother said.*

He was born in rural Alabama, a town called Linden. And his mother was a full-blooded Blackfoot Indian. His father was African American, Velina told me, not explaining whether she believed he was of pure African ancestry or a typically *multiracial* African American. Her father's father was a coal miner, she'd been told. He died from lung cancer. Both of her father's parents died before he was twelve.

"How did his mother die?" I asked her.

"She gave birth to fourteen children, which certainly would have been enough to kill me." Only six of the children lived. And all but one, a sister, acted as if Houston's father was dead when he married a "Jap."

When he did die, none of his siblings came to the funeral. "My Japanese grandmother liked and accepted my father," Velina said, but she had no extended family among her Black relatives. And little welcome from the African Americans around Fort Riley.

On the days Velina brought sushi to school for lunch, African American children teased her. But their mild teasing escalated to schoolyard terrorism: a group of Black girls pushing her down . . . bloodying her face, yelling "Nip-nigger" while they cut off her long dark hair 'cause "she swung it like a White girl."

"Even as I talk about that, there were African American girls who did not fit into that mold, ones who were curious about us and did not dole out that kind of oppressive abuse," Velina said. "Often, though, they were multiracial in the sense that they were usually light-skinned and had their own sets of problems with that African American enclave." She had a razor-sharp edge in her voice. "So there was some empathy going on there." I always thought Velina believed that, as a light-skinned Black, I had had similar experiences, and that that was one of my motivations for writing about her. She knew nothing about my family. And I can recall only two times in my entire life when someone

made an issue of my color to my face: a Tanzanian waiter in Dar
es Salaam who could not believe someone so much lighter than
he was not White, and a Haitian cab driver, who, spotting me in
the dark, reluctantly picked me up even though he thought I was
a European.

Velina momentarily took the razor out of her teeth. "White
teachers exploited the ethnic tensions," she remembered. The
Amerasian children were very studious. "The teacher would turn
to us to spell words or to give answers. And I remember that
the African American girls would just scream at the teacher: *We
know they know how to spell it. Why don't you ever ask us?* It
was a roundabout racism thing on the teacher's part. I remember
that very vividly."

Squeezed from all directions, Velina said, "we just didn't fit in.
And whatever recipe they *might* present for fitting in didn't appeal to us. It had nothing to do with us culturally."

"Was a recipe ever really offered?" I wanted to know.

She laughed nervously. "Well, none was ever offered to me. But
I remember, in high school, people began to judge you for what
you do rather than what you are. I was president of the National
Honor Society. I was a class officer. I was a cheerleader. The
people who surrounded me were overachievers, too, and whether
they were Amerasian or African American or European American really didn't matter to us anymore. There were groups of
other people who were angry about one's success or felt that
being successful meant copping out on one's culture."

But the most significant thing among her peers at this stage of
her life was sex. "We were all budding young adults, and romance was something new in our lives. I didn't have a high school
boyfriend, because my mother didn't allow us to date," Velina
said. "But for those who did date, the Amerasian women were
the favorites of both African American men and the European
American men." They were, in a sense, safe for the White men
who wanted to dare to have an *interracial* relationship, she assessed. And for the Black men, they were safer than White

women but exotic. So a layer of sexual competition was added to the mix, "though the naked cruelty of my childhood disappeared."

But it did a pretty mean striptease on one of L.A.'s main drags as she drove her son home one afternoon.

An Anglo in the rear hit the Italian in the truck. The Italian in the truck hit Japanese-African-Blackfoot Velina and her half Euro-American baby in the champagne-colored Honda sedan. Then two Black policemen came on the scene.

"You hit my car," she told the Italian. She knew he was Italian because he spoke with an Italian accent and wore a municipal employee name tag that read *Giuseppi Pira.*

"No, I didn't, lady. You're crazy," Pira told her.

"We saw everything," disputed a voice from a small crowd that had come out of a restaurant directly across the street from the accident.

Paramedics arrived, and one, an Anglo man, started joking with Pira as if they were old friends, Velina recalled angrily. "Maybe it was just male camaraderie. But they both started laughing about how upset I was," and when the paramedic walked over to examine her son, she shouted, "Don't touch us."

Then the cops came. Velina rushed toward them. "Officer, I'm so glad you're here." Kiyoshi, her twenty-month-old son, was crying and bleeding from the mouth. But the cops, she said, looked at her, looked at him, and walked off with the Italian. Eventually, one cop returned, took her license, and told her to wait. She wouldn't. "Something's wrong with this picture," she told the cop. "I want to get this guy's information. *He* caused the accident."

"I *told* you to wait over there," the cop instructed gruffly.

"But I want to get out of here. My son's mouth is bleeding."

"Did you let the paramedic look at him?"

"No, because —"

"Then it's just your own fault if you didn't let the paramedic examine him," the cop shot back while framing her and

Kiyoshi in an all-encompassing glare. Then he muttered in her face, "Half-breed bitch." The baby was screaming now. The cop walked away, shaking his head disgustedly. And Velina charged after him.

"I would like," she said defiantly, "the information on the other driver. I'm the only person not at fault here."

The cop spun around. "Stand over there on that spot." He pointed to a place about three yards away.

"Whaaaat?" came out of Velina's mouth. Her face telegraphed that he was nuts.

"I said stand over there on that spot, lady." Both cops were laughing at her now.

"I am not going to stand on any spot. Someone hit me. I would like his insurance information and I want to go home and attend to my son."

The hostile cop threatened, "You got three seconds to go stand on that spot or I am going to handcuff you to the car."

"Well, you can just go ahead and handcuff me, but I'm not standing on any spot." The cop grabbed her, pushed her against the car, and began to put on the cuffs.

"No, no, no." The other officer jumped in, realizing that things had gone too far. Besides, patrons from the restaurant across the street had called several of Velina's friends at her request. One of them intervened.

"Whoaaa, you can't do that," he said.

"Just keep her over there," the cop snapped.

"Why?" Velina's friend, a young White man, demanded. "What's your problem?"

"Because I don't like her face."

"I still feel the psychological reverberations of that," Velina told me the first time we met. It was that incident which had prompted her to call me after she'd read my stories about *multiracial* Americans.

Later, I would learn about one of the most painful episodes in her family's history. But it was not Velina who told me. Her silence, further evidence of the skepticism with which she viewed me, the distance that must be maintained with one who did not comprehend, she felt, her reality. The story was about George, her brother.

In 1957, George was eight and the only Amerasian child of color in an orphanage near Tokyo. Velina's parents adopted him.

"George came to the U.S. and became the classic misunderstood Amerasian," Velina once told another interviewer. The cultural limbo devastated him. He never got over trying to figure out his identity, his sister believed. There was no language, she said, to help him define himself.

In 1984, as Christmas neared, George disappeared, and no one has seen him since.

Undeniably, she would acknowledge, "I have a lot of rage. I have been oppressed by Black people, White people, and Asian people. Yet I've always had this hopefulness that minorities could get along. But throughout my life, history has proven otherwise. Color-against-color racism is a very strange animal to me. White racist attitudes I could feel. I always knew when I had a racist White teacher," even though it was hard to prove, because it was subtle. "But with the Blacks who didn't like half-Asians, it was more violent, more vicious."

"Why do you think that is?"

"I wonder sometimes if it is because groups that are greatly oppressed rechannel that oppression in ways that are darker and more violent. The oppressed seem to oppress more," she said grimly.

In 1903, when W.E.B. Du Bois wrote that the "problem of the twentieth century is the problem of the color-line — the relation of the darker to the lighter races of men in Asia and Africa, in America and the islands of the seas," he referred to the domination of Whites over darker peoples. This remains true. But that domination has bred an insidious offspring: internalized oppression; that is, the installing of the oppressor's values within the psyche of the dominated so that — in a system of structured inequality such as ours — the psychological dynamics that help to keep the system in place function on automatic pilot. In effect, the mind becomes the last plantation.

One wonders if the assertion of a unique *multiracial* identity — for a person of African heritage in the United States — is the ultimate expression of (or, through a synthesis of competing identities, an escape from) the divided consciousness that Du Bois claimed defined Blacks in the United States. For where, save in the United States, or as a consequence of the forces that created the products of its New World society, could a Velina be forged? Not just in the particulars of her ethnicity, but in the clear anguish, for many like her, caused by such an amalgam in an African-tinged package? Where else but in the United States does a slavemaster's economically motivated definition of identity so completely reign? Multiple souls, multiple thoughts, multiple "unreconciled strivings" warring "in one dark body, whose dogged strength alone," Du Bois wrote, "keeps it from being torn asunder."

Layers of complexity are added to what was a conundrum — at least for Du Bois and some since him — when confronted with the expanded riff on both "Black" and American identity that Velina embodies.

"My goldfish died on New Year's Day," she told me despairingly about a month after our talk in that café near the Pacific. "That is a *horrible* omen." It means an awful year ahead. "Most people would think that is crazy, but it's a Japanese omen," she said, her anxious voice spiraling higher. "The fish is a lucky symbol for the New Year, and mine died."

In her struggle to balance competing identities, she must also add to the mix of specific Amerasian concerns that of *multiracial* people as a whole, who do not always face the same tug of competing cultures or a foreign homeland. "If I am not supportive of the multiracial agenda and don't push it forward, then people who are somewhat like me will end up not having their politics addressed. They will get swallowed up into the African

American agenda or the Hispanic agenda or whatever the case might be, and their voice will get lost."

And she is adamant that the best way to press the cause of people like her is recognition of *multiracial* Americans on the census.

She underscored the point by telling me of her experience with the Department of Cultural Affairs in Los Angeles. "They want to award monies to minority artists. They have meetings to meet the artists in the community. They have a meeting for the Asian American artists, the African American artists, and so on. I send a friend to the African American meeting who is a multiracial Amerasian, and she can't even get her raised hand acknowledged to get a question answered. And all of the issues that come up from the African American artists are 180 degrees from anything that has to do with her artistic or political agenda. She simply does not fit in. They don't understand what she represents or who she is. They just want her to be quiet."

The same thing happens to Velina. "I go to the Asian American artists meeting and I have to rally to bring up the whole Amerasian or multiracial agenda. Because when the city looks at funding African American and Asian American artists, they don't remember the people in between."

She recalled when she first came to Los Angeles as a young playwright and asked the Asian-American theater group, East-West Players, to produce her work. "They looked at me and said, 'Gee, we've never really dealt with one of you before.' They could tell from everything I was that I did fit in as an Asian and in many senses was more Asian than they were. But it was hard for the mind to adjust to find a place to fit this person like me."

Then she went to the Negro Ensemble Company. "And they said to me, 'Well, your mom is Japanese, and your play is about Asian stories, so you really should go to the Asian theater.' And I said, 'No, my play is about an Asian woman and an African American man.' And they said no again." And round and round they went until the relentless Houston had *Tea* produced simultaneously by East-West and the NEC on opposite coasts in 1984. "But it was a fight to get my voice heard." And in the end, she insisted, the experience was a demeaning exercise in tokenism.

Highlighting the myth of the metaphor, Velina argued that in the land that supposedly embraces the notion of the melting pot, the people who embody it most are shut out and shut up everywhere they turn. Look what happens to her friends who are *multiracial* actresses, she added.

"An Afro-Asian woman goes in for a part and the casting director will look at her and say she doesn't look Asian enough — unless they're doing *South Pacific* and need a Polynesian girl. The same actress goes into an African American audition — and this happened to a friend of mine who is Chinese and Haitian. She goes in and they go, 'You're not Black.' And they send her away. She doesn't look like the cover of *Essence* magazine. So then she goes in for an audition for the part of a Vietnamese Amerasian who is half African American. And she is really happy going to this audition. She walks in and the whole room is filled with Filipino women and, quote-unquote, light-skinned African American women. And she walks up to the casting director and says, 'Hi, I'm here because I'm Amerasian and I want to try out for this part.' And the casting director, studying her head to toe as if she were a museum artifact, muses, 'Oh, so that's what one of you would look like.' Of course, she did not get the part. They cast a woman who was mulatto," Velina said, "because that's what they thought an Afro-Asian person would look like.

"There isn't a theater to represent me," Velina charged. "There's isn't a political representative speaking for my community." Without that representation, the "multiracial agenda falls right down between the cracks and we remain an unheard voice. As far as I am concerned, the civil rights of multiracial Americans must now be addressed. We have to be counted in order to access those public funds for our own political agenda."

CHAPTER 13

"PLEASE," I groaned, involuntarily. It triggered furtive glances from the people on line ahead of me in the L.A. supermarket. All through the Du trial — and when Latasha's killing sparked intrigues that lasted years beyond it, locking me in writers' prison — I continued to monitor developments on the *multiracial* front. Wondering whether we would ever extricate ourselves from the myths our current *racial* alignments perpetuated, I stared at a special edition of *Time* magazine devoted to THE NEW MULTICULTURAL FRONTIER. Along a continuum of ludicrous highs, I decided the national compulsion to deny the miscegenated American experience had hit a steep pitch in the mainstream media with the special edition of *Time* I held disdainfully in my hand.

The cover portrayed a woman with light brown skin, dark eyes, a softly rounded nose, hair a medium brown and straight — though possessing a hint of cotton in the texture — and kissable lips edging toward, but safely shy of being called, full.

She was described by the magazine's editors as the creation of a computer . . . a mix of several *races* . . . a remarkable preview of "The New Face of America. How Immigrants Are Shaping the World's First Multicultural Society."

This woman's "beguiling if mysterious visage," in the words of the editors, is 15 percent Anglo-Saxon, 17.5 percent Middle Eastern, 17.5 percent African, 7.5 percent Asian, 35 percent Southern European, and 7.5 percent Hispanic.

"It really breaks my heart," wrote one of the magazine's editors, "that she doesn't exist." This, *Time* lamented, "is a love that must forever remain unrequited."

Of course, this nonexistent beauty resembled every other Puerto Rican woman I've ever seen and about one in twenty so-called African American females.

Velina seemed equally content to accept the nation's portrayal of Blacks, referring to them as *monoracial*, despite asserting as a moral and political imperative the recognition of one's "biological truth." She and many other *multiracial* activists said they knew that Blacks were not *monoracial*, but since they perceived themselves as such it wasn't the activists' place to argue otherwise. "I have my own chips to carry," Velina said; it wasn't her duty to resolve the identity problems of African Americans.

My conversations with her drained me. I rarely challenged anything she said during our interviews, because I wanted to keep the lines of communication open. As a result, I often felt like a punching bag for her hostilities. I sensed she liked to Mau Mau me — the way Black people in the sixties tried to browbeat and guilt-trip White liberals. After all, I was just a Black liberal to her. But she was so bright and provocative, I found her an irresistible icon. I wanted readers to appreciate what it meant for someone to embrace subnational, national, and transnational identities as she had. I wanted to make psychological space in the culture for all the Velinas, for her lost brother, George, for my murdered cousin Jeffrey — while jettisoning the absurdity of creating yet another *racial* category, as she advocated.

Though I lamented Velina's alienation from Blacks, I understood her beef and did not distrust her motives for seeking a *multiracial* census designation. I felt very different about the mother who founded Project RACE, the grass-roots organization with thirty-five chapters across the nation, and the lobbying force behind recognition of *multiracial* citizens in Georgia.

A "mixed-race" category was a life-and-death issue, Susan Graham told me. "One of the things that Project RACE is concerned with is medical issues for multiracial people." That's when she zeroed in on the limited pool of *multiracial* donors for bone marrow transplant patients.

"We know that bone marrow can be transplanted across racial and ethnic lines." So it's not necessary for someone who is *multiracial* to have a bone marrow transplant from another *multiracial* person, she acknowledged. But just as the best match for any person is likely to be a sibling, the next best match would be someone whose "racial and ethnic genetics are similar," Graham said. And the problem is that the government does not target *multiracial* people for testing or for outreach when they conduct donor drives. "You hear of donor drives for African Americans and donor drives for Asians and Hispanics and Whites. But you never hear about donor drives for multiracial people." So, she concluded "if my children needed a bone marrow transplant, we would have a problem, because the donor pool would not be large enough."

Since the so-called *multiracial* population can be an infinite amalgam of human beings, an excellent argument should be made for specifically identifying and targeting members of such a group: Black-Hmongs, Korean-Ethiopians, Chinese-Armenians, Norwegian-Apache-Greeks — WE WANT YOUR BONE MARROW. But just because they weren't identified as *multiracial* didn't mean that people with that kind of genetic profile — a Japanese, African, and Native American person like Velina, for example — hadn't donated tissue that might match that of a *multiracial* person in need of a transplant. As people clamoring for a *mixed-race* category complain, the country is full of *multiracial* people who are not identified as such. And as scientists more broadly note, there are no pure "races."

When I asked Graham what her children's ancestry is, she answered, "I am White. And my husband is Black."

"That's hardly an exotic combination," I said. And when she added that her husband was Black and Native American, I told her, "that's basically the profile of the majority of African Americans." Fortunately, her children didn't need one, but finding a bone marrow transplant match for children like hers would hardly be an extraordinary feat, I argued.

I wasn't suggesting that outreach to *multiracial* Americans shouldn't occur, I told her. Rather, I wanted to underscore that *multiracial* identity was not the exotic phenomenon she and others pressing for the new census category chronically claimed it was.

Since Graham had made such of point of bone marrow transplants being a life-and-death example of the need to recognize mixed ancestry, I pursued that point. I called Dr. Craig Howe, the head of the National Marrow Donor Program.

Howe explained that, while it is true that matches for a bone marrow transplant patient are sought across all *racial* and ethnic lines, a match is first sought from those groups which most closely reflect the patient's ethnic and *racial* background. Since *multiracial* people are not recognized as such in health statistics, the process of finding a donor who is a combination of the accepted *single-race* groupings, and matching him with a *multiracial* bone marrow transplant recipient, is slowed, he acknowledged. But having a generic *multiracial* category would not be as beneficial, said Howe, as simply knowing the complete ancestry of all Americans.

People should be able to check off or write in all the groups that apply to them, I said, and he agreed. That would really expand the pool of recognized *multiracial* donors, I told Graham.

But Graham has testified before Congress that Project RACE prefers a generic *multiracial* category. Most of the time, Graham argued, the background of a *multiracial* person is asked unnecessarily. Marking two or more categories is a "mere invasion of privacy with no justification."

Then, elaborating her views, Graham told me, "I am not the racial police." She cannot tell other people how to identify themselves on the census. But if the *multiracial* category she desires becomes part of the census, it will not be meant for generically mixed ethnic groups like African Americans or Latinos. It will be for the first-generation offspring of people of different identities, like her and her husband.

She, specifically, is a European American of Polish and Russian descent. That's what one newspaper account said, she told me disdainfully. "But I prefer the term *White.*" And while some people may use the term *African American* in public to be politically correct, she said, in her house her husband is just *Black.* And her children are *biracial.* "That's the term we use in our home."

Since she said her husband is of African and Native American descent, doesn't that make him *biracial* and their children *multiracial?*

"They know they are multiracial," she answered, but she prefers the term *biracial.*

I wanted to hear her husband's views on all this, but she adamantly informed me that nothing about him was pertinent to the agenda of Project RACE. She allowed that he was a journalist and that she was a free-lance journalist who grew up near Detroit and moved to Atlanta from Michigan with her husband in 1988.

"As long as you persist in viewing your husband, a typically mixed African American, as monoracial," I argued, "you perpetuate the one-drop-in-the-bucket rule that advocates of a multiracial category claim to abhor. And in the health arena, just to cite the example you raised, your position makes it harder to identify an even larger pool of multiracial Americans as bone marrow donors."

She said she didn't get the point.

I heard her say she was from Michigan, but I suspected she'd attended biology class with my friend, Miss New Orleans — to whom I happily gave my back when my lab tests proved negative. Still, I persisted, using the nomenclature of racism to which she and all these other advocates of a *multiracial* category were so wedded.

"In other words, if you need to have a clearly identifiable multiracial population to expedite the matching of a multiracial bone marrow donor with a multiracial recipient, why not really identify all multiracial people — especially the oldest and largest multiracial group in the country, African Americans?"

"This is getting a little convoluted here," she finally answered
in exasperation. "Putting aside the African American community," she said dismissively, Blacks already have their category.
But her children don't. That's why she started Project RACE in
1990.

That year, a number of things all seemed to happen at once,
Graham told me. "I received my 1990 census form. There was no
place to classify my children. I was told that they should be
classified as White because the census takes the race of the mother
and I am White." When Graham asked why the *race* of the
mother was used, the woman answered, *sotto voce,* "Because in
most cases like these we know who the mother is but not the
father."

At about the same time, Graham said, her first child started
kindergarten. School forms came home for him and there was
nothing on them that described him. The school said: "Don't
worry, Mrs. Graham. No problem. Don't bother filling it out."
She found out later that her son's teacher was instructed to pick a
race for him — "based on her knowledge and observation after
knowing my child for about five minutes," his mother said seethingly. The upshot was that the same child was White on the
census, Black at school, and *biracial* at home, all at the same time.
Something was very wrong here, she decided.

She wrote an editorial about the problem for the *Atlanta Journal Constitution,* and the response was "incredible," Graham
said. "There were so many people facing the same issue. That's
how Project RACE started. People will say to me, 'You're doing
the wrong thing, Susan. You're perpetuating classification.' And I
don't feel that way at all," she asserted. "I would be shocked if
the government said there are going to be no racial classifications
in our country tomorrow. That would put a lot of statisticians

and demographers in Washington out of business. That's not going to happen. So as long as there are going to be categories, I want my children to be categorized accurately."

Her children are connected to the African American community, I said. Does she think about the implications of her agenda on that community?

She paused a long time. "You have me thinking about how to phrase this. One thing that upsets me is that people say the Black community is against this. We have people like Ralph Abernathy who have championed the cause. Multiracial pride is as important as Black pride."

That is not the point. If she is going to advocate such a category, why isn't the one-drop rule jettisoned for everybody, rather than just for children like hers? Generations of African Americans have been and continue to be misdefined by the Little Dab'll Do Ya School. What about them? Any moral authority in an argument to recognize *multiracial* identity in the United States is abrogated with the assertion that it apply only, in essence, to the Massa's kids — the old "mulatto escape hatch."

"I can't say whether African Americans would be better off if they were part of a multiracial category," Graham answered curtly.

"Would you mind if they were?" I asked.

"I don't know what it would do to the multiracial category as we are defining it," Graham said. "That may be a problem."

CHAPTER 14

"NONE OF THE LARGE so-called minority groups in this country are going to be happy about this new multiracial category, because it is just the opposite direction of what we are asking for. We are asking for more detail." The woman speaking was Linda Williams, a political analyst for the Congressional Black Caucus Foundation and a professor of political science at the University of Maryland.

For example, she told me, "I know the Asian Americans are not happy about the Asian designation."

There is no such thing as an Asian *race*, I pointed out. No one in Asia ever heard of such a thing until the U.S. government put it on the census, a National Research Council study documented. People in Asia identified themselves by nationality.

"Yes," Williams acknowledged, "Asians want to be identified by national origin here too. They want to have data that allow them to see what is happening to Japanese versus Cambodians, who are in entirely different financial situations."

The same with Hispanics, she noted. "They are very concerned that Cubans, perhaps, raise their socioeconomic ratings, while Mexican Americans, and particularly Puerto Ricans, are doing extremely poorly."

Black Americans are seeking more detailed information, as well. "You also hear this from West Indian Americans. They want to be able to see what is happening with the native-born Black versus the foreign-born Black. So the ethnic community is requesting data in just the opposite direction. This multiracial designation would be a very unpleasant development, I would argue, from the standpoint of the interest groups that would be captured by it."

But I told her that most advocates of the category are not constructing it to include *mixed-race* groups, like Latinos, African Americans, or Pacific Islanders.

"Then whom are they going to include?" asked Williams, who advises the caucus on emerging issues of concern to Blacks. "If you are not going to include the people who are African American and Hispanic, I can't imagine whom they are including."

As 1994 came to a close, she admitted that neither she, as a professor of political science, nor the caucus had paid much attention to the *multiracial* issue. I knew that. I'd called her because I thought there had been a dangerous avoidance of this issue by the national Black political leadership. There had to be a serious exploration of the political and social implications of creating a distinct *multiracial* category on the federal census. Political self-interest alone would seem to dictate that for these elected officials, not to mention the long-term political and social impact on their constituencies.

The designation is meant for the first-generation offspring of parents from different *racial* backgrounds, I explained.

"I guess it would have to stop at the first generation, because most people are mixed, whether they acknowledge it or not," Williams said. "And with Blacks, at least 75 percent of them are mixed."

One of the problems with this category, if it comes to pass, is that it will have to rely on a person's self-identification, she noted. Then, Williams confided, "I have always told people I have only African roots. I have no White blood in me, no Native American blood, blah, blah, blah. But my grandfather was half Native American and half White."

"Why do you deny it?" I asked, already knowing why.

"Because I see no virtue in saying anything else; I am Black. I am treated as a Black. I'll always be treated as a Black in this country for the foreseeable future." So in real life, it doesn't matter that a person with African ancestry is *multiracial*. "The old slave rule still operates." One drop in the bucket. "And if they can change how the old slave rule operates, racial classifications could change," she contended. "Actually, what this country really needs, and we are not in any position to get away from it yet, is to abolish the category of race. Period. Obviously," Williams said, "class would be the remaining big distinction between people if you didn't have race." But in the U.S., "race and class are inextricably tied, which is why we can't get rid of race. But if, first in public policy and in private actions, we could abolish the usefulness of race to people who want to oppress and exploit some people more than others, then we would have no need for the social construction called race."

But as long as that social construction exists, argue advocates of a *mixed-race* category, let's perpetuate the absurdity of *race* and the social divisions it encourages with a label that falsely distinguishes *multiracial* Americans from all others. In Edwin Darden, the vice president of the AMEA, the organization has an eloquent Black man pressing such an agenda.

A *multiracial* census category, as Darden's organization AMEA envisions it, wouldn't prohibit someone who is African American from choosing the designation just because it *wasn't* intended for him. But what this category does emphasize, Darden claimed, is an intention not to pull people out of the Black or African American category as so many fear it would. "I wouldn't, myself, want to go out of that category," he said. He wants to maintain the integrity of the Black category, not dilute its political strength.

Rather, the proposed category is intended to "document the rise in interracial marriages and the children of those unions. And there is not a category that reflects someone who is biracial or multiracial. We are basically correcting a flaw in the political vision," contended Darden, who is married to a White woman and the father of *multiracial* children.

While there may be some *multiracial* Americans who are hostile toward African Americans and see little common ground between them, Darden insisted that this attitude is rare. Further, as a Black man who can't be sure if he is *monoracial*, but perceives himself that way, Darden said he has no sinister motives for narrowly defining *multiracial* Americans. But he admitted that *multiracial* Americans have a social agenda that is different from, though not hostile to, African Americans. People who are the products of contemporary *interracial* marriages have a different social perspective from those whose ancestry may be mixed but generations removed, he contended.

African Americans, he went on, "hold tenaciously to the myth of monoracial identity because it has served them well as a unifying and galvanizing force politically. But in the last decade," Darden lamented, "the Black community has been turning away from the integrationist aspects of society and more inward — the Afrocentric trend. People who are involved in interracial relationships, though, where one partner is Black, like myself, can't afford to think in those singular terms. Your immediate partner is someone other than Black. But there also is a bigger issue at stake": that of seeing the Black community as "part of the whole."

Darden said he is an advocate of strong, independent Black institutions, especially ones that support Black economic development. "But these can be developed in a positive way that's been missing of late."

Black development is cast as "it's about us; it's not about you." And when people not Black, especially Whites, try to become part of the Black agenda, Darden said, they get pushed out. "There is a real cultural chasm there. And that kind of discussion is diametrically opposed to the multiracial community, which talks in terms of 'we,' not 'us' and 'them.'"

Certainly, Darden said of Black Americans, it is politically easier to set up a construct where "it is 'us' who have always, and in a very singular way, been discriminated against by 'them.' To acknowledge that 'them' is part of us means that you have to think in a much more complex way about what your feelings are, where those feelings hail from, and how you reconcile them."

But that last challenge — embracing shared identities and reconciling the contradictions they may elicit — must be faced by all Americans, not just African Americans who have been forced by history, time after time, to stake out an identity under siege. If, as a nation, we are connected by history, culture, and blood, then the dominant group, White Americans — especially those who so vocally denounce the balkanization of the United States they claim pluralism breeds — need to step up to the podium and make rhetorical perfume out of the phrase *the miscegenated American experience.*

Instead, the national narrative of choice insists that *if* the third president of the United States bedded the enslaved Sally Hemmings — the half sister of Thomas Jefferson's wife — it was an aberration and not the common practice that makes *Time* magazine's *New* Multicultural Frontier a joke.

Circumscribed generation after generation by these narratives of exclusion, we see the periodic flourishing of a compensatory Black nationalism asserting the myth of Black purity and superiority — this era's alarmingly vulgar version called Afrocentrism. Afrocentrics, generally eschewing any class analysis of social relationships, view everything through a *racial* lens, clanking, as they go, the chains of an oppressor's definition of reality.

I absorbed some things I think are sound from my schooling in the cultural nationalism of the late sixties and early seventies, and variously rejected or reinterpreted many of its elements. But by nature, background, and experience I took to heart the nationalist imperative undoubtedly worth keeping: the capacity to define ourselves and speak for ourselves as a people. And to the extent we are unable to conceive of a social reality outside the one created by our oppressors, we're just marking psychological time on the plantation.

People said Ralph David Abernathy III was bucking the Afrocentric tide when he sponsored the Georgia legislation that recognized *multiracial* citizens. "Yes, God," groaned the young state senator, recalling the Black outcry against it. "The fear in the Black community is that Blacks will become extinct." How could he? peopled chastised him. They told him his father, Martin Luther King's compatriot in the civil rights struggle and director of the Southern Christian Leadership Conference after King's assassination, "would turn in his grave."

But Abernathy, who is thirty-five, and inevitably, perhaps, falls into the cadences of a Southern preacher instructing his flock, said his sister is married to a White man. "She and we believe in integration. She believes her marriage is reminiscent of the struggle that Black and White come together as one."

A *multiracial* category, he suggested, "is the path to a raceless utopia. It may not be in my lifetime or my children's lifetime; it will take a metamorphosis," he offered, reaching for the rhythm and rhetoric of Dr. King *(I may not get there with you. But . . . we as a people will get to the Promised Land)*. "But eventually we will find everybody is the same, everybody is multiracial. And eventually this entire country will have only one race, that race. That's what will lead to the destruction of all these other categories. Because if you create a category that everybody fits into, then you have abolished the other categories, because no one fits in those."

The *multiracial* bill he sponsored in the Georgia legislature was passed in 1993 and enacted in July of 1994. Supporters of the legislation see it as a model for a federally recognized *multiracial* designation one day. The law requires all government and private institutions to include the category "multiracial" instead of "other" when collecting, for use within the state, or reporting to the federal government *racial* and ethnic information from people whose *parents* are of different *races*.

The primary effect of the bill — as AMEA and Project RACE want — is the recognition of *interracial* couples. The acknowledgment of *multiracial* identity is secondary, given the bill's failure to define who is *multiracial* after the first generation. The legislation does not, for example, make clear what happens when two *multiracial* people marry and have children. Does the child of a Sioux-Italian-Korean man married to a Sioux-Italian-Korean woman qualify as *multiracial*? Or do the component parts of the parents' mixed heritage have to differ for the child to be *multiracial*?

The bill does make clear, however, what happens when tabulations of *multiracial* people in the state of Georgia are reported to federal agencies, as is required under Abernathy's legislation, but the agency rejects the count because the federal government has no *multiracial* designation. The state will resubmit the data, but divide the *multiracial* population proportionately, reassigning it to the federally recognized *racial* and ethnic groups based on their percentage of the general population that is being tabulated. So, if there are ten *multiracial* children in a Georgia school district with a student population that is 60 percent Black, 30 percent White, 5 percent Hispanic, and 5 percent Asian, 60 percent of the *multiracial* population in that district would be counted as Black, 30 percent as White, and Hispanics and Asians would get a half a child each.

If enough states pass similar legislation, as Project RACE — which wrote the bill Abernathy sponsored — hopes, the pervasive use of a *multiracial* category could persuade the federal government to adopt it.

I asked Abernathy if his sister's marriage was the catalyst for his sponsoring the bill.

"We do look forward to having multiracial grandchildren and nieces and nephews in the family," he answered. And I thought: Doesn't this man know his family is probably already mixed? And he proved it later by telling me that his maternal grandfather was a full-blooded Cherokee chief. But the decision was more than personal, he assured me. It was "a political assessment, as well. I feel that it is important that every race of people be acknowledged in their independent right," he told me, contradicting his view of a color-blind millennium. "It is a violation of human rights for America not to acknowledge a multiracial individual as being multiracial or to relegate him to the negative term 'other.' Whites have shunned the fact that they have been intimate with the African American. As a result, if you are shameful of the act, you will be shameful of the result. [Consequently], America has turned its back and said these people don't exist."

That's when he pronounced that the recognition of *multiracial* Americans "is the next frontier for the human rights agenda." Reaching again for the rhetorical style of the civil rights movement, he said of the coming utopia that acceptance of a shared *multiracial* identity will "require a gradual metamorphosis. That's what it will take to change the bigots. We will not be able to march them to understanding. We will not be able to demonstrate them to understanding. [They will have to be shown] systematically in their own life, in their own lifestyles, that they are no different than we are."

One day, we'll look back, the preacher's son told me, and say: "In the 1990s they all had these race categories. But in the year 3001 everybody is all one, so race is not important. How stupid they were back then. Now we're all living in harmony. We're all one color."

I've never been fond of the notion that the obliteration of a distinct identity — either culturally or phenotypically — should be a prerequisite for the acceptance of any people's common humanity. And I tried not to slam the phone down on its cradle after thanking him for the interview.

Several months later, I checked with Abernathy to verify some information for a magazine article. I told him I might begin the piece with his utopian comments, but take him to task for his failure to acknowledge how divisive *multiracial* categories have been in other societies, as well as the long history of colorism in our own country.

He said he really hadn't researched the history of *multiracial* groups in societies like South Africa or Brazil or our own pigmentocracy.

"Why not?"

"This is not like the U.S. Congress," he told me. He doesn't have a staff to research issues for him. A group like Project RACE drafts a bill, gives it to him, and he determines its merits. "I really did it for the children," he defended. "Did you see Susan Graham on *48 Hours* [the CBS news magazine]?" he asked. I said I hadn't but had interviewed her and read about her.

"Well, she has a good sales pitch [with those kids.] That's what really moved me." When you see the children, you want to make life better for them, he explained. No one wants to see a child discriminated against because of his or her ancestry. Black people certainly relate to that, he said defensively. "But I wish I had talked to you first." If he had, he said he might not have sponsored the bill as passed.

"Talk to me! All you had to do was go to the library and read a few books. There are plenty there on comparative ethnic relations. You could have consulted with a few professors who are experts in the matter. There are a number of universities in the Atlanta area."

"Well, I certainly don't want you to think I am in cahoots with Susan Graham" to do anything to politically undermine Black people. That's when he told me about their conversation a few months earlier.

Around September of 1994, three months after Abernathy's bill became law, Graham told him the next step was a congressional bill just like it. Abernathy agreed, and told her he had the clout to help make that happen. But, he told me, Graham said no. She didn't think it was appropriate that a Black person be in the forefront of pushing national *multiracial* legislation.

That's when Abernathy pulled out his own *multiracial* ticket marked "Black-Cherokee" and laid it down. But Graham refused to punch it. The White captain of this *multiracial* cruise ship called her troops on board, said full steam ahead, and left Abernathy standing at the dock. They haven't spoken since.

CHAPTER 15

What this current discourse is about is lifting the lid of racial oppression in our institutions and letting people identify with the totality of their heritage. We have created a nightmare for human dignity. Multiracialism has the potential for undermining the very basis of racism, which is its categories.
— G. Reginald Daniel
The New Yorker, July 25, 1994

ILL-INFORMED and reactionary forces have seized an issue that held and still could hold such sanguine possibilities. When I and many others began heeding demands that the mixed ancestry of all Americans be embraced, we hoped it meant a new consciousness was abroad, not the perpetuation of an old one.

A fresh generation of multiethnic children, supported by an older one, and a flood of immigrants for whom a discrete *racial* identity was foreign, were actors on a stage ringing, during the last quarter century, with national rhetoric touting the country's cultural diversity. All this could provide fertile ground for a new view of U.S. identity. A view that could challenge both the polarizing Black-White *racial* bifurcation that exists, as well as the seemingly progressive vision of the U.S. as a cultural mosaic — diverse but carefully bounded. It could offer, instead, the icon of a nation as a tapestry of citizens joined by history, by culture and, yes, *blood.*

G. Reginald Daniel was among those with a similar view; though his belief that *racial* categories are the "very basis of racism," rather than an expression of the ideology of *racism,* misses the mark.

Daniel teaches a course on *multiracial* identity at the University of California at Los Angeles. He shared the stage with Velina Hasu Houston and others at the symposium I organized in 1990, and was among the first of those I interviewed in the 1980s about the emerging *multiracial* issue.

An ordinary-looking Negro, like me, Daniel shares a similar ancestry: African, East Indian, Irish, Native American, and French. In my case, substitute English for Irish (though relatives who have dug deeper into the family's genealogy now speculate that my great-great-great-grandfather, the pirate Sam Lord, may have been of Black Irish descent — his ancestors trekking from North Africa to the British Isles around the time of the Crusades).

Unlike me, his primary cultural identity is not Black. "I am not a *multiracial* African American. Sometimes I identify with my European ancestry more," Daniel said, and he feels more socially at ease with Whites.

When he says this, I infer that — like too many — the American in "African American" refers merely to geography, not the transformative reality of living in a New World culture.

Those things that he and others may see as distinctly "White" or European, I see as part of my heritage as a Western woman — whether I have any genetic links to that ancestry or not. It is part of, not separate from, my New World identity.

My syncretizing instincts certainly stem, in part, from my family background, but even more, I think, from my experience of music.

I spent childhood days on city playgrounds dancing, till my stomach ached, to "Fingertips," Parts 1 and 2, or mesmerized by opera once I'd been taken to the Met at the age of nine to hear Renata Tebaldi in *La Bohème.* Later, I would wake up to the sound of the shofar from the Orthodox synagogue next door, then rise from bed and look at my autographed picture of Judy Garland. Her likeness occupied a place of honor on my dresser from the time I was ten, when I won a contest for an alarmingly adult rendition of "The Man That Got Away," until I was a teenager. Rushing past Judy, I dressed and went to school to refine what teachers said was an instrument equal to Tebaldi's and just as capable — if I worked really hard — of approaching that of the "Divine One": Sarah Vaughn. She, with Miriam Makeba and Lady Day, became ultimate sources of inspiration — especially the latter two for their understated sensuality.

Of course, some would say that that is how it's supposed to be in the American melting pot. But the end product that metaphor classically insists upon is a homogenized thing, specifically an Anglicized one. You know, the same Big Mac you get here, you get in Oshkosh. The melting pot as ethnic smelter — an idea epitomized during World War I by Henry Ford's Ford Motor Company English School Melting Pot.

Ford — as Werner Sollors recalled in his important book on U.S. identity and culture, *Beyond Ethnicity* — used to have foreign-born employees attend his company's language school, which staged elaborate graduation rituals. With the hull and deck of an ocean steamship docked at Ellis Island as the backdrop, a gigantic cauldron with FORD ENGLISH MELTING POT SCHOOL painted on it stood center stage. The graduates — dressed in native costumes and carrying their Old World possessions tied in a bundle — marched down a gangplank into the cauldron, then emerged wearing American clothes and waving tiny versions of Old Glory.

Assimilation has occurred, will occur, is inevitable and desirable if we are to function as a cohesive society. No truly pluralistic society — large groups of people with completely different languages and cultures — could exist as a nation without extreme coercion; the former Soviet Union is the obvious example of that. But assimilation is not the one-way street too many Americans raised on the melting pot myth believe. In the tapestry of U.S. life I see four-lane boulevards everywhere, with traffic in both directions and stylish cultural jaywalkers always making their mark.

And while none of these categories is discrete, as some might insist, I'd argue that U.S. culture is composed of what is yours, what is mine, and what is ours.

As well as specific cultural practices that may be thought distinct, there is a body of experience that shapes our social perceptions and informs our individual subcultures. The attitudes, more than differing rituals — especially for ethnic groups with long histories in the U.S. — are what define and separate most U.S. citizens from one another, I think. And they constitute a broader definition of culture, not easily overcome.

Further, while polarized opposition exists in every dimension of U.S. life — pro-lifers in combat with pro-choice advocates, environmentalists slugging it out with developers — *race* has been the most intractable source of all our social woes. Though social scientists at the end of the twentieth century assert its declining significance and those in the hard sciences increasingly assail it as an amalgam of prejudice, superstition, and myth, on the whole the national dialogue seems locked in anachronistic rhetoric about its value. Perhaps it is the desperate utterance of a society whose moorings are about to be undone by the loss of a defining myth. I wonder, given the incredible publicity that surrounded Charles Murray and Richard Herrnstein's often spiritually eugenicist tract, *The Bell Curve.*

In it, they attempted to link intelligence — the measure of which is imprecise, often culturally biased, and changeable over time for the same individual — to *race,* a concept that falsely asserts there are pure, discrete divisions of humanity to which intellectual capacity, among other attributes, can be assigned. Having done so, they said that Blacks score lower on intelligence tests than do Whites and that the data they studied indicate the gap is largely genetic rather than environmental.

Even though Murray and the late Richard Herrnstein claimed

to reject the pernicious notion of *race,* it's the rotten plank upon which they built their case for nature over nurture in the realm of intelligence.

But to paraphrase the conservative Black economist Glenn C. Loury, for too long, the loudest voices of African American authenticity have insisted on viewing all experience through a *racial* lens. "These racialists are hoisted by their own petard by the arguments and data in *The Bell Curve.*" Indeed, these self-lynchings are the strange fruit we've often helped to cultivate.

As Angela Davis reminds us in Anna Deavere Smith's masterly theater piece *Fires in the Mirror,* about the Crown Heights riots, *race* was once synonymous with community for African Americans. But the rope attached to the anchor has become a noose, choking off social growth. It has become an "increasingly obsolete way of constructing community . . . I am convinced," she said, "that we have to find different ways of coming together, not the old coalition in which we anchor ourselves very solidly in our specific racialized communities, and simply voice our solidarity with other people." Though our own communities have to be the base from which we act, the rope attached to the anchor should be long enough to allow us to move into other communities.

"I have been thinking a lot about the need to make more intimate these connections and associations." A way of working with and understanding the "vastness of our many cultural heritages, ways of coming together without rendering invisible all our heterogeneity. I don't have all the answers," said Davis. "[But] what I am interested in is communities that are not static, that can change, that can respond to new historical needs."

As one of the oldest and largest populations of mixed ancestry in the U.S., and the most politically influential, African Americans, in the debate over *multiracial* identity, have an opportunity to forge an expanded definition of community for ourselves and the nation. But at the national level, African American politicians have been conspicuously absent from the debate, even though their constituencies have a significant stake in the outcome.

Black Congressman John Conyers from Detroit was the exception that proved the rule. In the wake of demands that a *multiracial* category be created for the 1990 census, he was among the signers of a letter to the OMB in 1988 protesting any changes to Directive 15.

Since then, Representative Sawyer's subcommittee hearings were held in 1993, the National Research Council made recommendations in 1994 that the government find ways to better document the increasing complexity of its population, and the OMB, that same year, directed the Census Bureau to field-test a *multiracial* question for possible use by the year 2000.

Shortly before and after the 1994 election, I called all the members of the Congressional Black Caucus to see what they knew about and thought of the proposed census category. Every one of their spokespersons told me that his or her boss either knew little or nothing about the proposal (that was most of them) or thought it too inconsequential to talk about.

"I read four papers a day," said the press secretary to one Northeast representative. "I've never seen anything about this issue."

"Meaning what?"

"Meaning that it's not even a blip on the radar."

Another press secretary told me that she wasn't aware of the proposal, didn't think the member of Congress she worked for was either, but she immediately saw its political significance. "I'm glad you're writing about this," said the press secretary, who I suspected was White. "I've always wondered who is Black in America. What does it mean?"

The press secretary to a Southern CBC member told me he'd read a lot about the issue himself but didn't know whether his boss had done so. "I worked for newspapers before taking this job, and there's been a lot in the news about multiracial children, their families, and the problems they're having. It's becoming a big issue. But my boss is reactive, not proactive. He's not forward-thinking."

"Isn't that the definition of a politician?" I half-joked.

"Yeah, most of the time."

When I polled them between August and December of 1994, not even CBC members from the state of Georgia, let alone the other members of the caucus, knew that the most sweeping legislation in the country recognizing *multiracial* Americans had been sponsored by Abernathy and passed in their state.

At the time I was polling the politicians, a *Newsweek* reporter called to interview me about the *multiracial* issue. On February 13, 1995, the blockbuster edition appeared with the cover story: "What Color Is Black?" When the magazine asked Americans: "Should the U.S. Census add a multiracial category so people aren't forced to deny part of a family member's heritage by choosing a single racial category?," a majority of Blacks, 49 percent, said yes, a minority of Whites, 36 percent, said yes. But a large percentage of Blacks were against adding the category; 42 percent of them said no. And more than half the Whites, 51 percent, said no to it.

Americans as a whole, however, did not want to see the category added. Thirty-eight percent said it "should" be added to population surveys, while 50 percent said it "should not," and 12 percent said "don't know."

Since then, advocates of the new *racial* category have grabbed front-page headlines with a Multiracial Solidarity March on Washington in the summer of 1996 to celebrate "mixed-race" identity and generate support for a federally recognized *multiracial* category. But some who might have been expected to participate are increasingly voicing the concerns that I and others have raised. "Many of these multiracial activists, both Black and White, want to minimize their child's African heritage," Candy Mills told one interviewer. Mills, who is Black and is married to a White man, is the publisher and founding editor of three magazines devoted to interethnic issues: *Interrace, Black Child,* and *Child of Colors.* Once a supporter of the new category, Mills now says, "We should resist all categorization. A multiracial category would give more credence to other categories when in fact we all know that there's no such thing as race."

This issue is not going to disappear, however, given the growth in *interracial* marriages — which doubled from 1960 to 1970, tripled from 1970 to 1980, and reached 1.5 million by 1990 — and the psychological abuse the children of these unions often face. Parents have a right to be spitting mad when their kids are trotted out for "racial" inspection, Gestapo-like, by a school's gene patrol.

But fearing the impact of Abernathy's bill, the lobbying efforts of Project RACE, and the continuing silence of Black political leaders as this issue has gained momentum for over twenty years, a coalition of civil rights organizations has stepped into the breach.

In the fall of 1994, the national offices of the Lawyers Committee for Civil Rights Under the Law, the National Association for the Advancement of Colored People, the Urban League, and the Joint Center for Political Studies, an African American think tank, wrote to the Office of Management and Budget to protest any changes in the nation's system of *race* classification.

Gary Flowers of the Lawyers Committee said the issue is simple: "We are concerned with the total and undiminished application of civil rights laws." Nothing should be allowed to jeopardize their ability to "enhance the potential for historically disadvantaged people, namely Blacks in this case, to exercise their constitutional rights in electoral and economic spheres."

Though the leading advocates of the proposal, Project RACE and AMEA, insist that targeting the first-generation offspring of *interracial* couples will not siphon off masses of African Americans from the Black category, Flowers is one of those who believe a substantial number of African Americans would jump the perceived group tugboat.

And even if they didn't do so deliberately, the same result may come about through confusion, the coalition fears. Suddenly confronted with a *multiracial* category, many Blacks, knowing their complex ancestry but unable to acknowledge it heretofore, might check it instead of Black or check both. Who knows? As it stands now, the census reports that many citizens identify themselves as South American because they live in Alabama.

But if the bill that Project RACE lobbied for and Abernathy sponsored is ill-conceived and regressive, so too may be the just-say-no attitude of much of the opposition.

It may be possible to accommodate the political uses of the census and to portray more accurately the identity of U.S. citizens. Statistics Canada, the equivalent of our Census Bureau, tested an example of this for Canada's decennial census in 1996.

They have an Ethnic Origin question that asks the person's ancestry. Fifteen ethnic or cultural groups are listed, not *races,* and Canadians are invited to check off or write in as many as apply.

Like the U.S., Canada has legislation that was designed to ensure equal opportunity for all its citizens; specifically, the Employment Equity Legislation of 1986. To better monitor the effectiveness of the law, the government added a new category, White or Black, in addition to the separate Ethnic Origin question. This allows the government to identify more clearly what it calls visible minorities: non-Caucasians, women, aboriginal people, and people with disabilities. Lamentably, says D. Bruce Petrie, assistant chief statistician for Statistics Canada, this generic White or Black category, listed among others that refer to national origin or a cultural group, is taking Canada more in the direction of the United States *racial* classification scheme.

"Race is not a term that gets used very often in Canada," he said. And the new categories were not meant to be construed as such. "But it resembles a race question; it's the closest thing in Canada we have to a race question; and that's how people interpreted it." There was a lot of resistance to it, and it was very controversial. "But we had to resort to a direct question," he said, "because we could no longer derive who was a visible ethnic minority from the answers to the ethnic and cultural origins questions on the previous census in 1991. People wrote in *Canadian.*"

At the time he and I spoke, the government had not analyzed the census returns and didn't know whether its citizens had checked off Black or White, continued to write in *Canadian,* or simply refused to answer that particular question. Still, unlike the United States, the Canadian government makes clear on its census that information derived from answers to the question is used only to enforce programs that promote equity, not as a means of identifying the ancestry of its citizens.

I would love to see the day when we abandon all these categories and deal with the class interests and conflicts they obscure. We *are* a national family linked by culture, history, and blood. But we are a dysfunctional one, fraught with inequalities, with members denying kinship. Canada's deracialized, two-tract system of ethnic identification suggests a feasible and more desirable way of dealing with this social reality in the U.S. It may be a means of accommodating the political uses of the census by maintaining the current, mutually exclusive categories necessary to monitor and enforce civil rights protections (recast in ethnic terms, preferably; though it may be necessary to retain the social construction of *race* here, because that has been the basis on which discrimination has occurred and legal remedies applied) and still recognize the complex ancestry of most Americans. This two-tract system should not prove abhorrent to *multiracial* people who celebrate the exotic cocktail they claim as their blood, or to *biracial* people who anoint themselves interpreters of worlds to which they are jointly and uniquely privy by virtue of biology — mistakenly thinking culture is in the genes rather than learned (a super-essentialist notion as deep among many *multiracial* advocates as it is among avid Afrocentrics) — but only check off the Black, White, Asian, Hispanic, or Native American box when it means a scholarship or job.

Their response to this last accusation, of course, would be that a *multiracial* designation would preclude such hypocrisy, which only brings us back to the lunacy of perpetuating *racial* classification and stratification. And acquiescence to the latter underscores that, ultimately, the last plantation remains the mind — a consciousness unable or unwilling to conceive of a social reality unbound by the calculated politics of ethnic division with which the nation's bloody *racial* history is rife. For despite the bogus rhetoric of a *multiracial* category taking us to the next frontier, the loudest voices addressing the *multiracial* issue prove that the old *racial* order is actually hardening, even as it seems to collapse under the weight of ethnic permutation.

There seems to be a political and psychological need in the U.S. for both the dominator and the dominated to maintain a permanent *racial* caste. One composed of a group taxed with a chronic disability stemming from a historical condition: slavery. As Toni Morrison noted in *Playing in the Dark: Whiteness and the Literary Imagination*: "The concept of freedom did not emerge in a vacuum. Nothing highlighted freedom — if it did not in fact create it — like slavery." Further, she wrote, "in the construction of blackness and enslavement could be found not only the not-free but also, with the dramatic polarity created by skin color, the projection of the not-me." Or, as the late historian Nathan Irvin Huggins put it, "Just as American freedom finds its meaning in American slavery, whiteness and white power found their meaning in the debasement of blacks."

It is, perhaps, this chronic need to stand in juxtaposition to the "not-me" and point a denying finger that compels many *multiracial* Americans, and their families, to demand that their biological truth be acknowledged, and exoticized, while persistently and falsely referring to African Americans as *monoracial*.

Lamely, many of the advocates of a *multiracial* category argue that since African Americans see themselves as *monoracial*, it would be presumptuous to challenge that self-definition. For African Americans, however, constantly under siege, the choices and chances for self-definition have been limited by patterns of dominance and inequality. Holding on to a slavemaster's definition of *race* has seemed a matter of political survival.

But it is possible and politically healthier to construct a strong group identity around the more fluid notion of ethnicity. Picture a very dark, African-looking person standing up at an academic conference in Atlanta in 1968 and saying, "'Given our diversity, Blacks should consider themselves an ethnic group.' The meeting collectively looked at him as some kind of traitor. What a 'bizarre' idea was the attitude," Ibrahim Sundiata, chairman of the department of African and African American Studies at Brandeis University, told me. People wanted to know, "'Where is this coming from?' But I think if people had accepted that idea earlier, it would have solved a lot of problems."

"Such as?" I asked.

"We hold on to this idea of pure races. But unless you are an essentialist arguing that the 'true folk' still exist on these shores after three hundred plus years, Blacks are not a race in any old-fashioned biological sense." But an identity constructed around ethnicity gives us much more latitude to accept the complexity of the group. As an ethnic group, people look different but have some commonality in terms of culture and maybe ancestry. We are already there physically, he said, "but psychologically, it requires retooling."

By making Black an ethnic category, he went on, "we can say what Henry Ford said of automobiles. You can have a Ford Model T in any color you want, as long as it's black." This sounded like the Black version of the melting pot as ethnic smelter. And it begged the question of what constitutes a Black identity.

As a child, my Jamaican grandmother never allowed us to move into a new apartment without first anointing the threshold with liquor, nor could one take a drink of rum at a party without first sprinkling a bit on the floor. Both gestures were an offering to our African ancestors. And when I'd tell some tale that seemed outlandish, my grandmother would balk, "Sounds like Anansi story to me." I always thought she was talking about Nancy, some lady I'd never met. I didn't know for years that Anansi was the famed character of West African folklore, the spider who spun tales, his stories still told by the descendants of Africans who'd been brought to Jamaica. Many things we said and did were African, I later learned, and so much a part of me that I took them for granted. But for many of my teen years and beyond, I wasn't Black enough because I sang opera. If my authenticity was questioned, where did somebody who ate sushi instead of grits for breakfast fit in?

Sundiata thought for a moment and then responded obliquely. "There remain a great many essentialists in the Black community espousing ethnocentrism. And African Americans on the whole have all sorts of tests of Blackness which ultimately become [politically] dysfunctional."

One of the things that concerns him about the *multiracial* proposal, should it come into being, is that there will be both a wholesale exodus of Blacks from the category at one end and a refusal to enter it at another. This is the pattern that has occurred elsewhere in the Americas where there are *multiracial* categories, "and I don't think the U.S. would be that different. I'm really concerned that we end up with this residuum," which is both color- and class-based — that darker-skinned brother in the hood standing on the corner who says: I am the true Black. And since color and socioeconomic status are linked in the U.S. to the disadvantage of the darker-skinned, the true Black becomes not only the most African-looking among us, but the poorest — with all the liabilities poverty invites for anybody.

"This person should become even more outraged," Sundiata suggested. And the angrier he gets — because his class position is not improved in this further stratified environment — the more likely he is to spark super-essentialist movements. One immediately thinks of the lure of the Nation of Islam and its successful appeal to the most marginalized of Black folk — convicts, addicts, prostitutes — many of whom can put the prefix *ex*- before these labels because of the salvation they found through the Nation's program of entrepreneurship and self-respect combined with racial chauvinism.

"We would start arguing among ourselves more and more," Sundiata predicted. And other groups, understandably, would go the other way. Potential allies would be loath to align themselves with us, and those who share a similar ancestry would increasingly distance themselves, in Sundiata's scenario, carving out their own social niche.

Within days of interviewing Sundiata at the end of 1994, I looked up at the TV in my Brooklyn apartment and saw a very dark-skinned woman offering a thirty-second commentary in support of a *multiracial* category for the 2000 census. The discussion of *multiracial* identity was far more salient in California than in the East, and the woman's commentary surprised me. I was about to catch a plane to L.A. when the program aired, so I stopped to call the television station and later tracked her down.

When I returned, I met Susan Manigault on a sparkling Sunday near her home in Westchester County, north of Manhattan. She'd grown up in the city's northern suburbs, the first nine of her thirty-seven years spent in Ossining. Home to the infamous penitentiary Sing Sing, the town was of significance to her only as the site of an ancient Indian burial ground.

Over brunch in a bright and pretty diner, the kind of comfortable, inexpensive, suburban establishment that lured families from the high cost and filth of living in the city below, Manigault handed me a poster. It had a big, black checkmark in a box next to the word: A M E U R O F I A N . Under it was written: "One Check Mandate has denied many people their true heritage, and reduced them to check 'other.' I am a combination of American Native, European, and West African. Statistical Policy Directive 15 is dehumanizing." And under that was written, in bold capital letters: R E E V A L U A T I O N   H E A L S .

When I asked her what the last phrase referred to, she told me

she'd read one of my essays that mentioned Re-evaluation Counseling. Taking it out of context, she slapped the RC reference to
the end of her poster.

In her existential quest for self-definition, Manigault, who
writes for *New People,* one of a burgeoning number of magazines
devoted to *multiracial* issues, has dabbled in Hinduism, Mor-
monism, Orthodox Islam, Buddhism, and "almost ended out in
Pennsylvania with a horse and buggy," thinking she'd become a
Quaker.

She went to flight attendant school after getting a liberal arts
degree, but that didn't work out. She was a data entry clerk for
years. But most recently she took a job as an administrative assistant at a Manhattan high school. She's lived in the North all her
life, but as she moved and spoke, she seemed a character conjured
up by Tennessee Williams. Though physically statuesque — two
more inches and she'd be six feet — she spoke demurely, and I
expected her long, tapering fingers to reach for a lace hanky at
any moment and dab her brow. After brunch, we went to the
place she shared with her mother. Primly serving tea from gold-
rimmed china cups in an apartment building that she, with carefully modulated irritation, described as looking like "the projects
now," she said, "I got married the same year Princess Di married
Prince Charles." And with equally disastrous results.

Her former husband was a Jehovah's Witness and a "border-
line genius," she said. He was a supervisor at a post office though
he could have been a college professor. "But the religion didn't
encourage higher education. It taught that all you needed was
a skill so you could provide for your family. Higher education
would lead to worldliness, which could lead to agnosticism,
which could lead to being an atheist." The sect's socially circumscribed, anti-intellectual world "made the marriage very stress-
ful. I lived in the hospital." Indeed, she seemed like a steel magno-
lia, long boxed-up and prone to the vapors her first days out. She
said she was on Prozac.

Since she was a teenager, she'd been struggling with three inner ethnic identities. Raised in an African American family as an African American, she was confused by the very dark and very light range of complexions in her family and all the different textures of hair she saw. She didn't understand why family members called themselves Black when they were obviously mixed. She said she particularly identified with her "American Native" ancestry, though she couldn't tell me specifically what it was. She never learned about Black history in school, she said, but she'd been taught a lot about Native Americans.

"Might that be the reason you identify with them, since you obviously couldn't call yourself White?"

"Yes, it could."

"How did you come up with the term Ameurofian? It doesn't exactly roll off the tongue."

She told me the obvious — American Native and European inspired two thirds of the word. And the *fian* was supposed to refer to African.

I told her it was pretty hard to ascertain the allusion to Africa in that word. "How do you feel about Black people?"

She averted her eyes and looked down at the floor near the dining table where we sat. "I am asked that question a lot. I hate that — I wish that they would stop saying the White man did this and the White man did that. There comes a point where you have to let go of the anger and move on. You don't forget what has happened but you learn and move on. Everyone has had their struggles — some more than others. All families have problems."

But you can't voice such opinions in the Black community without being attacked, she said. Then she complained: "Look at something as simple as a Black woman dying her hair. Women are very diverse; they dye their hair all the time. But Black people say a Black woman shouldn't dye her hair because that is less ethnic. It's so simplistic to say dyeing your hair is to escape your race."

Well, she was no cheeseburger — what Black folks call a dark woman with a bad blond dye job. Her hair seemed a natural dark brown. But I was looking at someone who for a variety of reasons fit into Sundiata's scenario. Rational or not, she was trying to carve out a social niche that allowed a fuller expression of her self-perceived identity. And the more I talked to her, the more evident it became that class was a factor.

"When Cosby came on, I loved it," she said, referring to Bill Cosby's situation comedy about an upper-class Black family in Brooklyn, *The Cosby Show*. But she was really surprised when a co-worker in her office dismissed the show as totally unrealistic. "And she was a college graduate," Manigault said with astonishment. She said Black people don't really live like that.

"But we're not all from the backwoods or cotton shares or whatever."

"You mean sharecroppers?"

"Yes."

Her father was an entrepreneur, she told me. He moved to New York State from Alabama after World War II, worked in an auto factory, then opened his own hardware store. Manigault's mother is an accountant. Her parents divorced but remain friendly, she said. Her mother is even close to her father's second wife, who is White. Manigault has a *multiracial* younger sister from her father's second marriage. And she said, "I guess it's all right to let people know I'm dating interracially" — a White man whom she had met at a family gathering.

While it is unlikely that Ameurofian will appear on the census any time soon, the social latitude that now exists for asserting *multiracial* identity means that, whatever her motivation, Manigault is part of an emerging critical mass that won't be easily silenced.

And whatever else one might dismiss, there is an aspect of her alienation from the Black community that is based on a potent point Darden of AMEA asserts, as does Sundiata. There are so many tests for Blackness in the African American community that it ultimately becomes dysfunctional. Many people tell him to "go slow" in elevating the *multiracial* issue, said Sundiata. "They say this category is not going through. But on the state level, it is

going through. And I sympathize with the parents who are pushing it."

Even though he voiced the National Urban League's objections
to the category at Sawyer's congressional subcommittee hearings,
the organization's director of research, Billy J. Tidwell, thinks the
proposal has merit and that a *multiracial* question may appear on
the census in 2010 or 2020. Would the African American community be any better prepared to deal with its consequences then
rather than now? He doesn't think so. Even if the federal government never puts a *multiracial* category on the census, the people
who perceive themselves as such exist and are multiplying. And
the social landscape is increasingly pocked by conflicts between
them and a Black population falsely described by itself and others
as *monoracial.*

For Tidwell this is not a minor issue. Resolving tensions between Blacks and *multiracial* people of African descent, especially, and the related problem of colorism "is key in my view,"
he said. "It is one of the critical challenges facing the current
generation of African Americans." In a fundamentally conservative nation moving farther to the right and attempting to dis-
mantle hard-won civil rights protections that are perceived as
threatening White privilege, "we have to bring these internal
frictions out in the open and discuss them within the context of
current political, social, and economic realities — realities which
render the long-term prospects for African Americans very uncer-
tain." Moreover, those who oppose a *multiracial* category on the
grounds that it is politically dysfunctional to the Black cause, said
Tidwell, have to address the issues that underlie the call for it —
the psychological pain, the social alienation, the lack of political
representation.

Attempting to marginalize this issue through silence, as Black
politicians seem to want to do, is to ignore a historical tide that
may well dilute Black influence. We could, instead, ride its cur-
rents to our advantage and, ultimately, the nation's by compelling
it to deal with its miscegenated past and present. We should be in

the forefront of the *multiracial* debate. We should never allow any *multiracial* person — either through ignorance or political calculation — to exoticize his identity at our expense. We should co-opt the position and assert that, as New World Blacks, we are multiethnic people; in doing so, we should make clear to ourselves and others that affirming our multiethnic ancestry and being "Black" are not mutually exclusive. Further, should the day ever dawn when a *multiracial* or multiethnic category appears on the census, Black politicians had better make sure that it is constructed in a way that includes African Americans. If African Americans are not included in the designation — and in a way that ensures our hard-won constitutional protections — there should be no such designation.

Thinking this way, as Sundiata put it, requires psychological retooling, and other groups have done better at accommodating their diversity. "For instance, I am studying the man who popularized the term Hispanics," the Puerto Rican nationalist Pedro Albizu Campos.

Albizu Campos was a complex character who was three *races* in his lifetime. He was a mulatto born under the Spanish in Puerto Rico in 1891. He came to the United States shortly before World War I, lived in Massachusetts for eleven years, went to Harvard to study law, and then joined the U.S. Army. "He was put in a Negro unit for, after all, he was the grandson of a slave and the illegitimate child of a mother who scrubbed floors," said Sundiata. He was thrown into the African American community. And whether he rejected it or vice versa, by the time he returned to Puerto Rico in the early 1920s, he had constructed a new identity for himself and his people.

He did this using the elite ideology of the plantation owners who called themselves *Hispanos*. "The term had a very distinct and limited meaning, referring to people who owned the land," Sundiata explained. But Albizu Campos took that and said no. All of us speak the same language, Spanish. And we are Catholics. This is the core of our identity, he asserted, the "transcendent power of the Catholic Church and the beautiful Castilian language." Of course the dominant elite laughed at him, Sundiata said. "This little brown man going around saying he was the same as they were. But he joined a party, the Nationalist Party, and continued this campaign — in some ways very violently — until his death, in 1965."

Of course, the term *Hispanic* is a highly contentious one. The Spanish-speaking community in the East is more accepting of it, while in the West, the preferred term is *Latino*. Actually, the preferred term is whatever one's specific national origin is — Nicaraguan, Mexican, Guatemalan. But I am interested here in the larger point: the idea of subsuming the phenotypical aspects of *race* with ethnicity.

Such an idea "would have seemed silly in nineteenth-century Puerto Rico," Sundiata continued. But it has worked out today that Puerto Ricans are an ethnic category. This, he reminded, occurred on an island where slavery was abolished ten years after the Emancipation Proclamation. And for a population that essentially mirrors the polygenetic ancestry of African Americans.

"I am not saying that racism in Puerto Rico is gone. But by emphasizing ethnicity rather than race — when dealing with outsiders, and to a certain extent on the island — ethnicity has triumphed. Politically, culture was exalted over race in Puerto Rico, exactly the opposite of what happened in the U.S."

While scholars, writers, and artists may be exploring the evolution of Black identity in the United States as the millennium approaches, the Urban League's Billy J. Tidwell lamented that "the rhetoric of the Black leadership in this country is on the whole fifty years behind the times. It is anachronistic in terms of its binary, Black-White construction of race relations, and lacks any serious comprehension of the place of African Americans in a social landscape transformed by vast demographic changes." The latter is evidenced in part by the emergence of multiethnic Ameri-

cans of partial African descent who have little or no connection
to the traditionally defined Black population — as well as the
Black-Korean conflict.

It would be unfair, then, to view the waxen figure of Tom
Bradley as singular as he offered political boilerplate standing
outside a fire-gutted Korean American market: "*We have to get
better mutual understanding of the differences in the cultures
of these two racial groups. And we have to stress that courtesy
in a market is something that is expected and demanded.*" Coming five months after Latasha's death, those were the first words
he uttered publicly about the long-standing Black-Korean tensions. Afterward, as he tried to glide to his car, that neighborhood
schoolteacher named Desira Ruggles hounded him, accusing him
of talking only to the elite, not to the people who patronized the
markets daily and felt their lives threatened as much as the Koreans felt theirs were.

But on Bradley's watch, this was the city whose Chamber of
Commerce propaganda trivialized multiculturalism as gastro-
nomic tourism, making diversity virgins out of visitors who never
swallowed a kosher burrito under smoggy L.A. skies. Businessmen and politicians in pre-riot L.A. could pretend that Los Angeles was either a paradise of separate but harmonious ethnic
groups or, in an updated version of Anglo-dominated assimilation, a zesty tossed salad served on the American flag. But too late
— amidst the smoke that rose from incinerated flesh and bones
and wood and steel that was Sa-I-Gu — the Sphinx of City Hall,
who took credit for L.A.'s friendly smorgasbord, would say he
had never seen an ethnic conflict escalate as quickly and turn so
bitter as the one between Koreans and Blacks.

CHAPTER 16

ON THE SECOND DAY of the *People* v. *Du*, a firearms expert for the Los Angeles Police Department testified that the gun that killed Latasha had been altered. It required far less pressure to fire the .38-caliber Smith & Wesson than the manufacturer's specifications demanded. It was the type of thing a quick-draw artist in the Old West might do to get the drop on his opponent, said Richard Leonard. The gun, Lloyd's co-counsel asserted, had a hair trigger.

But Billy Hong Ki Du testified that he didn't do it. The gun had been stolen, returned to him by police several years after the theft, and, other than checking to see that it was loaded, dusted, and kept under the sales counter, he had never touched it. His son Joseph said the same thing.

"I do want to go out and test it, fire it, but, you know, person who is working fourteen hours a day, I just — no way to find time to do that," the former Korean army major told the court, even though he admitted buying the gun ten years earlier for self-defense.

Du shifted from Korean to English throughout his testimony, despite the presence of a translator, until Karlin required him to speak only in Korean to make sure he would not be misunderstood.

When Leonard held up another weapon, a carbine rifle, Du said, "In the Korean army I gave training in this type of weapon, and also this was issued to the officers in the army." Then he said that particular carbine was his, and that he brought it to the

Empire Market because of gangsters who had burglarized and robbed his store. "They were threatening to kill my son." That is why his wife, who usually worked at the store the family owned in Saugus, north of the San Fernando Valley, was at the Empire Market the morning Latasha walked in.

The mother feared for her son's life and wanted to relieve him of his duties at the market that day. She and her husband arrived about eight A.M. But Billy Du, who had worked late the night before, testified that his wife told him to go to their van, which was parked in front of the store, and take a nap. Explaining why he was asleep, the husband defensively told the jury, "I am not an iron man."

When a sullen Joseph Du took the stand, he said he usually worked at the Empire Market from ten in the morning to ten, sometimes eleven, at night. His father opened the store around eight A.M., then traveled to the family's Canyon Bouquet Liquor store in Saugus.

Shoplifting was a daily occurrence at the Empire Market, he grumbled. "I see it every day. Forty times a week." And the place was burglarized too often to count. He, too, was robbed in the store, twice in the same week five months before Latasha's death. On December 16 a lone Black man robbed him, which he reported to police, he testified. Three days later, as he was about to close the store, "ten to fourteen" Black men rushed in, he told the jury.

The men who rushed in — "these people are going out of the store, they're taking items from the store, and they showed you that they had a gun. Why didn't you grab either the carbine or the handgun and try to stop these people?" Leonard asked him.

"Because I was not willing to engage in a gun battle and threaten my own life," Du replied.

"When you were working at that store, did anybody ever threaten to kill you?"

"Yes."

"How many times?"

"Too many times," he said grimly. When pressed, he finally put a number to the death threats — thirty — adding that gangsters had threatened to burn down the store, too, at least twenty times.

"Did you discuss this with your mother?" Leonard asked.

"I told her of it every day," he said.

"Why?"

"First of all, because she is my mother. Second, I want to emphasize how dangerous this business area was and that this was an area in which I cannot do business too much longer. I wanted to make sure we sell that store as quickly as possible and go elsewhere."

And despite the danger, he, like his father, insisted that neither had shown Soon Ja Du how to use a weapon. As his father put it, "She was a woman"; she would not have been capable of handling a gun.

Trying to chip away at his credibility, Carvajal challenged his account of the two robberies in the same week. Instead of a robbery on December 16, two men Joseph Du knew came in and demanded he give them jobs, but he refused, Carvajal said, adding that he never told police about a robbery.

"I did," he insisted.

"And isn't it true, Mr. Du, that you told the police officer that they threatened you and that you believed that one of the suspects was about to shoot you, so you removed your gun from your pocket and pointed it at the suspect?"

"Well, because he had — he had first grabbed the cash in the cash register, and then he was trying to take something from behind him. So I sensed that probably it was a gun. So I then grabbed the gun underneath the cash register and then I pushed the holdup button."

"But you told the police that you got the gun from your pocket."

"I cannot really recall."

"And, Mr. Du, you also told us that you did not use this gun, that you wouldn't use a gun, wouldn't show a gun, because you didn't want to engage in a gun battle."

"But this guy first came in and started to sort of slap me around."

"But now that you remember that," said Carvajal, "you did, in fact, use this gun on December 16, 1990?"

"Because I felt threats to my life. That's why I did so."

"When you went home that evening, did you tell your mother what had happened?"

"Yes, I did."

"Did you tell your mother that some Black man came in the store, hit you, tried to grab the money, and then you took out your gun?"

"Yes," he said, and repeated what he had told the court about the gang that rushed in to rob him a second time.

"Did your mother know where the gun was kept?"

"Well, she has eyes. So I'm sure she's able to see where the gun was."

"Were you worried about her working there?"

"Of course."

"And you didn't take the time to show her how she could protect herself with that gun?"

"No, I did not."

Then Carvajal asked him about an interview he'd given John Lee of the *Los Angeles Times*. A few days after the March 16 shooting, Du told Lee that his mother said Latasha was going for the cash register and was trying to rob the store of money. Under cross-examination, he told the jury, "That's not correct. I never said that before."

"What did you tell Mr. John Lee?"

"I did not say that she was trying to rob us. I said she was trying to steal money."

*   *   *

No, she didn't see any money in Latasha's hand. "I am a business operator," Soon Ja Du testified. "If she had the money, I would try to grab the money rather than the orange juice, since she already had the orange juice in this backpack."

The doctor's-daughter-turned-merchant told the jury of five Blacks, four Latinos, and three Whites that she had never touched any gun before the day of the shooting. In fact, until the moment she took the witness stand and the prosecutor showed her, Du said she didn't know that she had to pull a trigger to fire a gun. Further, there seemed to be no connection in her mind between the firing of the gun and the corpse in her store.

"When the gun went off, you had no idea what made it go off, right?" Carvajal asked.

"Really," the defendant answered. "I do not know. Korean women only take care of the house chores and domestic work," though her own mother had been a nurse.

She admitted that her husband had once offered to teach her how to use the gun, but weapons frightened her as much as the neighborhood. "You would understand it if you know about that area. I was always afraid and always scared, and fear was not just among Koreans. It was among all merchants, all people. And when I was hearing that some people were dying every day, I felt like they were my husbands. I felt like they were my sons, and I was very, very much scared."

She thought Latasha looked like the gang members her son described. She wore a cap, carried a backpack, which might have concealed a weapon, wore sneakers, and was Black. And she looked to her like a male at first.

"When was the very first point that you remembered being afraid of Latasha?" Carvajal asked.

"After I was beaten up," Du answered dryly.

Even though she told the jury she didn't know she had to pull the trigger to fire a gun, Carvajal pressed, "You realize that guns can kill people?"

"Yes. The gangster movies that we see nowadays shows that, if they put their arms in front of the gun, the guns go off." She demonstrated in court that she thought the gun would go off if she shook it up and down with her hand merely on the grip.

"You know that you have to point the gun in the direction of what you want to hit?" Carvajal pressed again.

"Yes. I've seen that." But she insisted that she had not aimed at Latasha deliberately. The teenager had battered her, the merchant had fallen behind the counter, and, as she was struggling to get up, she glimpsed the holstered gun on the counter beneath the shelf under bags, she said.

Before she grabbed the gun, she said, she threw the stool at Latasha, and the girl slammed her iron fist into Du's face again, saying, "Bitch, I will kill you." Du said she thought she was going to die if the girl hit her again or if she pulled some sort of weapon, a blunt instrument if not a gun, from her neon-bright, lime-green and orange backpack.

But the videotape showed that Du had already won the battle for the backpack — it was behind the counter — and that Latasha did not hit Du after she threw the stool. Latasha put the orange juice on the counter, then stepped back. In the video, the merchant knocks the container to the floor, fumbles to get the gun out of the holster, and points it at Latasha seconds after the girl turns and begins to leave.

With the videotape contradicting her, Du explained she was just panic-stricken. "She had already beaten me up senseless almost to oblivion, and I had already fallen twice. And under such circumstances, I thought I was surely going to die."

"When you took the gun and you had the gun in your hand, were you angry?" Carvajal demanded.

"I was scared; I was afraid. At that moment I thought I was going to die."

Then, stating what she would hammer home to the jury before their deliberations, Carvajal — sounding like no novice — asked incredulously: "This Black girl that you think is a gang member hits you in the eye, causes you a great deal of pain, and you were not angry?"

"It was beyond that point," Du told her.

Carvajal agreed.

CHAPTER 17

─────

I T W A S N E V E R a case of cold-blooded murder but of hot-blooded killing. District Attorney Ira Reiner overcharged the case, and Karlin ruled in favor of a defense motion to dismiss the first-degree murder charge against Du.

At most, the shopkeeper now faced a second-degree murder conviction, which carried the possibility of twenty-five years to life in prison, with an additional five years tagged on for the commission of a felony with a firearm.

Still on leave from the paper, I had the luxury of staking out the courthouse corridor on the fifteenth floor, where the jury deliberated. How aggressively a news organization chooses to cover a trial is a matter of editorial judgment that does not always include actual newsworthiness. And at even the biggest papers, that judgment is influenced by resources: there are lots of courts and lots of trials in L.A. County, and only so many reporters to cover them. While waiting in the courthouse press room for the verdict in the Du case, a court reporter was likely to be writing about another case, gathering background for the next case, or doing interviews for either or both.

Because I had covered state and federal courts early in my career at a small daily, I learned to be — because I had to be — everywhere. And I learned early, whatever I was covering, to hang out where the other reporters weren't; the pack was usually going the wrong way. This required long hours and a lot of energy, but I was younger then; about as young as the Radio Korea reporter, just out of Vassar, sitting across from me on the fifteenth floor.

Shiene Young Cho and I had spoken several times during the course of the trial. I knew she was an inexperienced reporter but an aggressive one whom Karlin had reprimanded for bringing a concealed tape recorder into the courtroom against instructions.

She sat across from me, reading, oblivious of the loud voices at the other end of the hallway, where a door led to a small, metal-enclosed balcony area. Melvin Belt, a Black juror, and Tito Andrade, one of the Latino jurors, were arguing, unaware that their voices, amplified by the metal surrounding them, could be heard in the middle of the hallway where I sat.

Belt was arguing that Du should be convicted of second-degree murder; Andrade was pushing for the lesser charge of voluntary manslaughter.

Of course, all jurors are routinely instructed not to discuss a case outside the jury room, and at first I thought the door to the jury room had been accidentally left open. "Why am I hearing this conversation?" I thought.

There were no other journalists around except Shiene, who seemed to be in another world, and no bailiffs. The jurors had been let out for their usual break around three P.M., and I walked casually toward the men, who stood in profile and were too engrossed in their argument to notice me.

Belt said it was an insult to his intelligence for Du to testify that she thought a gun would go off merely by her shaking it; and I saw his pink-shirted figure imitate Du, in court, jerking the gun up and down and sideways.

By now, I'd turned my back to the two men and was taking notes of what I could hear. I'd already seen Andrea Ford walking toward me and had beckoned to her. She heard much of what I heard, sat down on a bench in the hall, and was the first one to speak· "The judge is not going to like this at all." When I asked her if she was going to include the incident in her story, she hesitated, and then said her editor was not going to like this at all, either. The paper was very skittish about this controversial case and didn't want to do anything to inflame passions in the city.

She called her editor, Ardith Hilliard, and came back to tell me that Hilliard had groaned, "This situation is fraught with peril," and instructed her to come back to the newsroom. Ford told me that the editors were weighing whether it might be better to refer to the incident in a wrap-up story when the trial was over.

Now that would be responsible journalism, I thought. Wait until a verdict is in and report on an incident that might be grounds for a mistrial in this controversial case after the fact. My book was a frankly subjective account of the Du-Harlins matter. But were I covering it for the paper, I would have argued that good journalism demanded that we simply report the incident — after all two *Times* reporters were there — as either a separate short or in the context of the daily coverage of the case. Let the judge read it and let the chips fall where they may.

With hardly any sleep, I awoke early the next morning, got my paper from the front door, and found no reference to the incident involving the two men. I was ticked. It was a bad call journalistically and I was pissed as a citizen. In light of the high-profile cases that have come since, the public might now be equally outraged to think that a news organization had knowledge of possible juror misconduct and did not report it.

In a letter I handed to the bailiff, I informed Karlin of the incident, stated that Ford could corroborate my story — and hell broke loose on day three of the deliberations.

Deliberations were halted, and Karlin hauled Ford and me into her chamber for questioning, with all attorneys present. Ford called the paper and was told by the editors to say nothing until the *Times*'s counsel arrived.

While she and I traipsed in and out of Karlin's chambers individually several times, reporters, who'd been waiting in the courtroom because of a question from the jurors to the judge on a matter unrelated to what I'd seen, watched indifferently. This went on for more than half an hour, once with Andrea and the *Times*'s attorney marching into chambers together, before one of them asked, "Hey, what's going on?" These were journalistic instincts with which I was unfamiliar. And though other high-profile cases in California might suggest that the L.A. press is a school of piranhas, I would demur. It depends on whether it is a high-profile case — the rich and famous count as such, of course — and how much competition it generates. This is especially true of the broadcast media. The more dignified *Times* will choose to ignore an incident like the one between the jurors because it has no real print competition. In effect, I functioned as the competition and embarrassed the *Times* and left Shelby Coffey III, the executive editor, steaming.

I became the issue instead of the paper's bad judgment, which was discussed with amazement a few weeks later when I was invited to lecture to several classes at my alma mater, the Columbia University Graduate School of Journalism. Andrea could not invoke the shield law, which protects reporters from revealing their sources, because she had discussed the incident with me. She corroborated to the judge what I had heard. The prosecutor asked that both jurors be dismissed and replaced with alternates. Lloyd and Leonard objected. Karlin questioned the jurors, who, I was told, said they were arguing about baseball.

I'd paid particularly close attention to Belt during the trial; he seemed bored, dozed off a few times, and, I suspected, had been hostile toward Du from the start. But the judge decided that no damage had been done, admonished the jurors again, and the deliberations continued.

Meanwhile, back at the *Times Mirror* plantation, the bosses ran a carefully edited story that claimed I had reported the jurors' argument merely out of a sense of civic duty and was going to write about it in my book anyway, deliberately deleting my main argument: it was, journalistically, the right thing to do.

Later, a senior editor told me that the metro editor at the time, Craig Turner, privately tried to put the blame on Andrea. If she had told her editors the whole story, they would have reported the incident.

"I told them everything I heard," Ford insisted.

CHAPTER 18

THE VERDICT was voluntary manslaughter. The four days of deliberations inside the jury room were as heated as the one-on-one outside it, between Belt and Andrade. At one point, about half of the jurors were prepared to vote for a second-degree murder conviction but agreed to a lesser charge to preclude an impasse. Immediately after the verdict, several jurors told Carvajal that if they had been allowed to consider first-degree murder, they might have compromised on second-degree. But Cathy Buddemeyer, one of the White jurors I spoke to at length weeks later, told me she wanted to acquit Du but gave in.

Ultimately, the jury found that Latasha's slayer did not act with the premeditated malice a second-degree murder conviction required. Rather, in the heat of passion, she aimed the gun at Latasha, intending to kill her, and had to take responsibility for her actions.

The Los Angeles County Bar Association's future trial lawyer of the year — who tried surprisingly little of the case — was shocked by the defeat and the severity of the verdict, which was front-page news in the *Los Angeles Times* on October 12, 1991. But the banner, front-page headline that day read: HILL'S NEW HARASSMENT ALLEGATIONS DRAW ANGRY DENIALS FROM THOMAS and was accompanied by large facing photos of the man who would be justice and the University of Oklahoma Law School professor. Soon Ja Du and Latasha Harlins were again pushed to the margin by other news, but the bomb was ticking . . .

Between the October 11 verdict and the scheduled November 15 sentencing, over four hundred letters were sent to Karlin from citizens of Korea and from Korean Americans, asking for lenient treatment of the shopkeeper, who had never committed a crime before and was unlikely to do so again.

But the recommendation of the Probation Department was unusually harsh. Du had told the White probation officer who interviewed her on several occasions that she was frightened of and didn't understand Blacks, whom she'd never encountered before buying the Empire Market. "They look healthy, young . . . big question why they don't work. Didn't understand why got welfare money and buying alcoholic beverages and consuming them instead of feeding children." Later, she decided it was their culture, "their way of living."

Du showed no remorse for the killing, the Probation Department told the court. In fact, the merchant said that, under the same circumstances, she would do it again. Had Latasha come from a better family, Du said, the killing, which caused so much pain for the Harlinses as well as her own family, would not have occurred.

The White probation officer told the court that "within Du's character lie serious flaws." She admitted to a "regard for Black citizens tinged with suspicion, fear, and contempt. It was this attitude that caused her to set in motion a chain of events which led to the death of a fifteen-year-old child."

Sitting on the bench in the packed L.A. courtroom, six months from Sa-I-Gu, Karlin said she was rejecting the Probation Department's report. "This is not a time for revenge, and it is not my job as a sentencing court to seek revenge for those who demand it. There are those who have demanded publicly the maximum sentence in the name of justice as Miss Carvajal just did." Further, she admonished Carvajal, "to suggest that any sentence this court might give means that young Black children don't receive full protection of the law is dangerous, unjustified rhetoric."

She then sentenced Du to six years in state prison for the voluntary manslaughter conviction and gave her a four-year consecutive sentence for the use of the firearm, "for a total of ten years in state prison. [But] the execution of this sentence is suspended." Then she told the shocked spectators that she was placing Du on five years' probation, ordering her to perform four hundred hours community service, and to pay a $500 fine and any costs Latasha's family had incurred for her funeral.

Offering no basis for her opinion, Karlin told the spectators that the merchant's failure to express remorse to the Probation Department was a result of cultural and language barriers rather than an indication of a lack of true remorse. Further, Du posed no danger to society, had been law-abiding all her life, and was likely to remain so.

A .38-caliber handgun is normally one of the safest weapons in the world, Karlin said, and ordinarily it would take a great deal of pressure to fire it. "I have serious questions in my mind whether this crime would have been committed at all but for the altered gun." Further, the district attorney wants the court to ignore the very real terror that was experienced by the Du family before the shooting and the fear experienced by Mrs. Du on the day of the shooting, she said. "But these are things I cannot ignore."

The crime was committed under circumstances of "great provocation, coercion, and duress." In fact, if Latasha's pummeling of Du after the merchant grabbed her had not resulted in her own death, Karlin contended, "the district attorney would have relied on the videotape and on Mrs. Du's testimony . . . to prosecute Latasha Harlins for assault."

Then, like a schoolmarm admonishing a potentially rowdy room of children, Karlin lectured the African American community as to what their behavior should be in response to her choice of probation instead of jail time for Du: be quiet, go home, and stay quiet. *Tick, Tick, Tick* . . .

She then counseled all the colored people involved to reject the "intolerance and bigotry" some members of both groups have shown each other and, saying she agreed with Lloyd, advised that Latasha Harlins's death be used as a catalyst to "confront an intolerable situation by creating constructive solutions."

I'd thought the verdict fair. I neither expected that Du would get the maximum sentence, nor did I believe she deserved it. And given the sentencing latitude granted judges, a court of appeals, as expected, would ultimately uphold Karlin's decision. Still, throughout the legal profession and beyond, there was the sense that justice simply had not been done in this case.

Among the most eloquent who stated his concern at the time was a White professor of law named Samuel H. Pillsbury. "Nothing puts our government to the test like criminal justice," he wrote. "Decisions about guilt and punishment involve our deepest angers and fears and so challenge our commitment to moral principle." Du had committed a crime of violence whose seriousness should have been directly reflected in her sentence. We may never know what went through the merchant's mind when she raised and fired the gun. "But if we approach her situation sympathetically, as did both the jury and the judge, what seems critical is her fear. The case seems to rest on her fear of crime — and of Latasha. This raises the question, critical in our urban environment, of how we handle the terrors of crime. Do we keep it within legitimate bounds, or do we let it corrupt our relations with others?"

In the Du case, fear was driven by *racism,* and reinforced by class biases and stereotypes (those "model" hard-working Asian merchants, aren't they just like the Jews that preceded them, versus those "shiftless" Blacks) that pervade the nation, and to which Karlin, I believe, was not immune. Ultimately, in Karlin's courtroom, Latasha Harlins had been tried *in absentia* for her own death and found guilty.

CHAPTER 19

THE PEOPLE'S PRELATE, who shrouded self-interest in the capitalist credo of doing well and doing good at the same time, rallied his troops. About three hundred and fifty demonstrators who'd been chanting "Karlin Must Go" outside the Compton Courthouse, where she usually sat, surged inside when Bakewell told them to take their protests directly to her tenth-floor courtroom.

They swarmed past security guards, toppled a metal detector, marched into the lobby, and attempted to enter the elevators.

Orchestrated by Bakewell's Brotherhood Crusade, the Compton City Council, and several local churches, the demonstration was intended to "send a message that we as a people are strong and we're going to stand up and be counted," Compton's mayor and soon-to-be-representative, Walter Tucker III, told reporters. People knew that Karlin's sentence was "blatantly and egregiously wrong."

"I think a lot of people expect people to stay outside and that's not where I come from," Bakewell boasted. "We went in peacefully. We went in big numbers, but I don't think anyone was out of hand."

No one was injured at the chaotic scene, partly because leaders of the protest led the demonstrators back outside when they were confronted by deputies at the door leading to the elevators.

"There's no doubt about it, it was very volatile — and that was reflective of the sentiments of the community," Mayor Tucker told reporters. The veiled threat was lost on nobody.

The ten-minute courthouse siege in December 1991 was the most confrontational of a series of protests that had been mounted against Karlin since her sentencing of Du the month before. A Compton city councilwoman, Patricia Ann Moore, who was one of the organizers of the protests, proclaimed she would initiate a recall campaign to unseat the judge appointed by the governor just six months earlier.

As a 1992 New Year's present, Moore had a man, whom newspapers described as "community activist . . . Lauroi Gillory" — a name its owner varied with calculation, I would learn — serve the recall papers at Karlin's Manhattan Beach home.

It would be difficult, but there seemed so much multiethnic outrage over the sentence that supporters of the recall effort believed they could gather the 301,000 signatures necessary to place the measure on the June 1992 ballot.

On the first anniversary of Latasha's death, and the day before Soon Ja Du's daughter would celebrate her twenty-second birthday, about a hundred people marched in front of the boarded-up Empire Market. After prayers and statements from the Harlins family, many in the crowd held lighted candles over their heads during a moment of silence.

"We want to make sure the public is very clear about what this is about, and what this is about is a precious life," said Moore, an activist and politician whose substantial form and pretty face managed to get themselves on the *McNeil/Lehrer NewsHour,* as well as *Nightline,* because of her outspokenness on African American issues. "Precious life," intoned Moore, "you are remembered."

A Louisiana native, like Bakewell — but one who grew up much poorer, working in the fields with her parents as a migrant laborer — she wanted the power of the Pope of South-Central but was not smooth enough to pull it off. Maybe she couldn't because her early poverty made her too greedy, out of a visceral desperation, to feign enough do-gooding while doing well. Maybe, too, whatever the arena, women have it tougher. The hue of her flesh in the chocolate-bar range — Moore had that color thing going against her, too, in some quarters. She was coveted neither as a White woman might be nor as a light-skinned Creole queen. Still, if guys had nuts, she had guts. And I thought her a film-noir-style bitch that left the cinematic imitations in the dust.

CHAPTER 20

LEROY GUILLORY was one of those young guys who liked to walk as close to the edge as possible. So when he secretly married Patricia Moore, it seemed fated.

"People warned me about her; said all sorts of things about her. She was a Black widow. A coffin chaser. She slept with ministers and used their pulpit to get political support. But I didn't care," said the twenty-six-year-old Guillory, once a rising political star in the mostly Black L.A. suburb of Lynwood. "She didn't care what people thought of her, and I respected her for that. But after a while, when you realize the person you are with seems lower than you, well, that starts to turn your stomach."

They were sipping tea in their bathrobes the night his stomach first flipped, he claimed. It was about eight at night; they were preparing for bed — they always went to bed early; there was just so much to do. Just that day, Guillory claimed, *he* was the speaker who revved up the crowd before it stormed the courthouse where Karlin sat. The phone rang; Moore answered it and listened at length. She hung up, her raised eyebrow momentarily frozen in place as she muttered to herself.

"What did you say?" her husband asked.

"They're ready to pay," she answered.

"Who's ready to pay?"

"The Koreans," she told him.

"They're ready to pay who?" Guillory claimed to demand. And then, he alleged, she told him that a group of Korean merchants wanted to make restitution to the Black community for the death of Latasha. They wanted Moore to stop urging Blacks to boycott Korean-owned businesses. They wanted Moore to lay off Mrs. Du — she had been demanding that Du be charged with the federal violation of Latasha's civil rights. And they wanted her to call off the recall campaign she'd initiated against Karlin. If Karlin were removed from the bench, it would be an indirect slap in the face to Korean Americans and a political boost to their perceived ethnic antagonists, Blacks, who felt marginalized more and more by the growing political potency of the Latino majority and the economic clout of Asian Americans.

Guillory said he did not want to get involved with the recall effort at first. "I thought Latasha was a troublemaker who'd stolen from Du." But Moore convinced him of the justice of the recall effort. And by the time he served the recall papers at Karlin's home on January 2, 1992, "I was all the way in it. Long before the June 1992 primary I knew we had more than the 300,000 signatures necessary to place the recall issue on the ballot," he claimed. And he couldn't see selling out the community. That's when, in a variation of their usual pillow talk, Moore, twenty years his senior, told him: "Little boy, you don't know what politics is about. Let me be the politician."

And then she launched this "vulgar dissertation" of what a politician does, said Guillory: "'You get the issue, you don't take it personally, you win the sincerity of the people, you do what you can . . . and you have to make sure that your interest is met.'"

"'Your interest is the people's interest,'" Guillory supposedly argued.

"'Well, who's gonna buy my clothes, the people or me?'"

"She started trying to convince me that we should meet with them." Looking back, it seems that this had been her strategy all along, he said. As a dedicated coffin chaser, she was using the fallout from Latasha's death to generate publicity and money for her 1993 race for the California assembly.

In early 1992, Guillory claimed he went with his wife to several restaurants in Gardena, where she was given money by a group of

Korean American merchants. The merchants didn't trust him, he said. So at the first meeting, while they and Pat allegedly transacted business at a dining table, he was asked to sit at the bar. The players changed, but there was one constant, a Korean immigrant merchant who owned one of the largest swap meets in the county, Guillory said. He would not tell me the name of the businessman but said he had identified him for the Federal Bureau of Investigation, which had been looking into corruption among Compton politicians for over three years by the time Guillory and I first talked, in early 1993.

"It's confidential . . . I told the FBI that I was contacting you," he said to me, "and they don't want me to blow what they have going. So a lot of things you ask I can't answer."

This businessman, Guillory went on, supposedly made the initial call to Moore and continued to be the primary contact for all subsequent meetings with Korean businessmen. There were approximately six meetings of which Guillory was aware, either because he was present or because Moore told him about them, he asserted. He helped to spend the thousands of dollars he claimed were passed to her in a manila envelope at each of these meetings — approximately $5000 at the first meeting, then progressively more.

A prominent Jewish businesswoman also attended one of these meetings, Guillory alleged. There was an "extreme" amount of money involved this time. They wouldn't let him know how much, though he was present when the cash was exchanged. "They had the money in an attaché case, eel-skin; it was a gray, eel-skin briefcase . . . The briefcase was sitting on a chair in the restaurant. They opened it up . . . and it was a big package of money. It was in a manila envelope; it was a big one that filled up the briefcase and there wasn't nothing else in the briefcase but a few papers. And I distinctly remember the Jewish lady saying, 'We all have to work together, the Jewish, and the Korean, and the Black community. And this money is not to insult anybody's integrity. This money is to bring unity and to stop both communities from suffering.'" Guillory laughed dryly as he recalled the episode. "I just sat there and listened. And the Koreans were saying that they want their interests met too. The Jewish lady added that 'the Jewish community was going to stay behind Karlin and they wished that [Karlin] and Pat had been friends.' And the woman turned to Pat and said, 'You and I have been friends for a very long time. And I've always been supportive of you and always been supportive of what you've wanted to do in Compton. And we are going to continue our support. We just have to find a way to make all of this right.'"

"Who is this woman?"

He was more forthcoming about her. He told me the name of the business she owned. I checked business records, discovered the name of the owner of the company, and asked him to confirm it. He did. When I checked with a government investigator involved with the probe into corruption in Compton, the source knew of the woman and Guillory's allegations, but it was not relevant to the federal case being built against Moore, so the matter was never pursued.

Knowing it would be a classic case of he said, she said, I decided not to use the businesswoman's name. But I called her twice, the two calls over a year apart, the first time to find out if she even knew Moore.

"Patricia is a friend. I don't always agree with her views. How to put it, the only fault, it's not a fault," she clarified cautiously, "but she says her mind. And it doesn't always agree with people. It comes too strong. And as a politician, I think it is a loss if we lose her. Because I told her, I wanted her to be a Republican. I call myself a liberal Republican. I choose to be a Republican because I can do more in the Republican Party than in the Democratic [where too many people already think] like me. No prejudice. I come from the Jewish persuasion, so if you know *Schindler's List*, you know what I am talking about.

"And I swear to myself," she went on, "that I would never bring prejudicism to my home. And the funny thing is — and I told Patricia this — I have a granddaughter," she suddenly interjected. "She came to us when the riots was, and the people were talking about African Americans — and I don't really know what you are," she interrupted herself to say, "and I am not asking because it makes no difference, but I am going to tell you a story.

"My granddaughter, she comes to her father and says, 'Daddy, am I Black?' So it's such a nonissue that she didn't know what she was. Her best girlfriend in the kindergarten is Black — African American. She was adopted by Jewish people who think like we do, that color has nothing to do . . ." Her voice trailed off.

"How did you meet Pat?"

"How did we meet?" she mused. At one of her offices, in Compton, she told me, "in 1986." Whenever she opens a business, the woman explained, "I go to the city and say I would like to contribute something. Like I was with Mrs. Tucker, which is a wonderful woman," she said, referring to the mayor of Compton's mother. The woman said she contributed to educational programs for children in Compton. "So we just don't like to take. We like to give something back." Pat, she explained to me, was "very impressed" by that attitude and told her, "You have to talk like that to other businesses."

When I asked the woman if she supported the recall campaign her friend had launched against Karlin, she said, "I wasn't supportive. But I am supportive of her because she is a formidable woman and has potential. And if she's your friend, you don't have to agree with everything your friend says, [especially] if they are formidable." For any woman, especially a Black woman, to be as successful as Pat has been shows she is "formidable."

I asked her if she agreed with the sentiments expressed by Marlene Marx, editor of the *Jewish Journal.* In a column, Marx called on Jews to support Karlin because she was Jewish, even though the weekly had expressed concern that Du's sentence had been too lenient.

"I wasn't aware of it," the woman responded. "I didn't make it an issue. I thought it was a racial issue between the Korean and the Black people. I think what happened was a bit of jealousy [on the part of African Americans] over the success of the Koreans."

I asked her how her twelve-year-old business was going, and she said, "Up and down. Pat and I were talking about the riots, which I was greatly hurt by —"

I interrupted her. "How do you mean? Personally, your property, or both?"

"Property." She told her friend after the conflagration, "Patricia, if I were a politician and I was you, I would go on the front and I would go and say, 'My people, this is your chance. You have to vote for the politician — and I am not talking about myself — that can do something about your cause. You all have to pick up your behind, go left-right, left-right to the poll, and vote for the person you know can make the difference for you.' That's what I would have said," she told Moore.

I thanked her for her time and told her I'd be in touch again.

When I came to the *Times* I said I'd stay for five years; and almost five years to the day, in April of 1992, I resigned my staff position to write books and teach — though I became a contributing editor to the paper's Sunday magazine. I knew of the ongoing FBI probe into Moore and other Compton officials and told my editor at the magazine about it in 1993.

My interest was in possible violations of state election laws by Moore, a felony offense for which she could receive three years and a $5000 fine if she had, indeed, accepted bribes to ditch the recall effort. But the feds were after her and other Compton politicians for more serious offenses: extortion and income tax fraud, which could put them behind bars for decades. My immediate editor at the magazine showed no interest in having me pursue a story about the Du-Harlins-Moore-Karlin recall mess, and she made no attempt to pass on to either national or metro desk editors information about the federal investigation or the possible violation of state election laws. Early in 1994, when Bret Israel, at the time the magazine's top editor, discovered the infor-

mation I had gathered and told me he had passed it on to the
senior news editors at the paper, it was ignored; so the *Times* got
beat in its own backyard.

On March 24, 1994, the *Wall Street Journal* reported that federal prosecutors were considering criminal charges against Representative Walter Tucker III for alleged bribery while he served
as mayor of Compton in 1991 and 1992. Relying on tapes from
hidden video cameras and other material gathered during the
investigation, the U.S. Attorney's office and FBI were also "lean-
ing toward" seeking felony charges against Moore for bribery, as
well as against Tucker, recently elected to Congress.

The case could prove controversial, the *Journal* reported, because "both former city officials are prominently identified with
minority causes and have close ties to some of the area's most
powerful Black community leaders. Black leaders in the past have
criticized the Justice Department for what they claim is the unfair
targeting of minority officeholders for criminal prosecution." It
had been an investigation carried out under extreme secrecy, and
the U.S. Justice Department rushed to find the source of leaks to
the *Journal* and wrap up the investigation and seek indictments as
soon as possible.

Knowing that the "businesswoman" was Pat's friend and that
there was an ongoing criminal investigation of Moore and her
contacts, I did not raise the accusations made against her by
Guillory in our first conversation. When I did, in a follow-up
telephone call, she told me in a firm, calm voice: "First of all, I
don't even have an eel-skin briefcase. My briefcase is — I have it
now for maybe seven years — is a brown briefcase. The second
thing, I never carried a sum of money for nobody, not for Koreans, not for anybody. I don't carry money around, especially in
this neighborhood. I am scared stiff. The fact that I said the
Jewish and the Black community have to live together in harmony, I said it here in my office. But never in front of any Korean.
As far as I can recall, I never met Pat with any Koreans. I know

she wanted to introduce me to some, but I don't remember that it happened."

By 1995, Moore had been indicted by the Justice Department on bribery and extortion charges widely reported in the media, but Moore's friend told me, in January of 1996, "I really don't know what the alleged circumstances are that they're charging her with. I have no knowledge. I don't like to read negative reports about people I know. As far as I know, when she was here she was always very cordial. She never gave me any suspicion that I should be avoiding her. She was very supportive of me as a Jewish woman. She understood that it's hard to be a minority, any minority, and that's why I liked her." Whoever is making these accusations against her, said the woman, "I don't think says the truth."

"So under no circumstances, did you ever, whether it was in your office, whether it was in Pat's home, whether it was in a restaurant —"

She interrupted. "I never met her — I met her once with a man, a Black man, who was supposed to be her boyfriend or something, and they came to my place and looked around. But I didn't think I stayed there with them for too long. And there was another time that another Black man that was her boyfriend or her husband" — she didn't know what happened between them, but she met Pat with that man once. "And that was the only time I met her with another man." But under no circumstances did she "ever give her money to stop anything."

It could be that the person telling these lies is "her ex-husband or boyfriend who has something against her, but, *shhh*" — the woman blew air through her teeth in dismay — to bring such an allegation against her was absurd.

Unquestionably, Mr. Guillory, sometimes Gillory, sometimes Leroy, sometimes Lauroi, other times Leroi — it was helpful to confuse people about his identity — had a mega axe to grind. The man identified by court records as Leroy Joseph Guillory was banished to a town of a little over two thousand people near the Mexican border. You had to drive east from Los Angeles on Interstate 10 to get there, passing the rows of fig trees in the agricultural Imperial Valley, passing the inland waters of the Salton Sea, which looked like a shimmering blue mirage, surrounded by land that grew more dusty and barren — both of people and foliage — with each mile. Almost midway between San Diego and the Arizona border, Guillory sat with me in a visiting room of the Calapatria State Penitentiary. Two prison officials sat nearby. This was no ordinary maximum security prison, but one of the few in the country surrounded by a fence that warned prisoners and visitors that they would be electrocuted if they touched it. At a time of government belt-tightening, it certainly cut down on the need for guards in the now-empty towers overlooking the prison grounds.

Framed, he said, by his former wife for attempted kidnaping because he planned to charge publicly that she'd received kick-backs as a Compton city official, as well as bribes to sabotage the judicial recall campaign, he was doing fifteen years behind a hot fence in a town that looked like the backdrop for a spaghetti Western.

Their secret Halloween marriage in Lake Tahoe in 1991 deteriorated steadily after their fallout over the recall effort, Guillory claimed. By the summer of 1992, when he sent out a press release — intercepted by one of Moore's aides — calling a news conference to expose his wife's alleged wrongdoing, an unmistakable flushing sound marked their union. People who knew the couple said Guillory had been let into the inner sanctum, was privy to too much, and had to be eliminated.

Guillory's kidnaping victim, Andrew Valdez, was a Bahamian immigrant and a homeless man who sometimes slept at the home of Guillory's father and stepmother. In confidential court records, Valdez alleged to police that Moore arranged for him, and a friend named Wayne (Smokey) Gardner, to get a contract with the city of Compton to clean up graffiti, bypassing usual bidding procedures for such work. Statements from the victim in those same confidential records allege that Gardner was paying kickbacks to Moore for this contract. But Valdez told police after the kidnaping that his boss, Smokey, was delinquent in "paying his taxes," meaning kickbacks to Moore.

According to trial records, Guillory and three other Black men kidnaped Valdez and told him to page his boss, Smokey, to lure him in. When Valdez couldn't reach him, he was hit in the back of the head with a gun by Guillory and beaten up by the other men as Guillory looked on. Then, in the early morning hours of December 21, 1992, Valdez was driven around town in a maintenance truck, owned by the city of Compton, and beaten some more. When he awoke, Valdez, according to court records, said he found himself in Leroy Guillory's house in Dominguez Hills, one he'd never been in before, in a community near Compton.

Valdez said Guillory gave him a bottle of peroxide, told him to clean up his bloody face, and to stay there until he healed.

Guillory, whom Valdez had seen only three or four times before, had been talking "big," doing a goodfella's routine while he supervised the beating. Later that morning, he told Valdez that the only reason he was alive was because "he let you live," and pointed to the framed picture of a man on the desk in the room. "That's the big boss." Valdez told police the photo was of a male Caucasian, "possibly an Italian."

Guillory denies all this. He said Valdez was dumped at his door and that he placed a call to 911 to get help for the man — evidence that was never admitted in court. In fact — tried in the Compton courthouse he had helped to storm, in the city whose past and current elected officials he was helping to blow the whistle on — Guillory, who acted as his own attorney, claimed he was railroaded.

Looking back at everyone he claimed was exploiting Latasha Harlins's death, Guillory, a compact man with a dazzling smile and a misapplied lightning intellect, said he was the only one on the platform calling for Karlin's recall who wasn't getting paid.

"Because," he guessed, "I was young and stupid — no, I think I had some morals."

"Oh, please," I told him, laughing. "You are in a maximum security prison for kidnaping. You and Pat spent the money. Why should anybody feel sorry for you?"

"Yeah, well, right, right. If I was a little bit older and a little bit wiser, I probably wouldn't be here." Even though I called him on the fact that he'd helped his ex-wife spend the cash she'd allegedly received in those Gardena restaurants, that pittance wasn't enough to support the lavish lifestyle they were enjoying at one point.

Telephone company records showed that in December 1991, Patricia M. Gillory lived at 8449 Hollywood Boulevard in a home valued at almost $2 million. This was during the period she served on the Compton City Council, which paid each member about $26,000 a year.

And though I found no evidence that she was one, Department of Motor Vehicle records showed that a 1973 Rolls Royce was registered in Moore's name with the vanity license plate H E I R - E S S. I never found anything in Moore's campaign finance records or reported income to indicate she had the kind of money to support her lifestyle.

In a phone interview with me in December 1993, Moore hysterically denied even being married to Guillory, claimed she barely knew him, and called him a "nut" who'd been spreading wild rumors about her.

I didn't have a copy of their marriage certificate at the time, but I did have in my hand, as I spoke to her, a copy of the ceremonial certificate signed by her in Lake Tahoe, I told her. Further, it was well known that they had lived together as man and wife.

Robert Henning, the former mayor of Lynwood, now a councilman in that city and the man who was mentor and surrogate father to Guillory, recalled visiting the couple's lavish home in the Hollywood Hills. "He went on the wild side when he ended up marrying Pat Moore," Henning said. "It was just crazy. They, well, Pat bought some house up in Hollywood for one point something million dollars. I asked [Leroy] how much was the monthly note, and they were talking about $15,000."

I told Henning that records showed the monthly note was $10,262.

"Well, the way I got $15,000 was we added the insurance. Ten thousand was just the note; you got to have insurance on the place. I couldn't believe it." Leroy wasn't paying the note. He wasn't making $15,000 a month. "That's how he got on the wrong foot. She was in politics and somehow, I don't know if this is true, she was taking kickbacks. I have no proof of that. But some way there was a lot of money floating around." She was no longer on the Compton City Council and didn't have a job at the time, so "I don't know where the hell the money was coming from. To me there was no legitimate money coming in of that magnitude."

Henning said he knew that Guillory had gotten in "bad shape" chasing money, "and I was trying to convince him that that was not what politics is about — kickbacks and wherever the hell the money was coming from. But things went from bad to worse."

"How could you be so sure he couldn't support their lifestyle legitimately?"

"Well," said the fifty-year-old former mayor, "one day, he brought a sack full of money to the house and it scared the hell out of me and I got mad and went off on him. He was breathing hard coming through the door. Money was dripping all over the ground, and he was dropping hundred-dollar bills, and I said, 'What the hell are you doing?' I thought he'd robbed a bank. And he was telling me that the FBI was following him and Pat from Pasadena, where they'd just picked up a load of money from some guy. I said, 'Well, you take your money and get the hell out. Don't ever bring this over to my house.'"

Eventually, it was Henning who went with Guillory to the FBI to report the allegations of bribery and corruption against Pat Moore and other Compton officials. But the probe was initiated by a San Gabriel Valley businessman named John Macardican when he went to the FBI in 1989 and reported that Compton officials were soliciting bribes from him in exchange for their approval of a waste-to-energy conversion company he wanted to build in the city. Macardican went under cover for the FBI, helping in a sting operation that caught Tucker and Moore on videotape, soliciting bribes in exchange for their City Council votes.

Guillory claimed that when Moore wasn't on the take as a politician, she supported herself as a kept woman. The jealous husband once complained about his wife's behavior to Moore's long-time associate, former California congressman Mervyn Dymally. Supposedly, Dymally laughed at him and said, "Young man, you have a lot to learn. I like you, but you don't understand the nature of women and you don't understand the nature of Pat. She is thirsty for success and she will do anything to get there, including step on me. Pat has no sincerity or loyalty to anybody. Not even her own children."

When I talked to Dymally about Guillory, he sounded as if he was going to reach through the telephone and pull out my tongue for merely mentioning his name. "Guillory," he said, "is a known liar and con man."

Dymally, who was elected to Congress in 1980 and retired in 1992, sounded like a man who regretted that this woman out of a film-noir flick named Patricia Moore had ever entered his life. She'd once been on his staff, and he had, indeed, been her political mentor early in her career. Dymally said he'd "had several meetings after her indictment to try and help her with her case. But then it became quite clear that she had stated . . . or implied . . . to the grand jury that she gave some of the money" she had received in the form of kickbacks to Ken Orduna, "my former chief of staff," when Dymally was in Congress. "I ended up being summoned by the grand jury," he said disgustedly.

An activist and well-connected jackleg preacher in Lynwood whom Guillory called his former pastor told me, "Pat and Leroy are both opportunists. So if you have a seasoned opportunist and a neophyte as an opportunist, who will win out?" Charles Floyd laughed diabolically and seemed to ooze oil as he spoke.

"If Leroy was here, I'd tell him this; in fact I have told him this: 'Pat Moore placed you in the inner circles of the movers and shakers. And rather than you being mature enough to know how to comport yourself in that arena and to use it to your advantage, your [undoing] came because you really didn't know how to handle the power that the woman put in your lap.' Now, had Leroy been out about the business of supporting his wife and just being in the background managing her money, Leroy wouldn't be behind bars today."

"Does that mean you think he was framed?" I asked.

Evasive as a greased pig, he answered, "Well, let's put it like this. Leroy knows a lot on a lot of people. And Leroy will remain behind bars until Leroy either shuts up or can prove his allegations."

There seems to be evidence that will corroborate Guillory's accusations, I told him. His eyes widened in surprise, he shrugged, then offered cynically that, unlike a White politician, "a Black corrupt politician sooner or later goes to jail."

When asked if Guillory was a reliable source, a government investigator familiar with the probe into corruption among Compton officials said, "I am not saying that we have used any information from him," but "yes," his information has generally checked out. And "personally," said the source, "I think he was framed."

On December 8, 1995, the Democratic representative from the City of Compton, Walter Tucker III, was convicted by a federal jury of extorting $30,000 in bribes and cheating on his income tax while serving as Compton's mayor. After nine days of deliberation, the jury deadlocked on three other extortion counts, and the judge dismissed the charges. Facing twenty years in prison and a $250,000 fine on each of the seven extortion counts of which he was found guilty, and three years and a $100,000 fine

for each of the tax evasion charges, the minister-lawyer-politi-
cian, a mere thirty-eight, clutched a black leather-bound Bible
and told reporters: "I don't know why God has allowed this to
happen, but I trust him."

The one Black juror hearing his case issued a fretful postmor-
tem over the verdict. The government videotape showed Tucker
to be guilty, she admitted, but she believed him to be naïve, easily
led astray by the financial temptations cast before him. Wearing
tribal blinders, she refused to see him as a venal politician vic-
timizing his own community, as the prosecution argued. Even
though Tucker's lawyers initially claimed their client was the target of a *racially* motivated sting operation, they abandoned that
argument at trial. But it was going to be the bulwark of Pat
Moore's case. She was a victim of an FBI plot, she charged, "to
take down" African American politicians.

In November of 1995, she pleaded guilty to one count of extortion and to filing a false federal tax return. In a plea agreement,
she admitted taking a bribe of $9100 from Macardican's com-
pany, and she agreed to go under cover for the FBI in the ongoing
probe of political corruption in Compton. She was even willing
to wear a wire for them.

Expecting her to testify against Tucker in exchange for the plea
bargain, Compton's citizens turned on her, calling her a traitor,
threatening her with death, making her a prisoner in her home,
and compelling her to hide behind the door when the bell rang
and talk in a little girl's voice to disguise herself. In April 1995,
she withdrew her guilty plea, contending the government had
pressured her into it.

Fine, the government said, and raised the ante. She was caught
on videotape and audiotape soliciting as much as $100,000 in
bribes from Macardican's company, and actually receiving
$50,100 from it and another $12,334 from Compton Entertainment, Inc., which had sought city council approval to open a card
casino in Compton. The feds brought her to trial on twenty-three
counts of felony extortion. Each count carried a maximum pen-

alty of twenty years in prison and a fine of $250,000. As a bonus, they indicted her on two counts of income tax fraud, each carrying a maximum penalty of one year and a $25,000 fine.

Her trial, which began in the summer of 1996, was stalled numerous times by defense ploys, then came to a halt when Moore was ruled incompetent to stand trial because of severe depression and was placed under a seventy-two-hour psychiatric watch to keep her from killing herself. When the trial resumed, a tearful Moore told jurors she had been entrapped by an undercover FBI agent named Stan Bailey, who posed as a public relations representative for Macardican's company, then romanced her, persuaded her and some friends to invest $15,000 in a trade conference that never materialized, slipped her a Mickey in a cocktail of orange juice and 7-Up one night, then sodomized her and split.

Bailey said no, there had never been any romance between them. The ex-con, whom the FBI had used as an undercover agent before, had been hired strictly to mend a rift between Macardican and Moore so that the FBI sting would not come undone.

Macardican promised to reimburse her and her friends for the $15,000 Bailey had taken, and that was the reason, Moore claimed, that she had been captured on tape taking money from him and two associates, both of whom were undercover FBI agents, twenty times — and for a total of more than three times the amount Bailey took.

When prosecutors pressed Moore for records showing that she had reimbursed her friends with money from Compton Energy Symptoms for their losses in Bailey's investment scheme, the former councilwoman said all of her records had been destroyed in the 1992 riots.

One secretly videotaped meeting shown at her trial revealed Moore demanding $9100 from an undercover FBI agent, including $3000 that she claimed was destined for Compton's former congressman, Mervyn Dymally. Moore promised to line up political support on the Compton City Council and school board for Macardican's waste-to-energy plant. But besides the money she wanted for herself, she told the undercover agent, "Give me three thousand for Dymally at least. Give me three 'cause it's three different people I'm gonna need him to deliver."

Dymally said that if there had been any truth to her claim, the FBI would have acted on it. "This FBI sting was set up to get me, and you can rest assured that if there was anything to what she said, they would have been at my doorstep."

The government's secret recordings of Moore's conversations also gave credence to some of Leroy Guillory's allegations about his ex-wife, the "coffin chaser."

"I hope we recall [Judge Joyce Karlin]," a jury heard Moore say to Macardican. "But that's not my real goal. My goal is to keep the issue alive until the election." Explaining to Macardican that she planned to run for the California Assembly in 1992, Moore said, "I can't make a dime here" in Compton — but she was delaying the announcement because she wanted to be viewed as an activist rather than as a political candidate.

The notoriety she was receiving as leader of the recall drive was better than any campaigning she could do. She said that the press looks at you a lot more closely "as a candidate as opposed to an activist involved in a cause. So if I can keep this going as a candidate and run for the Assembly . . . I'll have more notoriety and more publicity than [my opponent] ever will."

The Harlins case, Moore said, was "the greatest issue" for a candidate because it "involves a Black child, and here's my district, predominantly Black, I mean you know it's the best." Nothing more about the recall issue was revealed at the federal trial.

On October 9, 1996, a jury convicted Moore of fifteen federal criminal counts, including extortion and income tax fraud.

She awaits sentencing.

On the unrelated matter of the recall petitions, Moore yelled that she was tired of being asked about those damn papers. Then, sputtering at me, she screamed the equivalent of the dog ate my homework: stored in her garage, the papers were destroyed by L.A.'s heavy winter rains in 1993.

No one will ever know if there were enough names to get the recall on the ballot in 1992, but three years before Moore's federal trial, when Denise Harlins dogged her demanding that she turn over the documents, the silver-tongued coffin chaser turned on Harlins after a community forum, as both left a place called the Cockatoo Inn. Moore whined indignation when Harlins accused her of sabotaging the recall and profiting from her niece's death. "How can you come in my face challenging me about those petitions? Aren't I the one who got this recall going against Karlin?" But Harlins would not let up, and Moore moved closer, whispering hotly in her face, "Let me tell you something. You know what happened to Latasha? Well, you mess with me and the same thing is going to happen to you."

CHAPTER 21

NO ONE is going to care about Latasha Harlins, Blacks and Koreans, and the L.A. riots several years after the fact, my former editor insisted. He wanted a book about color warfare in the Black community. But that was too narrowly focused on ancient intragroup pathology. It left White people comfortably shaking their heads like that copy editor at the *Times,* I knew, and I wouldn't do it. I was interested in something broader, deeper.

My healthy bank account dwindled as I pursued the intrigues surrounding the Du case, and four years after I started what I planned to be an eighteen-month project, the book was still incomplete. People died; I kept getting depressed; then sick and more broke. Finally, I changed publishers and got a much better deal. The manuscript required relatively little work by the summer of 1995, but the more hours I put in, the less I accomplished. Still, I could juggle long hours writing and editing, as well as the emotional fallout from family deaths and my recurrent ill health. But my brain went *tilt* when I added to the mix the responsibilities of teaching.

Rushing to class after a few hours of sleep and a long night of manuscript revisions, I had an out-of-body-experience. My mind insisted my body sped toward the building I aimed at yards away when, in fact, I'd keeled over and fainted on the grass.

For over five years, I'd felt as if I had a chronic case of PMS — constantly revved like an engine or paralyzed with fatigue. I was convinced that there was something amiss with the chemistry of my body. Certainly I was an intense person. Yet, despite the trauma of my childhood, I was not particularly neurotic. In fact, I was the type of person people called upon when rationality was demanded — unlike a brother invited to an intimate Southern California dinner party held, coincidentally, a week after Soon Ja Du was sentenced.

During dinner party chit-chat, the guest asked his two White hostesses the name of their cat. Between mouthfuls, one of the women said, "I hope this doesn't offend you, [but] my cat's name is Nigger." The man lunged at the woman, tried to choke her, then grabbed a knife and slashed the forehead of the other pet owner while the midnight-colored cat hid. Police nabbed the man as he attempted to drive away.

About eighteen months later, I was sitting on a downtown Manhattan bus. A foreign tourist delayed the driver to ask a question. It wasn't rush hour, but this was still New York City, and a minute-long exchange about the sights to see felt interminable. Finally, a Black woman told the tourist, "You're holding up the bus"; then she told the driver to get moving. Another passenger, a middle-aged White woman sitting across from the Black rider, scolded, "Really, you should be more patient."

With that, the Black passenger — a well-dressed, matronly woman — unleashed a tongue that went from 0 to 60 in three seconds and lashed: "You-White plantation-owning-slave-whipping-woman-don't-you-tell-me-nothing-about-patience!"

My jaw dropped, I sank in my seat, open-mouthed, and thought, Damn, why did she have to go there? That's a mighty old grudge to bring up under the circumstances.

Like the encounter with the nurse from the Big Easy, these were scenes from the tragicomic pastiche of daily Black American life. But unpleasant episodes seemed to enter my life with greater frequency. White men tried to run me off the road one night as I drove to Riverside, California, in 1992.

Six months after Sa-I-Gu, that same animus came at me, reeking of liquor, in the empty car of a commuter rail line between Chicago and Lake Forest. The White conductor bent down to inspect my stylish, Catwoman-style sunglasses. A yard away, I could smell the alcohol on his breath.

"Those are some glasses," he said. "Where did you get them?" I'd had my head buried in a book and was startled by the intrusion. "L.A.," I said, curtly.

Not many Black people got off in Lake Forest, an upper-class White enclave that was also home to the Ragdale Artists Colony, where I was staying that summer. The conductor wanted to know where I lived in L.A. "The middle of the city, not far from where they tape *The Price Is Right*," I said lightly. I was getting off at the next stop and started gathering my things.

"A lot of rats and roaches where you live, huh? You're on welfare, right?"

Evenly I said, "This conversation is over and if you don't get out of my face I'll report you to the railroad." Not a novel encounter, but ones like that for me are usually spread over months or years. Yet in the course of thirty-six hours a short time before the commuter line incident, three cabs in San Francisco refused to take me to a bookstore in predominantly Black Oakland, where I was to give a reading one night. The next morning, when the hotel limousine pulled up to take me to the airport, I entered, said good morning to the White man and woman inside, and was studiously ignored. They were facing me and moved as far away from me as they could on the other side. Then, minutes later, they began an animated conversation with the two new White passengers from Canada who entered next — strangers to them as I was. Big deal, right? Back in L.A., a few hours later, I decided to take one of the shuttle buses home. "Where do you live, Compton, South-Central?" the Asian-American driver asked.

"No, Park Labrea, behind the County Museum, in the middle of Los Angeles," I explained.

"You live Compton, South-Central." I didn't know if it was a question or an order.

"No," I repeated. Perhaps he was afraid to go to those Black areas after the riots, I thought. Once we arrived, however, he demanded, "Why you live here? You not good enough to live here."

Perhaps it was simply that youth had insulated me from the sense of *racial* vulnerability that suddenly overwhelmed me as I watched videotaped death freeze-framed . . . replayed . . . in the living room of the apartment complex in which my shuttle bus driver thought I was unfit to live. Unliberated regarding the matter of age, I now wrote "The Eisenhower Administration" under date of birth, and perhaps both the denial and oblique acknowledgment implicit in that answer meant I'd been on the planet long enough to feel the cumulative weight of both the subtle racism I'd long experienced and the brutal racism I knew of but never let define me. Pain and loss were humanity's companions. The grace with which one handled them was a test of mettle. By the nineties, I had to know why mine had worn so thin, catapulting me toward that moment of despair and irrationality when I believed, if even for a minute, that a gun could protect me in any sane way from the conventionalized evil that too often passes for civilization here.

"Oh, God, I'm so tired, I'm so tired . . ." That's all I seemed to be able to say. I usually wore my long braids elegantly swept into a French twist, with the ends forming tendrils that cascaded over the top of my head. I had it pulled back some kinda way that day just to keep it out of my face — and I know I had clothes on. I kept pulling my hair back from the temples as I gave the psychiatrist my life story in an hour and a half.

I went to the High School of Music and Art, a six-story Gothic-like structure. "My classmates used to joke that they'd see me on the top floor, then the first floor an hour later, and I was an entirely different person." But it was the party-giving that clinched it, the doctor later told me. I was either the hostess with the mostest for six months or holed up working obsessively and completely isolated the rest of the year.

I was a manic-depressive, all right, the kind particularly hard to diagnose. I never suffered classic manias — no intense, psychotic highs. I was hypomanic, the type of high-achieving, entertaining personality that the culture praises. And when I got burned out from all this Type A behavior, I crashed, got sick, developed crippling depressions. There were certainly environmental stresses that triggered the depression, but I had inherited the genetic predisposition for the disorder — a chemical imbalance in the brain. Not everyone with the genetic predisposition develops manic-depression — in my case, Bipolar Disorder II, to be exact, a milder variant of the disease. But combine the inherited tendency with early childhood trauma, and it's a good bet the disorder will develop. Because my condition had gone undiagnosed by all the psychologists I'd seen — therapists who assumed my mood swings were the result of environmental stress only and, unlike psychiatrists, eschewed drugs and focused on talk therapy — I was in danger of getting sicker. I was in danger of developing full-blown manias, the kind that put you in the hospital wearing paper slippers.

The day after I left the doctor's office, I began taking a mood stabilizer called Depakote, also used in the treatment of epilepsy, and all things considered — given the human condition — I have been well ever since.

I once seriously considered becoming a clinical psychologist after college and was ready to enroll in the New School for Social Research, until I realized I was just grateful to the profession for saving my life.

At sixteen, I'd sat in the kitchen where my father tried to take a hot iron to my mother's face, picked up a knife, and pricked at the skin on my chest, preparing to plunge it in. But I could not. I was preparing then for a career as a great singer, and I decided that the world could not afford to lose so great an artist. One might argue that such self-perception reflects a very healthy ego or hypomania. In any case, that's when I started therapy.

In all the years since, despite the psychological carnage that has claimed elements of my family, generation after generation, they, like many Americans, dismiss the mind as a locus for healing, whether it be an emotional disturbance or an organic brain disorder like manic-depression.

Many Americans are like the two grizzly bears seen chatting in the forest. Behind them, a familiar-looking, pale, thin, bearded man hung from a tree limb by his shirt. As the man dangled helplessly, one bear turned to the other, and said: "His name is Bradshaw. He says he understands I came from a single-parent den with inadequate role models. He senses that my dysfunctional behavior is shame-based and co-dependent, and he urges me to let my *inner cub* heal . . ."

"I say we eat him."

You may insist that at least one of the bears in that Brian Moench cartoon is your uncle in his grizzly disguise. But I'm just as convinced that both come from my neighborhood. Blacks are notoriously hostile toward any kind of psychotherapy — that stuff is for White folks, we keep on keepin' on, despite four hundred years of oppression. And when we fall by the wayside, there's always Jesus.

Ruth Harlins managed to put one foot in front of the other, despite death after death. Not knowing the gargantuan effort that took, Minnie Crews, the dean at Latasha's high school, wondered why the youthful grandmother was acting like "*this tired old woman — and she might have been tired, but it seemed like she should have had more energy or a little more time to deal with whatever was going on.*" If anyone had a right to be depressed, plagued as she was by defeats big and small, it was Latasha's grandmother.

When I last saw Ruth Harlins, it was evening. She had come home from work — home was still around the corner from the Empire Market Deli and Liquor Store. She sat alone in the twilight of her dim, always dim, living room. She had no telephone, but there were benefits to that. None of the endless calls for the Justice Committee that had disturbed her days and nights after Latasha's death. Denise and her daughter had moved to an apartment out of the neighborhood. Admitting that she'd been overwhelmed by all that had happened and that she unintentionally neglected Shay at times, Denise had done all she could to make up for it. Her daughter was now headed for West Los Angeles Community College and eventually planned to be an obstetrician. "And I have three nieces in foster care in New York that I am doing everything I can to bring here to live with me in California," said Latasha's aunt. Richard was rooming elsewhere. And without much ado, after Johnny Cochran refused to represent her, the courts had made Ruth the legal guardian of Latasha's brother and sister; but they were out at the moment, playing at the Algin Sutton Recreation Center. She was tightlipped about them. No matter how much I pressed, all she would say was that they were doing "fine." Jerry Foster no longer worked there, but only because of attrition. He had never been investigated. Ruth was slimmer now. And always looking to improve herself, she said she had read a lot about nutrition.

"You got to cut that fat out. Ah-huh," she added to underscore the point. There was a long silence, then she said, "Yeah, ah, er-ah, I like to sit here in the quiet like this. Or sometimes I come home and still listen to my gospel music."

"You still like 'Everything Is Going to Be All Right'?"

"Oh, yes," she told me. "That's still one of my favorites."

Confused and politically unsophisticated, the Latasha Harlins Justice Committee voted to endorse one of the three candidates running against Karlin in the June 1992 elections, while Denise Harlins voted for another. Committee strategist Gina Rae, a.k.a. Queen Malkah, reasoned that, since he was the only White man in the field — and a sure winner because of it — they should support Donald Barnett, a Century City lawyer who was voted "unqualified" by the county's bar association. Denise chose to back a Black attorney named Thomasina Reed, who also received the bar's "unqualified" rating.

Newspapers editorialized in favor of Robert S. Henry, a deputy state attorney general. He was Black and, like Karlin, was given a "qualified" rating from the bar.

A month after her pronouncement in the Crystal Ballroom of the Biltmore Hotel, Karlin squeaked to a 50.7 percent victory over her opponents.

Even if they agreed on little else, Denise Harlins could concur with Karlin when she told the attendees at the Biltmore that May night: "We have, today, politicians, bullies, and gangsters who are exploiting racial tensions in our community for their own personal gain. It's time to tell them that we are not going to be intimidated and we are not going to be bullied."

But how? How did a community organize in its best interests against self-serving demagogues within and gain ground in the struggle for economic and social justice in the face of an intransigent government when so many were so tired?

CHAPTER 22

LESS THAN A YEAR before Latasha's death, an article that seemed to anticipate the bombing of the Federal Office Building in Oklahoma City, the slaughter of commuters on the Long Island Railroad, the debacle in Waco, as well as the L.A. apocalypse appeared in the *Los Angeles Times*. It began: "The nation . . . is on the brink of a civil war."

Qualifying the assertion in requisite journalistic fashion, the writer added that that grim prediction didn't necessarily mean riots in the streets but a "combination of [individual] sociopathic" behavior and "intensified intergroup conflict." The quote was attributed to Richard Rubenstein, then the director of the Center for Conflict Analysis and Resolution at George Mason University. I was the reporter, and that piece, in particular, seemed to prompt more sneering than usual and more why-is-she-always-trying-to-stir-things-up comments at the water cooler.

Published as the twenty-fifth anniversary of the Watts rebellion approached, and the NAACP ended its annual convention in Los Angeles, citing police brutality as the most pressing concern among its members, the story focused on *racial* tensions, however, and ran under the headline: BLACKS: ENRAGED OR EMPOWERED?

Americans ignore, at the nation's peril, what may seem to be minor conflicts erupting around the country between Blacks and Korean immigrants, the article continued; and suggested that the seemingly intractable issue of police abuse of Blacks and rising conflict between marginalized ethnic groups would light the fuse next time. My reporting had led me to this conclusion long ago, and I sought out experts who could provide evidence for it. More important, I sought people who were framing, in innovative ways, the issues involved in conflicts within and between groups and were developing conflict-resolution models that linked the healing of these tensions to an agenda for social change.

If economic, political, and social inequities based primarily on color and class were at the root of most intraminority group tensions (my primary but not sole concern), the immediate trigger was often more basic: hurt feelings. And those feelings were not fleeting but long-festering wounds, often the product of long histories of subjugation. This was as true for Korean immigrants as it was for African Americans or Jews.

I saw it in the disproportionate rage of fifteen-year-old Latasha when she slugged Soon Ja Du after the merchant grabbed her. I saw it as the brutalized and fed-up merchant hurled the stool at the retreating child, then pulled out a gun, aimed it, and, as Latasha turned to leave, blew the girl away. The histories of Du and Latasha revealed two people whose humanity, like that of the communities from which they came, was commonly ignored, so they were always poised to defend or attack.

I saw it, too, in those resentful Black girls in a Fort Riley, Kansas, schoolyard who cut off the sushi-eating, Polynesian-looking Velina Hasu Houston's hair because she supposedly "swung it like a White girl." That psychic and physical battery helped fuel a deep, justified bitterness in the woman, one often inappropriately expressed in Black-bashing rhetoric whose influence may take public policy on *racial* classification in an even more regressive direction.

I came to believe that healing meant dealing with the profound grief at the root of this anger, exploding into homicide, "riots," and autogenocide — the self-mutilation of a people through drugs, alcohol, and murder. But for healing to be meaningful and lasting, we had to rationally understand how all of us got put into this box of social destruction. What were the personal and institutional forces that perpetuated estrangement and violence? How could we change ourselves and these institutions?

Pragmatists who looked solely to politics to change institutions often dismissed those who focused on the psychic wounds of oppression and social alienation as "touchy-feely types." And to a nation therapized to the max on talk shows and in pop psych best sellers, the notion has become so trivialized that if Americans hear once more why they should understand, for instance, the problems of the latest serial-rapist-murderer who was abused as a child by his club-footed-alcoholic-transvestite father, they'll throw up their hands and side with the bears: Eat him.

To dare to frame our social and political discourse in terms of the psychological or spiritual is to ensure that the perpetrator will be subject to the most vicious pre-dining preparations: hacked, skewered, and basted in vitriol while roasting. But there is absolutely a connection, I believe, between the panethnic alienation so many in American life speak of and the inability to mobilize a critical mass of Americans to make the progressive social change so many seek — a United States that has the political will to make education, health care, and the eradication of poverty paramount.

By even the most conservative estimates, at least 40 percent of those eligible to vote in the United States are allegedly too alienated from the political system to exercise their franchise. Overall, the percentage of adults who vote in presidential elections has dropped 20 points since the 1960s, according to the Committee for the Study of the American Electorate, a nonprofit research organization.

A marriage is needed between the so-called pragmatists who focus on the source of so much despair — social, political, and economic inequality — and those who comprehend that you must re-animate lives to get the critical mass necessary to make fundamental change in the face of entrenched resistance.

But who was doing this? And in particular, who was doing it in a way that might engage a woman like Ruth Harlins, representative of so many others in the nation? A spiritual woman who quested for knowledge, a way to improve her life and the lives of all those for whom she was responsible, she was weary but had yet to give up, despite the specter of death that hung all around her.

CHAPTER 23

THE WOMEN laughed and agreed: nobody goes around naming her daughter Jezebel. Eve got a bum rap as the mother of all temptresses. And the Philistine mistress who betrayed Samson, Delilah, is just a head-shearing whore to most. Yet, you've got to look at them and everything else in the Bible from a fresh point of view, they will tell you at Saint Paul Community Baptist Church in Brooklyn. Take the story of Rahab, a harlot, from the Old Testament.

"Rahab was a prostitute; she ran a house of ill repute — hey, sounds like a song," joked Rose Green. "You could easily turn it into a rap," another voice called out in a basement room of the low, sprawling modern church.

Congenitally animated, Green bobbed up and down, snapped her head back, and laughed. A systems analyst for an insurance company, she could write "The Eisenhower Administration" under her birthdate, too — the last month of the second one, I figured. "Her house was located on the outside of town. Rahab didn't get much respect from brothers, only when they wanted what they wanted. Okay?" She gave a knowing nod to the women gathered for the monthly meeting of the Sisters of Esther, one of the church's numerous Bible-study and support groups.

"And during the midst of all this here confusion going on, something political was going on. Joshua was about to invade Jericho City. This is where Rahab and them was living ... Jericho City, a section of Brooklyn," she embellished. "And Joshua was living in Jersey, just across the Hudson River. And they was gettin' ready to invade Brooklyn. And to do that, Joshua says he's got to send 'two of my top guys in to case out the joint.' So the two guys sneak into Brooklyn and hide on the outskirts of town — Rahab's house. You could *easily* disappear in there 'cause they so busy all the time." That ignited laughter and a chorus of "ehh-hmms."

So, "they all tell Rahab what they are all about." And Rahab says, "'I'll hide y'all anyway.' Word got back to the mayor that two of Joshua's spies were in Brooklyn. So the government comes to Rahab's house and asks, 'Have you seen these two guys?' Y'know" — Green did a quick take on Edward G. Robinson — "FBI type of thing. Rahab tells them, 'Naw, haven't seen anyone.' Later, she tells the two dudes, 'Okay, I lied for y'all. I save y'all's life, so to speak. What you gonna do for me?'

"They tell her, 'Okay, sister, I'm going back to my commander-in-chief, Joshua. Only thing I can say is that when we come back, if you stay in this house, you, all your kin folks, anyone close to you will not be destroyed. But if you step out of this house, I can't promise you anything.' She said fine, that's a deal. They go back to Joshua, tell him everything, the coast is clear, blah-blah-blah, and they come back and destroy the city. But Rahab and everyone in her house is spared."

"Now," said Green, wrapping up her exegesis, "what I got out of that was this: you cannot judge a person by their profession, because who would have thought that a prostitute would do something like that? Not only was she spared and spared others; she went off to live with Joshua and his tribe and wound up being linked to the lineage of Christ [one of his ancestors in the tribe of Judah]. So," she concluded, "you never know who's going to help you or where your blessings are going to come from."

They didn't call Saint Paul "Church Unusual" for nothing.

The Sisters of Esther was not my introduction to the church, however. It was, instead, through a book about its pastor, Johnny Ray Youngblood, called *Upon This Rock: The Miracles of a Black Church*. I was unacquainted with the author of the book,

Samuel Freedman, before it was published, but he'd read my memoir and invited me to speak to his students at the Columbia University Graduate School of Journalism, my alma mater.

When we did meet, I told him I was interested in groups linking psychological healing to pragmatic social change, and he insisted that I visit Saint Paul.

In the crime-ridden, apathy-beleaguered Brooklyn neighborhoods of Brownsville and East New York, Saint Paul, in coalition with others, has reclaimed swaths of an urban nightmare once dubbed "God's last Alcatraz."

They did not just create there the Nehemiah Plan — spearheaded by Youngblood, named by him for the prophet who rebuilt Jerusalem — and build 2300 owner-occupied, single-family homes for the poor, with 1300 more to be completed by 1997 and, in doing so, provide a national model for such housing. They did not just create a ministry to drug pushers, out-of-wedlock mothers, the surviving victims of violent crimes, or their most celebrated mission: the reclaiming of Black men alienated from the church, building a ministry around them because the pastor said America will never achieve its potential until Black males achieve theirs. The whole is more than the sum of its parts. These actions seemed to be evidence of a larger vision, a deeper comprehension.

Youngblood and the members of Saint Paul seemed to understand what I believed: if the poor are to be liberated from the hell to which the powers that be have consigned them in this nation, there must be a plan to wed aggressive community activism, which leads to social change, to a systematic program of education and spiritual and psychological healing.

Saint Paul is part of a fifty-member coalition of primarily religious organizations and two homeowner associations called East Brooklyn Congregations, co-led by Youngblood. Comprising Lutherans, Catholics, Jews, Baptists, Blacks, Hispanics, and Euro-Americans, the coalition functions under the umbrella of the Industrial Areas Foundation, the oldest institution for community organizing in the United States, founded by Saul Alinsky in 1940. The flamboyant Alinsky, who wrote the organizing bible for several generations of activists, *Reveille for Radicals,* created People's Organizations in the urban slums, most famously Chicago's Back of the Yards Neighborhoods.

After Alinsky's death, in 1972, IAF moved from ward politics to organizing primarily through churches — seeing them as the strongest institutions for community-based activism. With the iron rule *Never do for others what they can do for themselves* as its organizing mantra, IAF trains people to organize themselves and then take responsibility for solving the problems of their communities.

Experts who monitor the strategies and accomplishments of groups like IAF call them "the Sugar Ray Robinson of community organizers, because they are simply the best in their class," said Pablo Eisenberg, executive director of the Center for Community Organizations in Washington, D.C.

Upon This Rock focused national attention on East Brooklyn Congregations, but other IAF chapters have had notable successes, among them Southern California's United Neighborhood Organizations, the Southern California Organizing Committee, East Valley Organizations, and Valley Organized in Community Efforts. Better known by their respective acronyms — UNO, SCOC, EVO, and VOICES — they spearheaded the successful effort to raise the California minimum wage to the highest salary floor in the nation in 1987, $4.25 an hour, which became the federal minimum wage.

In 1978, within two years of its founding, UNO won widespread recognition for reducing auto insurance rates in the barrios of East L.A. by 30 percent.

With 2.5 million members in IAF's thirty chapters across the nation and nine more on the way in the United States, two already in England, and one planned for Soweto, South Africa,

IAF leaders know they scare protectors of the status quo. "They are tough, disciplined, and have a broad social vision," said Eisenberg.

"Even though we have a representative government, it really doesn't operate that way," said Douglas Slaughter, formerly an associate pastor at Saint Paul who left to become a full-time organizer for IAF in Jersey City. I'd heard that he did the real work of organizing people at Saint Paul while Youngblood took all the glory, but he shrugged off such assertions. Government, he went on, "basically operates as if politicians and people who hold public office are doing people favors."

But IAF is great at saying "no, no, no," to that. Government and the people have a "public contract, and public life is based on accountability, not on like or dislike. We teach everyday people that these relationships are based on mutual respect. And what's really exciting is that everything we have done for ourselves has been over and against the political machinery that has existed."

A classical scholar who reads the Greek that Christ spoke, Slaughter recounted a story about the struggle to get the first Nehemiah Houses developed. "We built them without a permit," he said gleefully, "because the city wouldn't give us a permit. We built them anyway. And they said, 'We'll have to tear them down.' And we said, 'Okay, you tear them down and we'll have the press there to watch you do it.' That's when the former mayor, Ed Koch, said, 'We're for Nehemiah.'"

Though, in the end, Congress's bills to fund similar projects were turned into a "pork barrel bonanza," virtually guaranteeing, Freedman wrote, that future projects would not benefit the poor, Saint Paul's efforts to reclaim souls and develop a cadre of activists has lasted. Eisenberg believes that the key to understanding the success of IAF affiliates is their philosophy of balancing the creative tension between an organizer's private and public life.

"Movements have tended, historically, to minimize the need to have a private life and a whole, richly developed private self," said Michael Gecan, one of the national IAF supervisors based in New York. As a person tackles the growth and development of her community, she has to feel confident and secure herself if she is to be an effective leader and take power on a consistent basis, Gecan asserted. "And we believe that the growth of the private side is in creative tension with one's public self."

A pragmatic expression of this was IAF's decision to become the first organization of its kind to give its professional organizers a regular salary and full health benefits.

But Youngblood seemed to have plumbed the meaning of that creative tension for Black people in America and understood that if Lazarus was going to rise in the slums, he'd need a mighty spirit to get him upright in the first place and, in the crucible of American life, some counseling to keep him that way.

So, undergirding the church's social action agenda are its numerous Bible-study and psychological support groups, as well as three on-staff psychotherapists and many more who serve as regular consultants. Many of the church's fifty staff members, hundreds of its six thousand congregants, as well as the pastor, tout its benefits. Given the tortuous New World Black journey, it is a crucial part of healing and empowering a people who, it is said at Saint Paul, are only the children of those who refused to die.

But I hadn't decided whether Youngblood's understanding was intellectual, visceral, or both. We'd yet to talk one-on-one. And when I first saw him, from afar, he bore little resemblance to the assured figure portrayed in the beautifully written ode to Saint Paul that was *Upon This Rock*.

CHAPTER 24

THEY CAME to the airy, cedar-beamed sanctuary of Saint Paul by the hundreds to celebrate the publication of the book in January of 1993. There was a book-signing. Publishing industry representatives were there. And everyone was invited to dine later in the lower level of the church. The forty-five-year-old preacher with the name like a blues singer's, the doctrinal orientation of a liberation theologian, and the dazzling smile and easy grace of a Motown Temptation — at least around Black people — fawned at the White guests. His neck seemed to shrink slightly into raised shoulders as he told the White folks not to be scared of the Black folks and for the Black folks to treat them nice. It was the type of nervous *interracial* aside that passed for humor thirty years ago. I looked around the sanctuary and heard several people near me ask, "Why is he acting like that?"

"Well, you know," a church staff member told me later, "he's from the South, and he still has a lot of baggage from growing up there." He was raised in a home where his mother taught him that White people were perfect and all-powerful, and in a town, New Orleans, where light-skinned Blacks looked down on him. Many others in the church would tell me the same thing about this immigrant from the bayous of Louisiana. But the bearded preacher stood confidently before his congregation on another day.

"Why," he mused out loud in one sermon, "are there bumper stickers about how beer drinkers, elevator operators, all kind of men are better lovers? Where's the bumper sticker that says,

'Spiritual men make good lovers'? And that means much more than sex. It means being a good listener, helping people, praying when it's time to pray."

And the archetype of a spiritual man, he preached, is Joseph. "What would Mary have done if that man, that kind of man, had not been in her life? Would Jesus have been born? How would she have gotten out of Bethlehem to Egypt? . . ." After all, how many men would have stood by a woman who denied him any intimacies but on the wedding night tells him she's pregnant and the Holy Ghost did it? The brothers in Brooklyn would have told Joseph he was being played for a chump. So, "thank God for Joseph. And remember, Joseph may not look like much while he's around. But ask any widow what it's like when Joseph is gone."

Faith is the generator of all they do at Saint Paul. But "God," said Youngblood from the pulpit, "is irrelevant if God can't deal with the face-up issues of life. Any y'all in here, if God can't deal with what we run into every day, you don't have to serve him. You tell him you got that from a preacher."

And God, he assured, was a Black man.

"When Jesus was sent to Egypt by the Father to have his life spared, he was sent to Egypt where he could blend in. You can find a White baby easy in Egypt. Does anybody know what I am talking about here?"

Jesus, he preached, was not meek. "By the time he left here, he was over that meekness. 'Cause he said one time as a man, 'I didn't come to bring peace; I came to bring a sword.'"

It was hard for men and women to accept this interpretation of Jesus at Saint Paul, said Charles Lewis, the church's media director and coordinator of the Men's Ministry. Tall and lean, he does not look his forty-three years nor does his face betray the hard years from which Saint Paul helped to claim him and so many others. A former journalist and political speech writer, he found his marriage collapsing eight years ago and began abusing alcohol. Attracted to Saint Paul's activism and progressive theology, he joined the church. Reluctantly, at the pastor's urging, he agreed to see a therapist, then returned to school, and is now studying to be a social worker.

"Pastor," he went on, "had to make Jesus and the disciples the real-life figures that they were. He had to convince them Jesus had a penis. He told them he and Peter took a leak behind a rock." After all, Lewis pointed out, "look at the guys Jesus hung out with. One of them — look at Matthew 26:51 — cut off this dude's ear when Jesus was about to be captured and taken to his death. Only reason he stopped is probably because Jesus told him he was outnumbered."

As I heard Youngblood himself put it, one night before the men of Eldad-Medad, Jesus and his crew were no "sissies," no "punks." The hundreds of men who come weekly to the church's Bible-study and support group for men, Eldad-Medad, are central to Youngblood's ministry, Freedman's *Upon This Rock,* and the author and pastor's celebrity at a time the nation was contemplating, with mixed emotions, Black men as an endangered species.

Eldad-Medad was named for two men who, it is told in Numbers 11:26, were in Moses' camp when the elders were called to assist him. Though Eldad and Medad were not called, the Bible tells us, the spirit that fell on the others fell on them. "So the idea is that everybody can't be an elder, but they can embody that spirit of leadership," Lewis said.

As with every Eldad-Medad session, that night's began with the deep, stirring sound of hundreds of men singing, *Draw me nearer, nearer, blessed Lord,* and the reading of Scriptures, that evening from the Gospel according to Matthew: ". . . but I say unto you, that whosoever is angry with his brother without a cause shall be in danger of the judgment . . ."

Toward the end of the evening, the pastor, ticked off with one of his brothers for cause, took over from Lewis. Someone had broken into the church, he told them, and stolen the wiring out of the heating and air-conditioning system. "We want to deal with him and make him a fucking example. That's $50,000 to

$80,000 worth of repairs. And whoever did it might get a hundred dollars for it," Youngblood said disgustedly. "I got a right to be pissed. We intend to send a signal to the street that we are not going to take this shit."

Later, a boy of fourteen stood with an adult member of Eldad-Medad. The youth, the older man told everyone, was to appear in court next week.

"What did he do?" Youngblood asked.

"Shoplifting," the kid answered wearily, then elaborated on the deed. He and friends stole several compact discs from a store, and they got away with it. But when they returned and lifted a $1.99 pack of batteries, they were caught. There was a chorus of disgusted snorts, chuckles, and the sucking of teeth. And he did it in Staten Island, the Whitest, most conservative borough in the city. More snorts.

"How much more is this going to cost you and your mother than a fucking battery? The world owes you something," Youngblood lectured, "but you got to be in a position to take it when payment comes due."

The unspoken consensus of these men — carpenters, teachers, accountants, the unemployed, the underemployed, many ex-felons, many former addicts: the boy should go to jail for sheer stupidity.

In the philosophy Youngblood claims to perpetuate at Saint Paul, the bottom line for the petty thief, the felon, anyone — no matter the environment in which he or she struggles to survive — is that the individual must accept responsibility for his or her actions. And the language he used to convey that to this youth is little different from what he says in the pulpit on Sundays — to the dismay of many.

"I call it imitating Jesus," said Youngblood, sitting at a conference table in his rectangular office, with the phone constantly flashing. "Speaking in the language of the hearers." Biblical scholars hold that Jesus spoke the common Greek of the masses,

Koine. He is dealing with "hard-core" people, Youngblood said and just using common street language. "I don't even call it profanity anymore."

He leaned forward, his voice raspy from cross-country sermonizing, raising three sons, trying to keep a troubled marriage intact, and the stress of frequent visits home to his native New Orleans to see his mother, who would soon die of cancer. "I'd never seen it done. So I read the Scriptures, doing what I call imitating Jesus. What I mean" — he paused — "the Scriptures, feminists say, is a sexist book written by men. But the thing I noticed is that the Black Baptist church was occupied and perpetuated by women. Yet Jesus never had a problem getting men. So I had to look at how he handled men. How he handled himself."

He looked at the Nation of Islam, too, he said, because he admired the discipline of its members, as well as the writings of Robert Bly and other leaders of the men's movement. Women in the church are "mad at me," because of it.

Youngblood is doing some important work that can't be ignored, said a former female member of Saint Paul, "but I could no longer accept him as my spiritual leader." He treats the church as if it is a "fraternity." The language he has used is "insulting to women; he is sexist," a man who leads by "intimidation."

The church's fiscal director, Leroy Howard, tried to laugh off such characterizations of his pastor, but conceded that he is a "dictator. But he uses the Scriptures to justify that. He always likes to tell us 'God never operated a democracy and Saint Paul is not a democratic society.'"

"Catty and conniving" is how Youngblood has portrayed females in meetings with women members of the church, said Rose Green, the natural-born *griot* who attends Sisters of Esther meetings. But she defended him, as did most of the female church members, by saying he is "complex." She continued, "I respect him. He is my spiritual leader. He challenges you with the Scriptures. He gives you the word but also compels you to study it and find out its meaning for yourself."

Having been a member of a cult as a teenager, a nationalist one called the Congress of African People, headed by a charismatic, really brilliant but volatile man named Amiri Baraka, a.k.a. LeRoi Jones, I recognized the signs. Though deeply disappointed and troubled by all this, I continued to visit the church, trying to find what good could be extracted from its example.

Look, Youngblood once explained to me, he'd been the pastor for nineteen years and "it is only in the last eight years that I have been targeting men."

The research and writing of his doctoral dissertation — *Beyond the Conspicuous Absence and Controversial Presence of African American Men in the Black Church* — shook his religious foundation, he told me. "I tell the story about a preacher who came here one night to preach. And from the pulpit he said 'honey' this and 'baby' that. For the first time," Youngblood said, "I realized that we as preachers are so geared to speaking to women that we leave men out unknowingly."

Further — and his raspy voice became more animated — "men who come to Christ are usually brought by their mothers. So I began to reflect on what that means. When we are brought to Christ by our mothers, there are ways in which God tends to be more reflected in our mothers than in our fathers. There's another thing. If you watch men in the average church, particularly Pentecostals, in terms of being responsive in the spirit, their responses tend to be more feminine than masculine." He sat back, his hands, palms up, extended like a supplicant's. "A man is caught up in the spirit and is almost transformed and says, 'Hallelujah.'" Still in the posture of the supplicant, he said, "There is something nonverbally emasculating about this."

And so, he reasoned, "the challenge for me became how do you introduce a man to Christ, teach him to make himself available to the Holy Spirit, and let him know there is no need for

castration or emasculation." Add these factors to the conception
of Jesus as meek, he told me, and "perhaps this is why the church
tends to be an incubator of gays."

There are many lonely women in the church who are lesbians,
said a therapist who used to work with Youngblood. They want
to be part of this spiritual community of Saint Paul and share
their burdens, but the pastor makes it a very uncomfortable place
for them.

And, as usual with Youngblood, said the therapist, if an abused
wife seeks spiritual counseling from him, the first thing out of his
mouth is: What did you do to make him mad?

Yes, he was a complex man. A charismatic, sexist, and homophobic activist-preacher whose life story, as idealized in *Upon
This Rock,* had been optioned for a film by Limelight Produc-
tions — which brought us *Boyz n the Hood.* A company spokes-
man told me that Youngblood's story would make an equally
great television series. Every week Johnny Ray Youngblood could
confront and resolve some crisis within his congregation. One
story might deal with the gay men Youngblood told me he called
into his office. "There are gay men, openly gay men, in my congregation, although I'm not about to start a ministry to gay
men," he put in quickly. Then, dismissing claims that he was
homophobic, Youngblood said that just the other day he had
summoned these two gay men to his office and asked, "Do you
think I am homophobic?" And without a trace of irony, Youngblood related that they told him, "No, pastor, we don't think that
at all."

I laughed out loud at the story, and the pastor looked at me,
amazed. I knew that he didn't like me. Staff members intimated
that he didn't like me because I kept challenging him on issues
like this. "He's a scripturally based man," said one female con-
gregant. If you don't talk in those terms, it's hard for him to
understand where you are coming from. I was an agnostic, so
there was no common ground there. But I admired much of what

the church had done and saw the sexism and homophobia as undermining its ability to do more.

I knew of his early, conflicted relationships with women, as portrayed in *Upon This Rock;* and when I posed the obvious question — Isn't the hurt and anger from those experiences reflected in his tense relationship with women in the church today? — he snapped, "That's why I put my Black ass in therapy."

The Youngblood who speaks in the "language of his hearers" from the pulpit of Saint Paul would be the devil incarnate in the church of his youth and the house of his two mothers, Ottie Mae Youngblood, a domestic who gave him life, and Mother Jordan, a Spiritualist minister, who ruled both of theirs. His father, a hard-working factory laborer, turned his paycheck over to his wife each week, kept a little for gambling and drink — and another woman, with whom he had a child. He left the raising of Johnny Ray to the women.

In Mother Jordan's Spiritualist Church — a New World syncretism of African beliefs and Christian ceremony like that of Cuban Santeria, Haitian Vodun, and Brazilian Candomble — drinking, cussing, and dancing were condemned. It was in this church that Youngblood began preaching and singing at the age of twelve. It was in this church that Mother Jordan, known for her left hook, used it with regularity on the gum-chewing, wisecracking Youngblood. It was in this church, one day, in front of the congregation, that she hauled off and hit him until he wet his pants.

What seems remarkable about Youngblood is not his unsettling but all too common sexual politics; it is his willingness to struggle with the personal demons that inform them. It qualifies as a miracle in most churches — especially Black churches — for the pastor to openly admit he's been in therapy, acknowledge that he and his wife see a marriage counselor, and institute a psychotherapy ministry in the church.

"My own life in Christ," he said during a sermon, "forces me to confess that even when you've got the Lord, every now and then you need somebody else . . . You need another piece of flesh and blood talkin' to you. It doesn't mean the Lord is absent, but, y'all, we're just not sure angels and divinities go through what we go through."

And there was a woman at Saint Paul who reinforced my initial belief something worthy was to be extracted from the church's model and incorporated in a healthier environment.

Her name was Sarah Plowden. It was she who convinced Youngblood to work with IAF after she'd attended one of its training sessions in the early 1980s. She was the church's administrator when I last visited Saint Paul, and had once headed the Women's Ministry. Some younger women in the church saw her as too passive, too willing to acquiesce to Youngblood. But Plowden was fifty and seemed a wise woman, one who I imagined could sit down with Ruth Harlins and talk easily over a cup of coffee in the dim, late afternoon light of her California apartment.

I told her that pragmatists would argue that the best form of therapy in blighted communities like hers was a good job. Slowly, she told me, "I had a breakdown in my marriage after twenty-two years that was totally devastating to me. While I was able to come out, come to church on Sunday, and shout and cry and feel an instant relief, I was left with the same condition. I was only able to move to the next step when I sought therapy."

The Scriptures, she said in a voice still shaped by the South of her youth, tells us "it is possible to live life whole. Dealing with therapy helped me to say I have the courage to live whole." But that's not easy to do "if you've lived in a wounded place so long that when the healing comes about you don't know how to live it out. But once you deal with the spiritual and psychological, you have to move outside and reach for the social — there will always be a need for social change."

Gently, she added, "I was just looking for a way to make

THE LAST PLANTATION ❦ 301

my community better when I discovered IAF. My children were grown, but I still wanted it better. But if I had not been able to come up out of my grief, I would be just another bitter woman sitting in church and not concerned with the larger world."

Still, the messiah complex that was part of the "cult atmosphere" at Saint Paul is a monumental concern, as is the sexism that plagues it and reflects the society at large.

I was a privileged female guest at the Eldad-Medad meetings. Women were generally barred, because, Youngblood said, sisters had their act together more than the men did, and they would intimidate the men if they tried too soon to hash out their feelings together. This policy was "wisdom," not sexism, he lectured from the pulpit one Sunday as I sat in the church sanctuary.

Constance Carr-Shepherd, a New York psychotherapist who helped to establish the counseling programs at Saint Paul but has no involvement there now, shakes her head. "There needs to be a setting where they talk to each other directly, not kept separate like in cell blocks. The one thing we can't repeat in the structural models we build is any kind of internecine war. The fratricide in our community is already horrible."

"Machismo," that's one of the main obstacles to organizing within the Black community, said Cornel West one chilly May day in his Harvard office, musty from abandonment. The popular peripatetic scholar was rarely there, and the space was crammed with books and so much unopened mail that it looked like the dead-letter section of the post office.

"Marcus Garvey used to say the major problem facing Black folk is disorganization. I take that quite seriously. What are the conditions under which Black folk could organize more effectively? Get rid of the deep color conflicts; address the shocking and unprecedented level of neglect toward Black children — historically the force behind our most progressive movements; and change the attitude of the brothers. If the brothers had a less machismo identity, then we'd have not just more women in leadership; you'd have different kind of men in leadership. Because a lot of brothers ain't in the machismo thing. They back off" — afraid they can't be spokespersons because they don't fit that kind of image. "Why not have a division of labor among the leadership? You don't have to have one phallocentric, messianic figure always up there, who presents a certain image that resonates with the larger patriarchal culture."

On that we could concur. But West, who co-authored a book with Michael Lerner called *Blacks and Jews: Let the Healing Begin,* admits he has not considered what healing really means in the context of social change. Yet he has said that our public conversations must address "how wealth is produced, power distributed, and status accrued. I don't think we can start thinking about fighting racism in America unless we ultimately talk about Black people gaining access to decent-paying jobs and resources. Which means we've got to talk about redistribution of wealth in some significant way."

I think that's a tall order for a nation that doesn't vote in droves and for a subgroup whose communities are littered with unresurrected corpses.

When I pressed West on the matter, he told me, "My good friend Jim Washington, who wrote *Conversations with God . . .* always argued that there has to be a psychotherapeutic dimension to the Black church that goes beyond spiritual rejuvenation . . . I hadn't thought enough about the psychotherapeutic and psychospiritual dimension."

"Is that because you recognize that the hard-core stuff — the structural issues of social and economic inequality — are what ultimately have to be addressed?"

"Emmmmmm." He paused, then laughed. "No. It's a defect. You know, it's just a defect basically."

Then he said, intensely, "My problem is that psychotherapy itself not only has a history, but it has a history that's been shaped by the experiences of those in Europe who have particular conceptions of spirituality *vis-à-vis* the secular. Whereas for me, when I think of Black psychotherapy, I think first and foremost of Black music, which is to say, the attempt of Black people to soothe and caress scars and bruises . . . Now just how Black music, at its best, has done that is a question I don't know how to answer. But it seems to me that when we transpose psychotherapy within the Black context, and specifically within the Black church context, we are talking about forms of counsel and advice, forms of sustenance that can keep us going when we're radically . . . against the odds."

I shook my head. "That's an oblique approach. It's similar to the spiritual renewal that the church itself traditionally provides. I know, growing up, my mother was a lapsed Catholic and, though my father was a Marxist and atheist, I would stumble upon him crying when he heard Mahalia Jackson sing —"

"See?" said West. "Something profound was goin' on there."

"I know." As my father did, I respond to the Black church and its music as part of my culture, a part that stirs my core. But not because I literally believe in the Bible; I even doubt the existence of God, I told the theologian. I wish, often, that were not so. I had the gift of a great voice, studied to be a musician most of my life, and in the absence of formal religion, music became that for me. If there is a God, I told him, that was my connection to him.

"That's how it is for most Black folk," he said.

"It was and it is. But I don't think that's enough."

"In one sense, nothin's ever enough." West laughed. "You know what I mean? That's why sometimes you need to be silent, have a drink, and crack a smile or somethin', because the human condition, in general, is just overwhelming in so many ways."

I could second that emotion.

But using West's own words on nihilism, consider what the nation confronts unless we find a way to systematically ameliorate the despair in our midst generated largely by the inequalities in our society.

Nihilism, he wrote, "is to be understood here not as the philosophic doctrine that there are no rational grounds for legitimate authority. It is, far more, the lived experience of coping with a life of horrifying meaninglessness, hopelessness, and, most important, lovelessness. The frightening result is a numbing detachment from others and a self-destructive disposition toward the world."

West was talking about Black nihilism and said that only recently had this phenomenon surfaced in the larger society.

I thought not, especially as I watched for the fifth time — even before it came out on video — my favorite film of the decade, *Unforgiven,* then revisited *Menace II Society* for an essay I was writing. The latter film was one Denise Harlins hated. It opens, you will recall, with Caine and his psychotic homeboy, O-Dog, entering the store of a Korean American man whose wife suspiciously follows them through the aisles as they shop. After some verbal jousting, the youths put down their cash and turn to leave, but O-Dog overhears the merchant mutter, "I feel sorry for your mother."

"What did you say about my mama?" O-Dog snaps. And in that moment, the taunts of the playground, *racism,* xenophobia, poverty, ignorance, machismo, and greed combust in the head of a youth who might as well have been raised by wolves. O-Dog is compelled, as Caine looks on in shock, to murder the merchant and rob him. And because the merchant's wife is too slow to turn over the surveillance videotape that captured the killing, she gets blown, and blown and blown away, too.

By a national audience, even a local one, more preoccupied with the beating of Rodney King, the nomination of Clarence Thomas, and the trial of bank swindler Charles Keating, Denise believed Latasha would be dismissed as one of those menaces to society.

A fine film, *Menace* suggested the kind of nihilism that West described — though its narrow vision fed the racist national obsession that Black men and their community are the central locus of the American scene of violence. Rendered with an artistically impressive verisimilitude, the gangstas of *Menace,* nonetheless, were not representative of the Black community — despite your local five o'clock news. Their behavior was foreign to most Black people except as victims of it.

While exposing the mythology of the old West, *Unforgiven,* like *Menace,* deglamorized violence. But without a didactic second, it suggested, unlike *Menace,* the broad landscape of American violence: sexism, racism, police brutality.

Paradoxically, the film encourages us to empathize with a violent thug, Clint Eastwood's character William Munny, an ex-gunslinger, reformed alcoholic, pig farmer, and widowed father of two. Such empathy is easy, for he is, for a price, avenging, first, abused women and then his Black partner, killed while in police custody (familiar scenes of American violence). He acts out the maxim of a Sister Souljah rap that once ignited controversy: Two wrongs don't make a right, but it sure does even the score.

If the Eastwood persona is allowed to play out this equation with apparent approbation by American audiences, why not a Sister Souljah? Is it simply a matter of who the (political) actors are and whose wrong is made right? What are the moral consequences of such nihilism?

We are enthralled and aghast as Eastwood's Munny, in an inevitable and affecting star turn, comes into the saloon to confront the sheriff who let the dogs of chaos loose in the first place. He let justice go undone for a cut-up whore whose assailant is fined the loss of a horse instead of imprisoned, thereby ensuring no peace. An enraged sisterhood of prostitutes pools its pennies to hire Munny and company to kill the john.

Munny's co-terrorist from the old days, Ned, is played by Morgan Freeman. He comes out of retirement to join Munny, then backs out before the deed is done. But it's too late — he's beaten to death by a sadistic sheriff reminiscent of many a police chief come, gone, and here. Ned and Munny are spiritually analogous to the punks in *Menace.* And like any other knucklehead, what does Munny do when his homeboy is taken out? Even the score. But how deludingly palatable when this classic scene of American violence is played out thusly:

"I guess you are Three-Fingered Jack out of Missouri, killer of women and children," said the sheriff, played by Gene Hackman.

"I have done that. Killed women and children," answered a slightly drunken Munny, whose years of sobriety are busted when he learns that Ned's whipped-to-death corpse is displayed on the street in an open, upright coffin. (In this town, they fine White men but make a sideshow of a Black corpse as a social example of the price of lawlessness.) "I have killed most everything that walks or crawls an' now I have come to kill you, Little Bill, for what you done to Ned. Now step aside, boys."

And like the payback violence that wipes out much of the posse in *Menace*, Munny murders nearly everyone in sight. And when he emerges from the gunsmoke, stumbling into a night that grows bleaker, frame by frame, tears run down his cheeks; and, behind him, the fuzzy image of a slowly undulating American flag can be glimpsed, as he yells, "You boys better bury old Ned right . . . and you better not carve up nor otherwise harm no whores . . . or I will come back an' kill more sonsabitches, hear?"

Hear?

Is this not the ongoing scene of American violence: murdered Black men on display, women whittled? Is William Munny's cry not Sister Souljah's maxim? And didn't seven out of ten of you root a silent *yeah* when he played out its meaning?

Many people tell me that they missed the image of the Stars and Stripes in that scene. They missed the clear suggestion that such violence has characterized the nation's landscape throughout its history and that the targets of it have disproportionately been people of color and women.

From the vantage point of the 1990s, we see in *Unforgiven*, as well, the loneliness engendered by the American ethos of rugged individualism. It is an individualism that allowed then, as it does now, children like Munny's two tiny ones (they're tough; they'll survive) to be left "home alone" as he rides off for the reward from a final killing that will free them from hardscrabble poverty.

One can argue that issues of class and psychological abandonment are at work here. Do such children grow up to be alcoholics and thugs like Munny? Do they grow up to be the gangstas in *Menace*?

There is a connection between the larger social disorder and personal pathology that many refuse to acknowledge. And the social claustrophobia of a film like *Menace* obscures the engendering sites of American violence.

Yet, in certain respects, *Menace* may be the more honest film, because it never romanticizes any of its thugs. Watching *Unforgiven*, we fearfully catch our breath when an innocuous figure crouched in an alleyway contemplates immortality by killing Eastwood's notorious badman, only to say finally, "I ain't no deputy."

His death would have been a fitting end, especially if we are intent on hammering home the platitude that crime doesn't pay and enforcing conservative notions of domestic tranquillity. But he rides off, returning, we are led to believe, to the reformed life from which he lapsed. And aren't we glad? At some point, haven't most of us wished to avenge wrongs with this neat, nihilistic symmetry? It's not new to suggest, of course, that this is the slippery slope down the path to endless social vengeance.

Wasn't that the knowledge in the tearful eyes of William Munny? Had that cipher in the alley shot him, he would have expected it and thought it deserved. But it was unnecessary. Munny's wretched countenance was the mask not merely of death, but of spiritual suicide.

The punks of *Menace* and *Unforgiven* are the spawns of multiple scenes of American violence that overlap class, ethnicity, and region. The dominant players in this landscape demand law and order but refuse to control guns, and then murder presidents, rock stars, and nonviolent Christian martyrs in public with numbing regularity. In these scenes we find the spiritual pump for the nihilism infecting the American soul. And we invite the landscape of social doom with an often unforgivably arid national heart that seems willing to sacrifice democracy rather than allow true equality.

I wonder at the fate of an unhealed child, like Latasha's brother, in such a nation. I still think of the brooding boy, informal ward of Latasha's alleged lover, sitting in the dusky light of his grandmother's living room, staring at the grainy news photo of his sister's killer.